Contemporary Psychology

Contemporary Psychology:
An Introduction

Edited by

Clive R. Hollin

Taylor & Francis
Publishers since 1798

UK   Taylor & Francis Ltd, 4 John St., London WC1N 2ET
USA   Taylor & Francis Inc., 1900 Frost Road, Suite 101, Bristol, PA 19007

First published 1995

Library Catalogue Record for this book is available from the British Library

ISBN 0 7484 0191 1
ISBN 0 7484 0192 X

Library of Congress Cataloging-in-Publication Data are available on request

Series cover design by Amanda Barragry.

Typeset in 10/12pt Garamond
by Best-set Typesetter Ltd., Hong Kong

Printed in Great Britain by Burgess Science Press, Basingstoke on paper which has a specified pH value on final paper manufacture of not less than 7.5 and is therefore 'acid free'.

Contents

Contents

List of Tables and Figures

Preface

Why, one might ask, another introductory text? A stroll around any academic bookshop or a glance at a publisher's brochure will reveal an abundance of introductory psychology texts. There are introductory texts by famous psychologists and by psychologists who are, shall we say, rather less well known; there are introductory texts for degree students, A-level students, and even for those doing psychology just for fun at an evening class (I admit to joint authorship of the latter type of text, *Psychology and You*); and there are introductory texts in specialist areas of psychology, such as abnormal psychology, developmental psychology and social psychology. Given this glittering array, what more could there possibly be to say?

This was the very question Ray Cochrane put to me when we were discussing his Contemporary Psychology Series. I had just finished writing *Criminal Behaviour: A Psychological Approach to Explanation and Prevention* for his series, and we were thinking about new projects. 'Why not have an introductory text?', I asked. 'What more could there possibly be to say?', Ray replied. Then I had the idea: in a Contemporary Psychology Series, why not an Introduction to *Contemporary Psychology*?

The distinguishing feature of introductory texts is that they assume their readers know very little about the topic, and so set out to offer a broad view of their subject. This broad view typically includes a historical perspective on the topic at hand, an overview of the literature accompanied by a description of some of the landmark studies, and perhaps a discussion of the relevant methods of study. All these topics are important and contribute to the reader's general awareness of the field. However, this style of introduction says very little about what is *currently* occupying the thoughts and energies of psychologists working to advance their own area of study. For those learning about psychology, an appreciation of contemporary research seems to me to be as important as a broad knowledge of an area. Indeed, when given the opportunity, it is my experience that students will very much want to know how research is done, the problems researchers are actively engaged in solving today and what they think they are going to be doing tomorrow.

An introductory text along these lines seemed a reasonably novel idea; who, then, could contribute?

With a research reputation on an international scale, The School of Psychology at The University of Birmingham is home to one of the largest and most productive groups of psychologists in the country. We felt, therefore, that we really needed to look no further than our own back yard to discover what was occupying the attention of contemporary psychologists. Of course, in the time it takes to collect and edit a work such as this, the world moves on. While all the contributors to this volume were either academic staff at Birmingham or actively researching with academic staff when the chapters were commissioned, some have moved on to pastures new. In two cases, Kevin Howells and David Wales, to the other side of the planet! Indeed, the peripatetic academic is becoming more a feature of contemporary psychology.

When looking to content, even a brief glance at the page of contents shows how wide a range of topics has been included. It is true that contemporary psychology is in the midst of a cognitive revolution, and this is reflected by the three chapters here on perception, reading, and knowledge and problem solving. As many lecturers will testify, students often complain that cognitive psychology seems difficult; a complaint that often invokes the response that it seems that way because it is! Hopefully the cognitive chapters here, by Mike Harris, Glyn Humphreys and Ros Bradbury, and Koen Lamberts, will go some way towards convincing students (and some lecturers) that cognitive psychology can be both understandable *and* interesting.

The study of human development has long been a topic of psychological research and continues to be one that engages many modern-day psychologists. The chapter by Gillian Harris shows how difficult the task is of understanding even some very basic infant abilities. Despite, for example, a decade of research on face recognition in babies, developmental psychologists are still challenged by the complexities of the tasks achieved by the youngest members of our species. One of the immutable facts of life is that little children grow into bigger ones, and bigger children turn into adults who grow older then die. With the exception of the study of adolescence, psychologists' interest in life-span development is perhaps of rather more recent origin. The chapter by Kevin Browne and myself considers some recent concerns in the literature: accepting that it may say more about us than the real world, there is a distinct feel of unease around many topics we cover. It is sad that topics such as family violence play such a prominent role in today's society and are correspondingly of concern to many contemporary psychologists.

In any field of study topics go in and out of fashion with regard to their popularity among academic researchers and teachers. In psychology, the best example of this is what was traditionally called 'History and Theory': once to be found on just about every course in the land, I suspect one would be hard pushed now to find many psychology degrees with such a course. At the risk of sounding like an old reactionary (which I'm not), I think the loss of History and Theory courses is a major mistake in the evolution of the teaching of psychology. While not moribund to the same extent as History and Theory, there is a sense in which Individual Differences and Learning Theory are seen in some quarters as the topics of yesterday's psychology. The two chapters here, by Patrick Tyler and Glyn Thomas respectively, show that nothing could be further from the truth. The ideas and concepts from both ways of thinking about human action can be applied usefully and constructively to many contemporary issues.

If cognitive psychology is difficult, for those students without some background in biology Physiological Psychology can seem like meddling with the occult! The two chapters included here illustrate two quite different faces of contemporary Physiological Psychology. The first, by Philip Terry, examines some basic ideas from psychobiology and shows how methods of study have changed as technology moves apace. The second chapter, by Jane Riddoch and Glyn Humphreys, focuses on what might be conceived of as the area where thinking meets grey matter – cognitive neuropsychology. In contemporary psychology it is very much the case that the cognitive revolution has influenced studies of brain and behaviour. The chapter here gives an excellent insight into the concerns of those currently active in researching this field.

When I was an undergraduate I recall being asked by one of my tutors why I was studying psychology. I said that it was because I was interested in other people's behaviour. 'Well,' he replied, 'you've picked the wrong subject, you should be reading for an English degree.' While my tutor's sentiments may have been a little on the cynical side, it would be a reasonably safe bet to wager that it is the subject-matter of social psychology that continues to draw many students to the study of psychology. The two social psychology chapters here, by Raymond Cochrane and Christine Griffin respectively, show precisely why other people are so interesting. Ray Cochrane's chapter looks at the intricacies of interpersonal processes, while Chris Griffin takes a broader perspective in considering the social processes when young people move from adolescence to adult status.

Many people come to the study of psychology with the aim of becoming a practitioner of one sort or another. While there are several varieties of applied psychology, the two chapters here have been selected to cover areas that are always popular with students. David Wales and Kevin Howells offer an overview of clinical psychology; my own chapter gives an overview of forensic psychology, perhaps one of the fastest growing areas in applied psychology. (It is perhaps important to add that all three of us are active practitioners as well as writers and researchers.) On rereading these chapters, it is striking how they depend so heavily on theory and empirical research to formulate understandings of real-life issues, then use this understanding to begin to inform practice.

So, here it is: an introduction to contemporary psychology. Certainly my own appreciation of contemporary psychology increased as I read my colleagues' work; I'm sure the same will be true for you. My real hope is that the text itself is both enjoyable and stimulating, so providing a platform for further exploration of psychology.

Clive Hollin
Birmingham, 1995

Part I

Cognitive Psychology

Chapter 1

Perception

Mike G. Harris

Since this is intended as an introductory chapter, it begins with the assumption that you have either never thought much about perception or, if you have, that you don't consider it a particularly difficult or interesting problem. Perhaps, like most people, you think that the main problems of vision, for example, are essentially those of forming a faithful image and then transmitting it directly to the brain. The aims of this chapter are to show you why this view is wrong and to offer alternative, more appropriate and much more interesting ways to think about perception. It consists of a broad introduction to perception and a general description of the main contemporary approaches to its study, followed by specific examples of each of these approaches. These examples are taken from vision because that is the sense that we know most about. However, the principles illustrated are equally relevant to the other perceptual modalities.

The problem of perception

Imagine a group of children throwing things into a pond. As each object lands it creates a characteristic pattern of expanding circles on the surface: large objects create large waves with considerable distances between them, while small objects create small, closely packed ripples. When several objects land at once, their ripples intermix to form a complex, ever-changing, two-dimensional pattern on the pond. Now imagine that you are blindfolded and deafened so that you cannot see or hear the pond and your only contact with it is through your two index fingers, which you can hold a few inches apart and dip into the water to feel the ripples drifting past them. Given only this tenuous contact with the pond, how would you go about recognizing what the objects were and where they had landed upon the surface? Are these tasks even possible?

This imaginary situation offers a simplified analogy with hearing. Sound sources are just mechanical disturbances that set up waves of pressure variation in the air, rather like the pattern of ripples on the pond, except, of course, that they are three-dimensional spheres rather than two-dimensional circles. Instead of fingers, your only contact with these pressure variations is through two small membranes, one in each ear, which vibrate as the waves drift past. Yet, from this impoverished stimulation, you recognize and locate, apparently effortlessly, all the complex and different sounds around you.

The first point of this analogy is to emphasize the important fact that perception is very difficult – it just seems simple because we are very, very good at it. The second point has to do with *why* perception is so difficult. Distance senses, like sight and hearing, have no direct contact with the world. Instead, information is brought to them indirectly, by things like light or pressure variation, and the pattern that actually reaches the sense organs is *nothing like* the objects that produced it. Yet we perceive a world of things, not a world of ripples, so somehow, from this unpromising start, the brain reconstructs the rich perceptual world in which we live.

You may at this point suspect that I have cheated by deliberately offering an analogy with hearing, rather than, say, vision. After all, the visual equivalent of our pattern of ripples is an image, or rather a continuous stream of images, formed upon the light-sensitive retina in each of our eyes. Unlike patterns of ripples, images seem a rather good representation of the external world and, indeed, they are used as a powerful means of communication in our everyday lives. But light is really just like the water in our analogy. Objects may stamp their imprint upon it but, ultimately, images are just patterns of light like the ripples on a pond. They *seem* like direct representations of the world only because we each have a visual system that is very good at making sense of them. This point is illustrated by Figure 1.1, which presents an image in an unusual form.

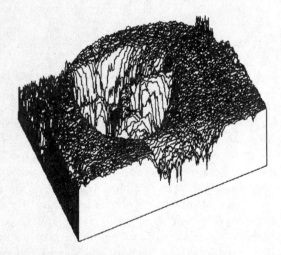

Figure 1.1 *The image as a pattern of ripples*
Note: The amount of light at each point in the image is represented by the height of a surface. Although this representation contains the same information as a conventional black-and-white photograph, our visual systems are not equipped to make sense of it in this form and we have great difficulty in working out what the image depicts. (It is actually part of the Mona Lisa.)

To emphasize the indirectness of images, try comparing a simple object like a cube with the image that it creates. It may help actually to write down a brief definition of a cube and, alongside it, a simple sketch. If an image is a good representation of reality, then a single description should apply to both these examples. Put another way, if images are easy to perceive, then we should be able to derive a description from the sketch that immediately captures the defining characteristics of the cube that it represents. The most obvious problem in doing this is that the two representations are in different languages – one in words, the other in terms of spatial relationships. Fortunately, translation between the two languages looks fairly simple: the verbal description uses terms like 'edges', 'corners' and 'surfaces' and, for each of these, there is a simple graphical equivalent – 'lines', 'junctions' and 'regions', respectively. So, perhaps all we have to do is to derive a verbal description of the sketch, and then substitute the appropriate terms: 'edges' for 'lines', and so forth.

Unfortunately, you will quickly find that this just doesn't work. A cube consists of six square surfaces joined at eight corners, each consisting of three surfaces at right angles to each other. The important terms here are 'square' and 'right angles' since these are really what define a cube. Yet your sketch does not consist of squares and, depending on how you've drawn it, may not contain even one right angle. Images are *not* good representations of the world because they don't preserve even the most obvious defining characteristics of the objects that they depict.

Different approaches

How do we derive a world of objects from a world of light? In recent years there have been two different approaches to this problem, each stemming from a different view of the complex relationship between objects in the world and the patterns of light that they produce.

The first approach is called Direct Perception and stems from the work of J.J. Gibson (e.g. 1950, 1979). It is impossible to convey the subtlety of Gibson's arguments in just a few sentences but the central theme is that, although patterns of light are obviously not the same as the objects that produce them, they none the less contain all the information needed to account for our visual perception. In terms of the pond analogy, every perceivable feature of an object has *some* effect on the pattern of ripples and so, in principle, a complete description of the pattern of ripples contains within it a complete description of the perceivable features of the object. This approach thus views perception as essentially a direct process of 'picking up' the relevant information from the environment.

Again in terms of the pond analogy, Gibson shifted attention away from the instantaneous arrival of a fragment of the pattern at the fingertips towards the whole evolving pattern of ripples upon the surface of the water. Thus, rather than thinking about a single image, Gibson thought about the 'optic array', which is the complete three-dimensional bundle of light rays that impinges on any given point in the world and which has, imprinted upon it, information about the physical layout of the world from that viewpoint. Since there is a slightly different optic array at each point in the world, the observer can move about and sample these different arrays, so building up a picture of the complete pattern of light in the environment. In doing this, the observer will find correlations between the light and the external world that reliably signal the useful properties of objects. Gibson termed the relevant properties of the light ''invariants' and the properties that they signalled 'affordances'. Since invariants reliably stand for affordances, visual perception can be regarded as a direct process conducted through the medium of light.

Gibson made great contributions to the study of perception by emphasizing the amount of information potentially available from light and by stressing the role of the perceiver as an active participant, able to control the pattern of stimulation by moving round the world. But the approach has two important limitations. First, Gibson saw the 'pick up' of information from light as a straightforward matter and was not interested in the neural processes that underpin it. So, traditionally, strong Gibsonians neither learn from nor tell us anything about how the brain physically works. Second, since all the information is available in the light, Gibson saw no need for any form of internal representation of that information. Yet it is clear that human beings *do* generate and manipulate internal representations of the world, for what else is thought? And it is equally clear that perception often goes well beyond what is immediately available from the senses; when we hear a voice, for example, we have immediate access to all kinds of knowledge about the speaker and about our previous experiences of people in general. The Gibsonian approach gets us no closer to the important links between perception and this more general kind of cognition.

The alternative approach to that of Gibson, popularized most recently by Richard Gregory (e.g. 1972), is called 'Indirect Perception' and regards perception as a much more active and difficult set of processes. It maintains that much of perception inherently requires some matching of the immediate stimulus with a pre-stored internal representation of the world, a process implied by the very word re-cognition (i.e. knowing again). Perception, according to this approach, is best thought of as two stages, the first providing a description of the stimulus, and the second requiring active inference to work out what kind of object could have produced the stimulus. The final result of all this – the percept – is a hypothesis that accounts for the stimulus data.

There are really two flavours of the indirect approach. The first 'top-down', or 'concept driven', approach is more obviously different from Gibson's because it holds that our knowledge of the world is deployed at a very early stage in the perceptual process. The second 'bottom-up', or 'data driven', approach is much more like Gibson's, holding that perception does not require such expectations, at least in the early stages. The distinction between top-down and bottom-up processing is like solving a jigsaw, where the initial data are fragmentary and do not provide enough information for useful perception, and where there are two possible strategies. You can look at the picture on the box and then use the knowledge of what you are looking for to try to find pieces that might fit in with these expectations. This would be a top-down approach. Alternatively, you can try to group similar pieces together, for example all the green ones, and then try to join together just the resulting sub-set. This is a bottom-up approach because it makes no use of expectations but simply uses physical descriptions of the individual pieces, in this case their colour. Having solved a small part of the jigsaw by this bottom-up approach, new descriptions will emerge, like the shape of the resulting cluster or its texture, which are not available from the individual pieces and which are potentially much more useful for working out what the jigsaw depicts.

Although the distinction between top-down and bottom-up processing is useful in thinking about perception, it does not really make much sense to claim that perception is generally *either* a bottom-up *or* a top-down process because, according to the indirect approach, both types of processing are clearly involved. In fact, their relative importance will depend upon the precise context and stimulus. When faced with a new and unexpected stimulus, for example, you may need to derive a rich and sophisticated description before you can make much sense of things, relying in this instance heavily on bottom-up processing. But when entering a familiar room, you have detailed expectations of its contents and may need only a cursory description to confirm them. Here perception would be predominantly top-down.

The distinction between top-down indirect perception and Gibson's direct perception is fairly clear in that the former is all about storing and using internal representations of the world, while the latter denies their very existence. However, the distinction between direct perception and bottom-up indirect perception is much less obvious. Gibson regards the extraction of information from the stimulus as the ultimate goal of perception, while the indirect approach regards this only as an intermediate stage, but both are centrally concerned with understanding the relationships between light and objects in the world and, in particular, in deciding which aspects of the light are useful for solving specific perceptual problems. In fact, however, there are at least two practical differences between the two approaches. First, whereas Gibsonians are generally happy if they understand the solution to a problem in principle, those working on bottom-up perception tend also to be concerned with how these principled solutions are actually implemented within the brain. Second, because Gibsonians emphasize the active role of the perceiver in manipulating a visual stimulus that is both very complex and very subtle, they believe that perception can only be studied by observing people or animals moving freely in their natural environment. In contrast, those favouring a bottom-up, indirect approach maintain that useful information can be gained by studying perception using simple, and often very unnatural, stimuli in a carefully controlled laboratory environment.

An overview

Is perception a direct or an indirect process? You will be in a better position to answer this question to your own satisfaction when you have read through the specific examples that follow. But you may well decide that the direct/indirect debate is rather like the top-down/bottom-up debate. For some perceptual tasks, like navigational guidance, sufficient information is directly available from the stimulus so that there is no need to propose any additional knowledge. For other tasks, such as object recognition, it is difficult to explain the richness of our perceptual experience without recourse to some form of indirect inference-based or internal knowledge. A more promising question may be first to decide what would constitute a good account of perception and then to ask which of the various approaches is most likely to lead to such an account. There are, of course, many definitions of a good account, but all should contain at least the following ingredients:

(a) *Specification of the problem:* It is a great, but common, mistake to think of perception, and particularly vision, as a single task. If you were to lose your sight, a great variety of apparently simple tasks would be affected, from maintaining your balance, through guiding your movements, to recognizing important features of the world. Vision is not a single task, but a service industry that is involved in most of what we do. And, since different tasks require different types of visual information, we must first be very clear about which aspect of it we are trying to explain.

(b) *A principled solution:* Only when we have identified a particular task can we begin to consider what visual information might be relevant to its solution. Return to the pond analogy for a moment and consider the specific task of working out the direction of an object. Which aspects of the pattern of ripples might be useful here? The difference in time of arrival of a given ripple at the two fingers seems one obvious candidate, although, if you think about it, it is not quite sufficient unless you are also allowed to move your hands. Another, more subtle, candidate is the way in which the height of the ripples decreases with distance from the point of impact, and there are no doubt others. Whatever the details, it should be clear that there are potentially several ways to solve even a very specific problem, so that we should not necessarily expect to find a single 'correct' account of even simple perceptual tasks. It should also be clear that a proper understanding of any perceptual task requires a proper understanding of how objects and events affect the environment by creating, for example, patterns of light or pressure variation. Finally, we should also note that, for some tasks, we can propose complete solutions. In the pond example suggested above, for instance, it is quite possible to think of simple calculations based on easily measured properties of the surface ripples that would yield a single number specifying the direction of the target relative to the current position of your hands. Other tasks, such as object recognition, are much more complex and we cannot reasonably hope to find simple and complete solutions although, in such cases, it may be possible to break the problem down into a series of sub-tasks, each of which is itself more tractable.

(c) *A plausible implementation:* Principled solutions to specific tasks should identify a particular aspect of the stimulus that is relevant and needs to be measured. In the case of object location in the pond example, we have suggested that it might, say, be the relative time of arrival of a given ripple at the two fingers. You may be content to leave the analysis there, which is essentially the position developed by Gibson. On the other hand, you might wish to go a little further and consider how the required measurements might be made by plausible neural mechanisms. The issue here is not only about your level of interest and whether or not you want to know about biological brain function. For, faced with a number of possible solutions, it may well be that a knowledge of neural processes can narrow down the realistic candidates. In general, just as an understanding of the physics of light or pressure variation can provide theoretical constraints on a problem, an understanding of the biology of the brain may impose equally useful practical constraints.

(d) *Supporting evidence:* Any useful theory of a perceptual task must, at the very least, account for the known perceptual phenomena: explaining the conditions under which perception works effectively and where and how it fails, for example. To be a proper scientific theory it must also go beyond this by making testable predictions. Suitable tests may take several forms, including observations of animals or people in natural or nearly natural surroundings, or controlled experiments in laboratories which, although they may sacrifice the naturalness of the situation, allow firmer conclusions to be drawn about what is really causing the observed results. In those tasks that are complex and have to be broken down into a series of interdependent sub-stages, it may even be necessary to resort to building computer models to show that a theory is actually capable of accomplishing the task for which it was designed. Such models may then behave in unexpected ways, suggesting observations or experiments that can be performed using human or animal participants. Each of these different approaches is illustrated in the examples that make up the remainder of this chapter.

A Gibsonian example: the guidance of movement

As we move about the world, how do we know that we are heading in the right direction? How do we time our actions so that we don't bump into things? How is it that our perceptual systems, which evolved to work at a natural maximum speed of about 20 miles per hour, allow us to drive reasonably safely at much higher speeds?

The first of these questions is obviously complex, if we include the planning involved in selecting even a simple route. But we can illustrate the principles of the Gibsonian approach by considering the simpler task of maintaining a directional heading once it has been selected. The type of visual information that might be useful here is illustrated in Figure 1.2. The left and middle frames represent two consecutive views as we move towards a house: as we get closer to the house, its image just gets bigger. Of course, instead of just two stationary glimpses, the image will actually grow smoothly and continuously as we approach and, consequently, individual points in the image will gradually change their positions. This is represented by the rightmost frame in Figure 1.2, in which the solid arrows illustrate the smooth movement of just the six points corresponding to the visible outside corners of the house. (We could do the same for any other point in the image.) Note that all of the arrows can be extrapolated backwards, as shown by the dotted lines, to cross at a single point. Gibson termed this point of intersection the 'focus of expansion' or, later, the 'focus of radial outflow', recognizing the important property that, providing we are moving in a straight line and keeping our eyes still, this point corresponds exactly with the direction in which we are heading. In Figure 1.2, for example, we are heading slightly to the right of the door. Thus the position of the focus of expansion is a visual invariant that can tell us where we are going and which can easily be obtained from the motion of points in the image. Specifically, an estimate of its position, and thus the direction of heading, can be obtained from just the directions of any two moving points, although three or more points would provide additional useful information about the accuracy of the estimate.

Although common experience suggests that animals and people are very good at detecting and controlling their direction of movement, there is little directly relevant quantitative evidence. Early attempts requiring people to estimate the direction of heading from natural film sequences proved disappointing and the most promising recent work, at least for human participants, has resorted to much less natural stimuli (Warren and Hannon, 1988; Harris, 1994).

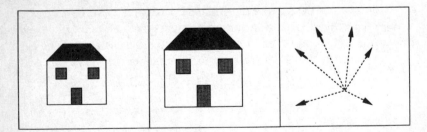

Figure 1.2 *Visual information relevant to the task of controlling locomotory heading*
Note: The leftward panels show two images as the observer approaches a house. The right panel shows the typical motion of a few points in the image. When the directions of these points are extrapolated backwards (dotted lines), they intersect at a 'focus of expansion' that specifies the locomotory heading.

These generally consist of random-dot kinematograms: patterns of randomly positioned dots, normally presented on a computer screen, which are made to move as though they were placed on a surface, such as the ground over which the observer is travelling, and which thus depict a rather stylized fragment of a normal image sequence. In these circumstances, people can accurately estimate the direction of heading suggesting, at least, that image motion is sufficient for accomplishing the task. The specific importance of the focus of expansion, however, remains less certain. People may still perform well, for example, when the display is made more complex by including the effects of simulated eye movements. In this case, the focus of expansion no longer coincides with the direction of heading and the task, though theoretically solvable, is much more complex. The finding that people can deal with this more complex (and natural) situation indicates that they can make use of more sophisticated strategies than that outlined above (Royden *et al.*, 1994).

What about the second part of the problem? How do we time our movements so that, for example, we know when to stop? Relevant information for this kind of task is also available directly from image motion. Figure 1.3 shows a schematic side view of a situation similar to that in Figure 1.2. Here the observer is moving towards the right in a straight line, at a constant speed, and without making eye movements. The observer's viewpoint is represented by the point, P, and is moving at a speed, v. Everything to the right of the viewpoint represents the world, in this case a very simple world consisting of a single object, O. Everything to the left of the viewpoint represents the observer's retinal image, so that the image of O is represented by the point I_o, and the point F in the image represents the focus of expansion, corresponding to the direction in which the observer is moving. Although the most obvious information for the observer to try to extract from this situation might seem to

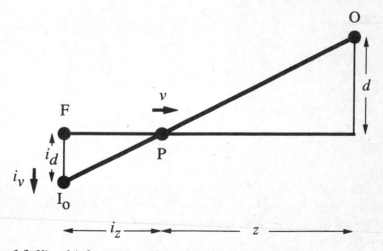

Figure 1.3 *Visual information relevant to the timing of actions*
Note: See text for explanation.

be z, the distance to the plane containing the object, this is actually very difficult. However, something much more useful, the time needed to travel that distance, can easily be extracted. This is in many ways a more appropriate measure on which to base behaviour because actions tend to require a fixed time and thus need to be initiated at different distances from a target, depending upon the speed of approach. Indeed, sensitivity to time required rather than to distance may underpin our ability to deal with high, and thus unnatural, speeds of travel.

The calculation needed to estimate time required is the one you do when stuck in traffic: if you are travelling at 5 mph and are still 10 miles from your destination, you will take another two hours to get there. In general, you can extract an estimate of the time required by dividing the distance by your rate of travel, in the case of Figure 1.3 given by z/v. How can such an estimate be derived from things directly available to the observer in the changing image? The easiest way to answer this question is mathematical. Those of you who hate equations can safely skip the next bit. As the observer approaches, the image expands, so that I_o moves away from F at a speed i_v.

Through similar triangles:

$$\frac{i_d}{i_z} = \frac{d}{z}$$

which, on rearranging, gives:

$$i_d \cdot z = i_z \cdot d$$

Differentiating with respect to time, using the product rule:

$$\frac{d(i_d)}{dt} \cdot z + i_d \cdot \frac{d(z)}{dt} = 0$$

or, by definition:

$$\therefore \qquad i_v \cdot z + i_d \cdot v = 0$$

which, on rearranging, gives:

$$\frac{i_v}{i_d} = -\frac{v}{z}$$

Non-mathematicians can open their eyes now. The equations just show that we can estimate time required by measuring, first, the distance of a point in the image from the focus of expansion and, second, its rate of motion away from the focus of expansion.

Casual observations of, for example, the landing behaviour of flies confirm that even comparatively simple animals are extremely good at timing their behaviour. More formal observations (Lee and Reddish, 1981; Lee *et al.*, 1982) suggest that such animals, and also people, do make use of time required, rather than distance, since they tend to start their actions a constant time before the target, irrespective of their speed and distance of approach. However, as with work on the focus of expansion, this type of observational study does not provide direct evidence that the behaviour is based on the specific solution outlined above. People presented with artificial random-dot kinematograms depicting motion towards a surface can make good estimates of the time required before they reach the target, demonstrating that image motion is sufficient for this task. But when the stimulus is manipulated to remove or distort the available information, the picture that emerges is one of flexibility (Freeman *et al.*, 1994). Rather than using one fixed strategy or solution like that outlined above, people seem able to make use of whatever information is available, even when this might only be useful within the specific experimental context. Of course, it is exactly this type of interaction between a theory and the experimental results that it provokes that allows scientific progress.

A bottom-up example: finding edges

If asked to sketch a scene, you will probably begin with an outline drawing rather than by filling in blocks of colour or shading. You do this partly for ease of reproduction but, more importantly for our purposes, because outline drawings efficiently capture the essence of the scene: we have no difficulty in recognizing single, static, black-and-white line drawings, even though they are quite unlike the moving, coloured images projected on the retina of the eye. What are the essential features of the scene that are so effectively captured by a line drawing and how might we go about extracting them from real retinal images?

The first of these questions is fairly straightforward. In general, the lines in a drawing correspond to the edges of objects or to places where the shading or colouration abruptly changes, which are obviously important and informative features of the scene. The edges of an object characterize its shape (or, at least, as much of it as can be captured in a two-dimensional representation of a three-dimensional thing), while the shading and colouration changes provide a description of its surface markings. Both of these aspects will provide vital clues in helping to recognize the object.

If for simplicity we ignore colour, how would you decide where to put the lines corresponding to object edges and surface markings in, for example, a black-and-white photograph? If you actually try this exercise, you will find yourself tracing around the places in the image where the amount of light changes fairly dramatically from one place to another. So, if you want to know about object edges and surface markings out in the world, and your only contact with it is a pattern of light, a good strategy is to look for places in that pattern where the amount of light abruptly changes.

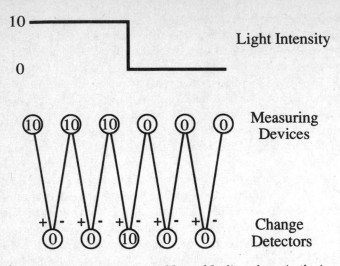

Figure 1.4 *A simple solution to the problem of finding places in the image where the amount of light changes abruptly*
Note: Figures represent the amplitude of response of the various devices. Change detectors subtract the responses of neighbouring measuring devices. Only the change detector located at the 'edge' responds.

How, in principle, would you go about building a device that could locate the places in an image where the light abruptly changes, and which would thus give you access to the arrangement of edges and surface markings in the world? You might start by measuring the amount of light at each place in the image, the more closely spaced the measures the better. Then, you could look for places at which there is a large difference between the measures at adjacent locations. You could accomplish all this very simply and efficiently by using a whole set of measuring devices working in parallel, and by wiring together neighbouring pairs so that the output of one is subtracted from the other as shown in Figure 1.4. Figure 1.4 illustrates the principle involved but, because it shows a one-dimensional cross-section, it contains an important oversimplification. In reality, we need to wire together rings of devices, as shown in the top view depicted in Figure 1.5, so that we can be sure to locate changes in any direction: no matter the orientation of the edge, one pair of devices will always be across the change and so will pick up the difference in light intensity.

So far we can detect a change in light intensity at any individual point in an image, but there is one further property of natural images that we can usefully exploit. Edges tend to be elongated and continuous so that, if there is a change in light at one point, there ought to be other changes at nearby points. One way to make use of this would be to combine the outputs of groups of simple 'change detectors', as shown in Figure 1.6. Notice that each of these new combination devices will be more sensitive, because it sums several sources of

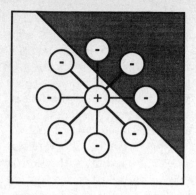

Figure 1.5 *A detector capable of detecting a change at any orientation: the responses of a ring of measuring devices are subtracted from the response of a central measuring device*

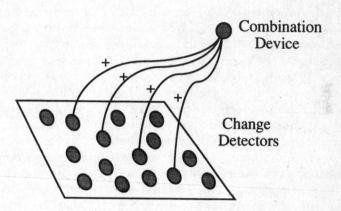

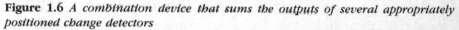

Combination Device

Change Detectors

Figure 1.6 *A combination device that sums the outputs of several appropriately positioned change detectors*
Note: This device would respond best to an 'edge' in the image at one particular orientation.

information, and will respond best to the particular orientation at which the edge is aligned so that it activates all its component change detectors. By looking at the pattern of activation across a set of these new devices, each preferring a different orientation and each appropriately labelled, we can not only detect an edge but also say something about how it is orientated.

Thus far, although the topic is different, the style of this approach is much the same as that encountered in the previous section, identifying a task and proposing a theoretical solution. Here, however, the proposed solution goes a little further by proposing an explicit way to implement the solution. This greater detail goes hand in hand with a much better understanding of the relevant neurophysiological mechanisms. In this case, in fact, much of the neurophysiology was known (e.g. Kuffler, 1953; Hubel and Wiesel, 1959, 1962) before detailed implementations were proposed and this greatly aided the account summarized above.

Figure 1.7 shows a simplified and highly schematic cross-section through a typical primate retina. At the top is a set of closely-packed receptor cells, each of which responds proportionally to light, and which thus corresponds to the required set of measuring devices. Below this are three layers of interneurones which combine the outputs of the receptors in various ways. Some of these interneurones are excitatory (causing an increase in the response of the cells to which they project) while others are inhibitory (causing a decrease in response), so that the network of cells can implement the additions and subtractions needed in the proposed scheme. The bottom layer of cells, termed retinal ganglion cells, constitutes the output of the retina. The axons of these cells make up the optic nerve which projects eventually to the visual cortex located at the back of the head. These retinal ganglion cells have the properties required by the proposed 'change detectors'. They have a background level of response which can be either increased or decreased by appropriate stimulation. When small spots of light are shone upon the retina, the properties illustrated in Figure 1.8a are revealed. Each cell responds only to light in a small region of the retina, termed the cell's receptive field. This receptive field is made up of two concentric, antagonistic sub-regions: light in one sub-region is excitatory and causes an increase in response, light in the other sub-region is inhibitory and causes a decrease in response. This arrangement is just an elaboration of the crude ring of connected measuring devices shown in Figure 1.5. Uniform illumination of the whole receptive field causes no change in response, since the excitatory and inhibitory influences cancel each other out. Under natural conditions, retinal ganglion cells will respond only when a change in light falls within the receptive field, so that the excitatory and inhibitory influences do not balance. They thus act as real biological implementations of the theoretical solution outlined above and the pattern of output in a set of retinal ganglion cells, one at each retinal position, is closely akin to a neural line drawing of the scene.

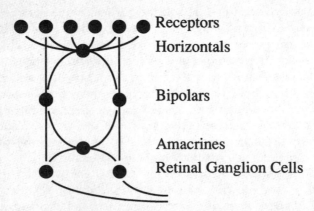

Figure 1.7 *A schematic cross-section of a small section of typical primate retina*

(a)

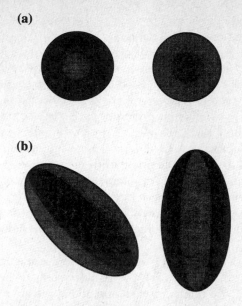

(b)

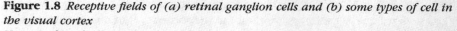

Figure 1.8 *Receptive fields of (a) retinal ganglion cells and (b) some types of cell in the visual cortex*
Note: Darker shading indicates excitatory regions of the receptive field that, when stimulated by light, cause an increase in the cell's response; lighter shading indicates inhibitory regions causing a decrease in response.

In fact, the details of the receptive fields of typical retinal ganglion cells and an understanding about how human performance depends upon such things as line width and orientation allow us considerably to refine the theory. For example, how many receptors should contribute to each ganglion cell? Should they all contribute equally, or should those more distant from the central point contribute less? How big should the gap be between the central sub-region and its inhibitory surround? Varying these arrangements makes the cells more or less able to distinguish real edges from chance variations in light, and makes them more or less sensitive to edges of different sharpness (Marr and Hildreth, 1980). The optimal arrangement will depend upon the detailed properties of the natural images with which the system has to deal and, as our understanding of these images and their relationships to the external world increases, and as we find appropriate mathematics to describe both images and neural processes, so our understanding of retinal physiology also improves. And as this understanding improves so does our grasp of just how beautiful and efficient the system is: in this case Nature has proved an excellent engineer.

The story continues when we shift our attention to the first stages of the visual cortex. Many cells here have receptive fields like that shown in Figure 1.8b, which is just an elaboration of the scheme proposed in Figure 1.6 and, indeed, these cells do seem to combine the outputs of several retinal ganglion cells in the suggested way. These cortical cells have localized receptive fields so that they analyse just one small region of the image. For each image region, there are many thousands of cortical cells, all neatly arranged close to each other in the cortex, and with neighbouring regions of the retina represented by neighbouring groups of cortical cells (Hubel and Wiesel, 1977; Hubel *et al.*, 1977). The cells in each group show a wide range of properties, including a full range of different orientation preferences. Thus, the pattern of response across a set of neighbouring cells, all looking at the same region of the image and each optimally sensitive to a different edge orientation, provides all the information needed to extract the orientation of any change in light falling on the appropriate retinal region. Again, a detailed knowledge of the physiological properties and of related human performance allows us to refine the theory by asking detailed questions about how long each receptive field should be, and how cells looking at neighbouring regions of the image should influence each other.

Before leaving this section, it is appropriate to ask one further, much more difficult, question. An image without a visual system to interpret it can be thought of as an array of numbers, each specifying the amount of light at one location. Similarly, all the mechanisms and processes we have described just deal with numbers, each representing the response level of one mechanism. In fact, you might want to argue that all we have done is to complicate the problem by taking the single number at each position and converting it into many thousands of numbers representing the response of the many relevant cortical cells. Now a line drawing can also be represented as a set of numbers, but it is much more convenient to describe as a set of *symbols*: an edge orientated at 36°, at horizontal position 12 and vertical position 25, joined at an angle of 47° to a second edge, for example. This is the kind of representation we seem to need and, though the processes discussed may actually be regarded as making this fundamental step easier, we have not specifically discussed how it might be done. Historically, the bottom-up approach has not been very good at answering this kind of question, at least partly because contemporary neurophysiological techniques, which concentrate on the properties of individual cells, do not seem appropriate. Although there are many theories, we cannot yet say which is correct or even which are really neurally plausible. It is clear that no single cell described so far can by itself 'detect' an environmental feature, and thus provide a symbolic description, because no cell is specific enough to respond only in the presence of one specific feature of the image, still less the external world. Rather, we need to take into account the pattern of responses of many cortical cells, and the particular cells we choose to include will no doubt depend upon the task in hand. Even if, at some later stage of cortical processing, we find individual cells that respond only in the presence of some feature of the world and of a corresponding conscious percept of that feature, this in itself does not provide a useful explanation. We also need to know how that cell derives its properties and how these exploit the physical relationships between the world and its image.

A top-down approach: recognizing objects

Even deriving a complete symbolic description of the image would not provide a complete account of the complex process of object recognition because, as pointed out in the opening sections of this chapter, a description of the image is not the same as a description of the object that produced it. The top-down approach tackles this problem by regarding the description provided in the initial stages of perception as raw data that are used to mobilize pre-stored knowledge about the visual world. In effect, we develop and test a theory, or hypothesis, of what object might have produced the visual data and, instead of perceiving the image, or even a symbolic description of the image, we actually perceive the successful hypothesis. Our conscious experience is thus a mental model of the world.

This approach provides an appealing account of simple visual phenomena such as the Necker cube, shown in Figure 1.9. This is an example of an ambiguous figure, where either of the two shaded faces can be seen as 'in front' and, with a little practice, you can flip between the two interpretations at will. What changes when your interpretation flips? It is not the image or, consequently, any description of the image alone. The top-down account proposes that there are two indistinguishably good three-dimensional models of the two-dimensional data, corresponding to a cube in two different poses, and that the flip reflects a change in the perceptual hypothesis that you currently hold.

Two obvious problems for this account, of course, are how we store information about all the possible things that we can see and how we manage to locate appropriate information from all the thousands of alternatives. How might knowledge about objects be stored in such a way that it can be easily and reliably accessed from the kind of information available in images? There are many object features that might be useful including, for example, characteristic colour or movement patterns but, because in the previous section we concentrated on static black-and-white line drawings, we will continue this theme. Line drawings tell us only about object shape, so to understand them we first need a way to represent and store a three-dimensional shape. There are a number of possible approaches but all of them share the idea of a limited set of solid

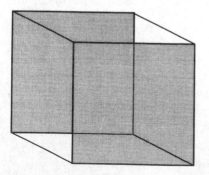

Figure 1.9 *The Necker cube: an ambiguous figure in which either of the two shaded faces can appear to be 'in front'*

building blocks from which objects can be made. We need to find a reasonably small number of blocks from which a reasonably large number of natural objects can be made and we need to ensure that specific blocks can easily be identified from the image. We will consider one particular scheme, proposed by Irving Biederman (1987), because it gives a good account of both these problems.

Biederman began with a simple idea, first proposed by Marr and Nishihara (1978), that building blocks can be described in terms of their axis and cross-section, as shown in Figure 1.10a. He also noted that some simple properties of images reliably signal three-dimensional features of the world. For example, a straight line in an image almost certainly corresponds to a straight, rather than a curved, edge in the world; a symmetrical region in the image almost certainly corresponds to a symmetrical, rather than an asymmetrical, surface. Such simple dichotomies, which can easily be extracted from an image, can be used to characterize the axis and cross-section and so produce a limited set of specific building blocks, which Biederman termed 'geons', as illustrated in Figure 1.10b. Just a few simple dichotomies, all of which can easily be extracted from an image, lead to a complete set of less than 40 types of geon. Notice that each type is not a specific shape, it just has specific properties, like a straight axis and a curved cross-section; there is no need to specify the amount or form of the curvature and, consequently, no need to measure this in the image. Thus,

(a)

Cross-section   Axis   Block

(b)

Curved cross-section,   Straight cross-section
straight axis   curved axis

Figure 1.10 *Representations of solid objects: (a) simple building blocks can be described in terms of a cross-section and an axis at right angles to this cross-section; (b) examples of 'geons': types of building block that can be distinguished by simple dichotomous descriptions of their axes and cross-section*

specific types of geon can easily be recognized in the image. It turns out that a very large number of common objects can be distinguished from each other just by describing them as being composed of a few geons in a limited set of relationships to each other, as illustrated in Figure 1.11. Thus, this scheme provides one efficient way to describe and store information about objects in a way that can easily be accessed from an image.

Biederman's scheme is obviously attractive but it is difficult to know whether it would actually work. This kind of question cannot be answered mathematically or by any other current formal analysis, and so it is best tackled by making a model and testing it on real images. Thus, much of the work on the top-down approach involves building computer models of theories, which forces the theorist to say precisely what information is needed and how it is stored, and exactly how the process works. Such models, if they work, show that a theory is adequate but they do not, of course, show that it is a correct account of how people or animals see. However, a detailed understanding of the model and of the circumstances under which it breaks down allows precise predictions to be made about our natural perceptual abilities. Such predictions can be tested using conventional experimental or observational techniques.

The scheme outlined above does not provide a complete account of object recognition in a number of ways. Its main strength is in suggesting one way to go from an image to an idea of the kind of object that might have produced it. This might be enough to allow us to name the object but it is not enough to allow us to interact with it because it doesn't tell us the precise shape or pose of the object: knowing only that an object is a cup isn't enough to allow us to pick it up, for example. However, getting from an image to an idea about a specific type of object is a very important step (in fact, so important that it is unlikely that we have only one way to do it). Once we know that a part of the image might depict a cup, rather than, say, a frog or a ham sandwich, then we know what other questions to ask of the image data. These questions will probably depend upon our particular requirements at the time, and the data needed to answer them may be very different from those that originally suggested a cup. Thus, it is important that the bottom-up stage of perception

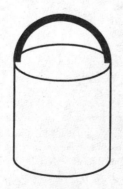

Figure 1.11 *Different object types can be formed from different spatial relationships between the same component geons*

should be able to provide a rich and varied description of the image for later processing.

A second limitation of the approach is that it knows only about individual objects. People and probably many animals can make use of rich and structured knowledge about complex events and situations involving many objects in particular relationships. When we enter a room, for example, we have expectations about what we will find in it and about what people are likely to do in it. These general expectations must considerably aid perception and so it is important for top-down theorists and computer modellers to know how information about individual objects is built up into more complex representations.

Finally in this section, since the top-down approach is based upon pre-stored knowledge, it is important to ask how that knowledge is acquired in the first place. It seems very unlikely that babies come into the world with knowledge about specific objects and so we must ask just what knowledge they do need in order to be able to learn to make sense of the world, and about the principles that govern that learning.

Figure 1.12 *The importance of high-level knowledge in perception*
Note: At first glance this picture appears to be a black and white jumble. With persistence it will suddenly make sense and you should make out a Dalmatian dog snuffling among leaves. A description of this image, no matter how sophisticated, can only deal with black-and-white blobs; to make sense of that description you need knowledge about dogs.

Conclusions

This brief review of examples should be enough to convince you that each of the different approaches to perception has something useful to contribute to our understanding. They are not mutually exclusive, but each tends to look at different tasks and to use different techniques. Thus, for example, a Gibsonian may emphasize that perception is largely a matter of direct description because that is all that is required to solve the perceptual tasks in which he or she is interested, while a top-down theorist would maintain that other tasks, particularly those requiring object recognition, also require indirect inference. The differences in practical approach are at least partly caused by technical limitations. Until very recently it was not possible to generate and control sufficiently sophisticated natural stimuli in a laboratory, and it is still very difficult indeed to allow the active interaction with these stimuli that a strong Gibsonian would require. Similarly, neurophysiological techniques do not allow us sensibly to ask the kind of questions that might establish the neural plausibility of a typical top-down theory, although recent interest in computer-based neural networks, which are based on excitatory and inhibitory connections between many neurone-like elements, look promising.

Finally, this chapter has concentrated on basic ideas and broad approaches and has omitted almost completely the vast range of information available from direct experiments and observations on human and animal perception. Interest in perception has a very long history and there are probably more experimental data available on vision alone than for the rest of psychology together. However, as Figure 1.12 illustrates for the case of perception, data are meaningless without some idea of what produced them. The same, of course, is true of science.

Further reading

Bruce, V. and Green, P.R. (1992) *Visual Perception: Physiology, Psychology and Ecology*, 2nd ed., Hove and London, Lawrence Erlbaum.

A very good account of different approaches to visual perception.

Marr, D.C. (1982) *Vision: a Computational Investigation into the Human Representation and Processing of Visual Information*, San Francisco, W.H. Freeman.

A classic account of one important approach to vision.

Sekuler, R. and Blake, R. (1994) *Perception*, 3rd ed., New York, McGraw-Hill.

A good all-round summary of perception.

Spillman, L. and Werner, J.S. (Eds) (1990) *Visual Perception: the Neurophysiological Foundations*, San Diego, Academic Press.

An excellent review of relevant biology.

References

BIEDERMAN, I. (1987) 'Recognition by components: a theory of human image understanding', *Psychological Review*, **94**, 115–45.

FREEMAN, T.C.A., HARRIS, M.G. and TYLER, P.A. (1994) 'Human sensitivity to temporal proximity: the role of spatial and temporal speed gradients', *Perception and Psychophysics*, **55**, 689–99.

GIBSON, J.J. (1950) *The Perception of the Visual World*, Boston, Houghton Mifflin.

GIBSON, J.J. (1979) *The Ecological Approach to Visual Perception*, Boston, Houghton Mifflin.

GREGORY, R.L. (1972) *Eye and Brain*, 2nd ed., World University Library.

HARRIS, M.G. (1994) 'Optic and retinal flow', in SMITH, A.T. and SNOWDEN, R.J. (Eds) *Visual Detection of Motion*, New York, Academic Press.

HUBEL, D.H. and WIESEL, T.N. (1959) 'Receptive fields of single neurons in the cat's striate cortex', *Journal of Physiology*, **148**, 574–91.

HUBEL, D.H. and WIESEL, T.N. (1962) 'Receptive fields, binocular interaction and functional architecture in the cat's visual cortex', *Journal of Physiology*, **160**, 106–54.

HUBEL, D.H. and WIESEL, T.N. (1977) 'Functional architecture of macaque monkey visual cortex', *Proceedings of the Royal Society of London, Series B*, **198**, 1–59.

HUBEL, D.H., WIESEL, T.N. and STRYKER, M.P. (1977) 'Orientation columns in macaque monkey visual cortex demonstrated by the 2-deoxyglucose autoradiographic technique', *Nature*, **269**, 328–30.

KUFFLER, S.W. (1953), 'Discharge patterns and functional organization of mammalian retina', *Journal of Neurophysiology*, **16**, 37–68.

LEE, D.N., LISHMAN, J.R. and THOMSON, J.A. (1982) 'Visual regulation of gait in long jumping', *Journal of Experimental Psychology: Human Perception and Performance*, **8**, 448–59.

LEE, D.N. and REDDISH, P.E. (1981) 'Plummeting gannets: a paradigm of ecological optics', *Nature*, **293**, 293–4.

MARR, D. and HILDRETH, E. (1980) 'Theory of edge detection', *Proceedings of the Royal Society of London, Series B*, **207**, 187–216.

MARR, D. and NISHIHARA, H.K. (1978) 'Representation and recognition of the spatial organization of three-dimensional shapes', *Proceedings of the Royal Society of London, Series B*, **200**, 269–94.

ROYDEN, C.S., CROWELL, R.J. and BANKS, M.S. (1994) 'Estimating heading during eye movements', *Vision Research*, **34**, 3197–214.

WARREN, W.H. and HANNON, D.J. (1988) 'Direction of self-motion is perceived from optical flow', *Nature*, **336**, 162–3.

Chapter 2

Understanding Written Language

Glyn W. Humphreys and Ros Bradbury

Introduction

In literate societies the written form of the language is an important and much used form of communication. For many centuries people who could read and write have been able to receive and pass messages across space and through time, enabling knowledge to be transmitted more easily across generations and different populations than if language was just spoken. Although modern technology now enables us to record and send spoken messages to each other, being able to read remains one of the most valuable skills that people learn.

Reading is a complex skill that can be shown to involve a number of cognitive processes. If you read a set of words, whether a line of poetry, a newspaper headline, a personal letter from a friend, or a longer piece of text such as this chapter, whether machine-printed or hand-written, you will need to be able both to recognize the letters and words, and also to assign a meaning to them so as to understand what the writers have said. Our aim in this chapter is to describe some current explanations and scientific evidence about how those operations are achieved.

Processing single words

The skill of reading is typically acquired only after people have first learned the spoken form of the language. Consequently, one prevalent view of how the meaning of single printed words is derived is that words are first translated into their associated sound form (their phonological form) and that our understanding of word meaning is based on its sound. There is considerable empirical evidence that supports this view. For example, if people are given a task in which they have to verify whether a written sentence is meaningful or not, they make more errors in rejecting meaningless sentences such as 'tie the not' relative to meaningless 'control' sentences such as 'tie the now' (Baron, 1973). The sentences that create particular difficulty in this instance are ones in which an appropriate word ('knot') has been substituted by a word that sounds the same but that has a different meaning (this is termed a *homophone*); in the control condition the substitute word looks similar to the target word but does not have the same sound (a *spelling control*). Since people find it difficult to reject incorrect homophones, it would appear that their assessment of the meaning of the sentence is based on the spoken form. Similar results have been found when the task requires people to verify whether a single word matches a previously given category name; for example, more errors are made with incorrect homophone stimuli such as A FLOWER? ROWS than with their spelling controls (A FLOWER? ROBS) (Van Orden, 1987). Such effects are not confined to when we judge the meaning of whole sentences, suggesting that the meaning of even single written words can be based on the phonological rather than the written form.

The problems people have in rejecting phonologically appropriate but visually incorrect stimuli also generalize from cases in which incorrect word substitutions are made (as above) to those in which 'non-word' stimuli are substituted for correct words (i.e. the substitutes are meaningless letter strings). For instance, when people are asked to read through passages and to mark any spelling errors they notice, they tend to miss phonologically appropriate non-word substitutes (termed *pseudohomophones*; e.g. in sentences such as HE USED THE HAMMER TO HIT THE NALE) more than phonologically inappropriate non-words chosen as spelling controls (HE USED THE HAMMER TO HIT THE NALT) (Van Orden, 1991). Results such as this extend those found when phonologically appropriate word substitutions are made, since they suggest that the phonology used to access the meaning of the written form does not depend on the visual recognition of the form, since it can be derived from a visually unfamiliar non-word as well as from a visually familiar word. For example, the phonology may be derived by translation of the letters (or of groups of letters) into their sounds, sometimes called a *non-lexical* translation process, which will work as well for a visually unfamiliar non-word as for a visually familiar word. On this view, access to word meaning requires non-lexical translation of words into their phonological forms.

However, while English is a language with some degree of regularity between the written and spoken forms of words, there are also many examples of words for which the most usual translation of the letters will not produce the correct spoken form. Consider words such as YACHT, PINT and BREAD; if the individual letters are given their normal phonological form, then YACHT and PINT become non-words and BREAD might be misunderstood as having something to do with having offspring! These words are *irregular* in the relations between their spelling and their sound. In order both to understand their meaning and to pronounce them correctly, we may have to recognize the words as familiar visual forms and to associate the meaning and pronunciation of the word with the visual memory of the words. Such visual memories are said to be represented within a *internal lexicon*, and the process of reading by accessing the visual memory of words is termed a *lexical* reading process.

There is also a good deal of psychological evidence indicating that skilled readers of English use a lexical as well as a non-lexical process to understand word meaning and to read words aloud. For example, when people are simply asked to name words or closely match non-words as quickly as possible (e.g. PINK and PIND), they are faster at naming the word than the non-word. They are even faster to name the words if the non-words and the words have the same pronunciation (NAIL and NALE) (McCann and Besner, 1987). Such 'lexical advantages' for words over matched non-words should not occur if both are translated into sound by a single non-lexical translation process.

Thus the evidence points to word recognition and pronunciation in English being dependent on two processes, a lexical and a non-lexical procedure for translating letters into sounds. Skilled readers seem to develop both procedures, and it may be that reading normally depends on a 'race' between the two procedures to determine whether lexical or non-lexical processes determine access to word meaning and pronunciation first. Interestingly, non-lexical phonological processes seem to determine performance more strongly for less skilled, younger readers. Given tasks of verifying whether written sentences are meaningful or not, younger readers make proportionally more errors in homophone and pseudohomophone errors than in matched spelling controls (Doctor and Coltheart, 1980). In slightly older children, the errors in pseudohomophones are decreased, while there remain proportionally high errors in incorrect homophone substitutions. This pattern of results suggests yet a further complication to our account. For errors to be greater on homophone substitutions than on their spelling controls, access to meaning must at least sometimes be based on the phonological form of the word; on the other hand, for such errors to be proportionately greater for homophones than for pseudohomophones, there must be more efficient access to the phonological form of a word than from a non-word. We can explain this set of results if phonology can be derived in a direct lexical way, by associating the visual memory of the word in the lexicon with its pronunciation. Sometimes access to word meaning might then be based on lexically derived phonology and not on either non-lexically derived phonology or on lexical association between the visual memory of the word and the word's meaning. Figure 2.1 gives a framework that outlines these different procedures for going from print to sound in English. The studies of how children detect anomalies in written sentences suggest that these procedures might normally develop at different rates, with perhaps the procedure by which visual memories of words are directly associated with their meaning being slowest to develop.

Word processing in other languages

English is a language with so-called mixed regularity in the relations between its spellings and its sound, since it contains a good number of irregular words as well as words that follow a regular pattern of spelling–sound translation. The degree of regularity between the written and spoken forms of words, however, varies considerably across different languages. Serbo-Croatian, for example, has an extremely regular relationship between the spelling and the sounds of the

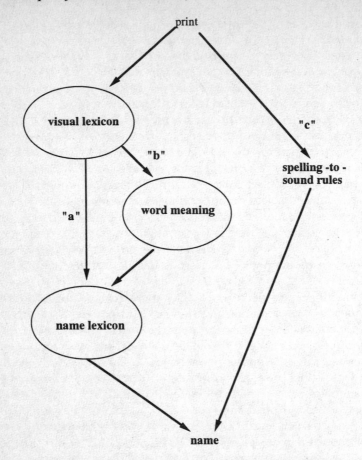

Figure 2.1 *A framework illustrating possible relations between different processes in going from print to sound*
Note: Route 'a' involves visual recognition of the printed word (by matching the word to a stored item in the visual lexicon), and association of the written form of the word 'directly' with the spoken form. Route 'b' involves retrieving the meaning of the word after recognizing its visual form, and then retrieving the name from the meaning. Route 'c' involves a set of 'non-lexical' procedures for associating the spelling of the word to its sound, without visual recognition of the word.

words, whilst Chinese has an opaque relationship, since the written forms of Chinese words were originally derived from pictures which bear no systematic relationship between their form and their name. A language such as Japanese encompasses both extremes via its use of two different spelling systems. Kana is a very regular spelling system, in which symbols have an exact association with a sound. On the other hand Kanji is a highly irregular script, which evolved originally from Chinese. These differences in the ways in which the relations between spellings and sounds are realized in different languages raise the question of whether the mental 'architecture' of the reading system varies across languages. Do languages with regular spelling–sound relationships rely solely on a non-lexical reading procedure, and languages with highly irregular relationships rely solely on recognizing the meaning of words by association with their written form? Do readers of different languages develop reading systems with different architectures?

Recent work on this topic indicates that, despite the superficial differences in the relations between spelling and sound, readers of different languages may still develop similar reading systems. We can illustrate this point with reference to work on Japanese. When skilled Japanese readers are asked to name either familiar Kana words or non-words written in Kana, they are faster to name the familiar words than the non-words (Besner and Hildebrandt, 1987). This lexical advantage for words over non-words resembles that found with English readers (McCann and Besner, 1987; see above), and suggests that the readers are using a lexical procedure for word pronunciation in addition to any non-lexical procedure even though for Japanese Kana there is a highly regular relationship between the spelling and the sound of the stimuli. In addition, studies of the reading of the highly irregular script, Kanji, demonstrate that word meaning is not always derived solely from associations with the written forms. When skilled readers of Kanji are given a category-verification task of the type used in studies of English (A FLOWER? ROSE), they too find it more difficult to reject incorrect homophones of the correct words (ROSE) than matched spelling-control words (ROBS) (Wydell, Patterson and Humphreys, 1993). The difficulty in rejecting homophones fits with the meaning of these symbols sometimes being accessed from their sounds, though for this script it is likely that the sound was itself accessed by a 'direct lexical' route rather than non-lexically (route 'a' rather than route 'c' in Figure 2.1).

Since these results with the two scripts of Japanese mirror those with English, it appears that the word processing system develops a similar architecture despite the variations across languages.

Dyslexia

A word processing system with an architecture such as that illustrated in Figure 1 might also show a systematic pattern of breakdown if parts of the system are damaged (see Riddoch and Humphreys, this volume), or a systematic pattern of disturbance if some procedures prove difficult to develop for some children. The term *acquired dyslexia* is used to refer to people who were formerly skilled readers but who acquire reading problems after having a brain lesion. Different types of acquired dyslexia can be distinguished, with the pattern of breakdown in accordance with the model of word processing we have suggested.

The term *surface dyslexia* is used to refer to people who have particular difficulties in reading words with irregular spelling–sound correspondences in English. For example, given a word such as BREAD, they might pronounce it as

BREED and say that it means producing offspring (see Patterson, Marshall and Coltheart, 1985). This form of reading error fits the pattern we might expect if reading were dependent solely on the non-lexical spelling–sound translation process, with access to both the meaning and pronunciation of the word based on non-lexically derived phonology. Surface dyslexics can also have difficulties in discriminating pseudohomophones from their parent words, and homophones from one another, because these stimuli are phonologically equivalent.[1]

A contrasting form of acquired dyslexia is termed *phonological dyslexia* (e.g. Funnell, 1983). In phonological dyslexia there appears to be an impairment in using the non-lexical procedure for translating words and non-words into sounds. This is most easily detected by using the task of non-word reading, since words may still be read correctly using the lexical reading process. Phonological dyslexics show severe impairments for reading non-words.

These different forms of acquired dyslexia may also provide models for understanding developmental difficulties in learning to read. For example, difficulties in acquiring adequate procedures for visually based word recognition may lead to the symptoms of surface dyslexia, in which children find it particularly difficult to read irregular words; similarly, difficulties in developing non-lexical procedures will produce symptoms of phonological dyslexia in which non-words are especially difficult (Castles and Coltheart, 1993; Coltheart *et al.*, 1983).

Given that independent lexical and non-lexical reading procedures may normally develop, we might ask whether it is important that children have difficulty with a non-lexical procedure. Does it matter if children fail to read non-words providing they can use a lexical reading procedure to read words? Current evidence says that it does indeed matter. For example, whether children have phonological abilities that enable them to code and manipulate phonological segments in words is a strong predictor of reading success (in fact it is a stronger predictor than age or general intelligence; Goswami and Bryant, 1990). Also, at the time that children acquire phonological segmentation skills they start to make errors that suggest that they are developing a visual memory system for words that can operate in a flexible way, enabling words to be recognized from spelling segments (Stuart and Coltheart, 1988). Thus phonological skills can be important for developing visual procedures in reading, so that the development of a non-lexical, phonological reading process may be crucial also in the development of a visual-lexical reading process.

Eye movements and reading

If you watch someone reading a passage from a book, you will notice that their eyes do not make a series of smooth movements but rather a series of short jumps (*saccades*) followed by static *fixations*. Little visual information is processed during each saccade, so that during each fixation we must process the information leading to word recognition as well as processing any information about the forthcoming text.

By measuring the average length of saccades and the time taken to fixate during reading, experimenters have learnt a good deal about the factors determining eye movements during reading. For example, skilled readers of English are disrupted if fewer than about 15 letters are available to the right of fixation or fewer than five to the left of fixation (Rayner and Pollatsek, 1987). This indicates that we use the ('parafoveal') information away from the exact location where we fixate either to help guide future fixations or to extract some information about the forthcoming text to facilitate future word recognition. Interestingly, the greater use of information to the right of fixation is not an inbuilt feature of the visual system. Skilled readers of Hebrew, which is read from right-to-left rather than left-to-right as English, show an opposite asymmetry, using information further to the left than the right. Also, the magnitude of this asymmetry increases in readers of English as their reading improves (see Rayner and Pollatsek, 1987, for a review). Thus we learn to use information about the forthcoming text to help our reading.

What kinds of information are used from the parafovea during reading? A fascinating experiment by McConkie and Zola in 1979 addressed this issue. They asked subjects to read through texts in which the words were printed in MiXeD cAsE. Every time that an eye movement was made from one part of the text to the next, the experimenters changed the displays so that letters that were originally in lower case then appeared in upper case, and vice versa (e.g. MiXeD cAsE became mIxEd CaSe). Their surprising result was that this apparently gross change in the visual properties of the displays had absolutely no effect whatsoever on either the mean length of each saccade (the number of letters between fixations) or the mean fixation times. In fact, the subjects reported that they failed even to notice that any changes to the appearance of the text occurred during the experiment (note that case changes took place during each saccade, when visibility is greatly decreased). This finding indicates that the information extracted from the parafovea during reading must be coded in a relatively abstract way, so that changing the actual appearance of the letters makes little difference; for instance, readers may encode the identities of upcoming letters but not their physical shape. The result also suggests that visual word recognition in skilled readers may be based just on the identities of the letters rather than on the overall shape of the word (which was of course changed between each fixation).

Context effects during reading

During reading we are obviously doing more than processing each word at a time, and using information about forthcoming words on the page to influence future word recognition; we are also trying to understand the meaning of each word, of the sentence and of the text as a whole. Studies have examined how word processing is affected by the context in which words appear using so-called priming procedures, in which experimenters examine how the efficiency of responding to a target word is affected by a preceding 'prime' word.

Meyer and Schvaneveldt in 1971 first showed that the efficiency of word recognition could be improved if a target word followed a prime word that was semantically related to it. For instance, the time taken to decide whether a target such as DOCTOR is a word is reduced if the target is preceded by a related word such as NURSE relative to an unrelated word such as TABLE. This 'semantic priming' effect has since been replicated on numerous occasions, under many different circumstances. Early accounts were built around the view that word recognition involved the activation of the stored visual representation of the word in the mental lexicon. Semantic priming might then occur because the prime 'pre-activated' the representations of related targets, so that less activation was required for the target to be recognized when it occurred subsequently. Such an effect might occur if activation spreads automatically from one representation in the lexicon to the representations of other related items. Subsequent work has clouded this simple account, however. In particular, it is now clear that some priming effects are based on specific expectations that readers develop about forthcoming words, and such effects are not based solely on the existence of previously learned semantic relationships between primes and targets (see Neely, 1991). One way of distinguishing automatic context effects from those based on specific expectations is to vary the times between the context and the target word; automatic effects occur rapidly, while effects dependent on expectations require longer time periods for the expectations to develop. In addition, while automatic spreading activation facilitates the identification of related words, expectations can produce both benefits and costs on performance – benefits when the expectation is correct but costs when the expectation is violated by the target word. When such violations occur, people are actually slower to read words than if no context had been given.

Research by Stanovich and West (1981) also indicated that priming effects on word identification are found when people read sentences as well as when they respond to word pairs. Responses to words at the ends of sentences are facilitated if the sentence contains words that are semantically related to the targets. Depending upon the speed of reading, these effects may be either automatic or influenced by expectations generated from the sentential context. Which kind of context effect occurs during the reading of sentences also seems to vary as a function of reading skill. West and Stanovich (1978) found that the context effects shown by skilled readers seemed to occur automatically, whilst those shown by less skilled readers were based on specific expectations generated from the preceding context. For example, only less skilled readers showed slowed naming times to words when they were preceded by an incorrect context relative to when they were preceded by a 'neutral' context (the word 'the'). This result suggests that, during reading, less skilled readers may be slowed by generating incorrect expectations, a factor that ought to be considered when designing passages for children's reading books.

We now move from considering processes that seem specific to reading, involving word recognition in isolation and in context, to the more general processes involved in understanding texts, which may be common to language processes in general and not just confined to reading.

Reading for understanding

Consider the following example sentences:

1. An important difference between the body chemistry of seawater fishes and their freshwater relatives is caused simply by the difference of salt concentration, and hence density, between seawater and freshwater. (Cox, G.F. *Tropical Marine Aquaria*, 1971)

2. Messages slipping out from the usual political sources this week have John Patten second only to Norman Lamont on the hit-lists of colleagues and commentators searching for scapegoats for last week's disasters. (*TES* Editorial 14 May 1993)

3. The table was arranged neatly with spaces between each group.

All the words in example 1 will be familiar to competent readers but to understand the author's biological idea it is necessary to recognize the correct meanings of the individual words and how they are related to each other. Example 2 also contains a set of recognizably familiar words but if the people and events which are mentioned were unfamiliar to some readers then their understanding of the sentence would be limited by their knowledge of the topic. Example 3 is shorter than either 1 or 2 but more difficult to understand than even 2. Is 'the table' one that is laid for a meal or a conference, or is it a set of data laid out in columns and rows? The question cannot be answered without additional information and it seems that the correct meaning of the word will depend on its context.

These examples suggest that reading a piece of text involves more than recovering the meaning of individual words, and more than being able to pronounce the words correctly – the topics we have considered hitherto: it involves discovering the message of the passage and understanding its content. If asked, after a lapse of time, what they remember about something they read previously, people will provide a summary of the ideas, what seemed to them to be the gist or the essential message of the text, and only rarely will they produce a verbatim recall. Authors seeking to convey their ideas must use the tools of language, that is, the words (lexical items) and the rules by which they are combined and ordered (the syntax of the language). Readers must apply their cognitive tools to analysing the elements of a text and derive a mental representation of the meaning (the semantics) of the text as a whole.

Linguistic structures, syntax

Do readers make use of the ways in which sentences are structured? Consider examples 4 (a) and (b):

4. (a) That that is is not that that is not is that it it is.
    (b) Mary where Jane had had had had had had had had had had had the teacher's approval.

These sentences are undoubtedly difficult to understand and in the case of (b) it is hard to keep track of the number of times the word 'had' appears. Nevertheless both strings can be parsed, that is the words can be grouped into sub-units or phrases which, when marked by punctuation, result in the following:

(a) *That that is, is not that that is not. Is that it? It is.*
(b) Here it is helpful to imagine that Mary and Jane have taken a test in English grammar and their answers are being compared, so we get:
    Mary, where Jane had had 'had', had had 'had had'; 'had had' had had the teacher's approval.

Thus it is possible even in these rather unusual cases to discover that the words are grouped into phrases within the sentences. Once the groups are identified the meanings of the sentences become clear because the groups have been organized in a way that complies with the grammatical rules of the English language, and as experienced users of the language we are knowledgeable about those rules even though we might not be able to state them precisely. Furthermore, as a consequence of that knowledge, we have no difficulty in judging that the two examples 5 and 6, although appearing to be similar, have very different meanings.

5. Peter said that the apple was not ripe.

6. Peter did not say that the apple was ripe.

People will also be very confident that while example 7 is a proper and meaningful sentence, 8 is not.

7. The black cat climbed the apple tree.

8. The cat black tree the apple climbed.

Example 8 demonstrates that the order in which certain types of words are placed in a sentence is important in English and the order, which here is subject–verb–object (actor–action–object) allows us to recognize the particular relations between the different people or objects mentioned. Thus:

9. parents hug children

without doubt describes what parents do to children, whereas

10. children hug parents

depicts children carrying out the activity.

There are other rules of sentence construction, such as agreement of number and tense, that help us to understand what we read. For instance, consider:

11. Jacob chased the cat: (a) it jumped over the fence;
                      (b) she jumped over the fence;
                      (c) he jumped over the fence.

Whereas in (a) and (b) we can discover who jumped over the fence, (c) is ambiguous unless we know already that the cat is not a male. Readers are not helped if the rules are ignored as in 12.

12. The students went to the cinema with their friends. They liked the film.

It is crucial that, in order to comprehend sentences, the correct meaning can be identified fairly easily because under normal circumstances people do not recall the exact wording of a passage of prose, but rather what they believed was its content or meaning. This was demonstrated by Sachs (1967) in an experiment where even after a fairly short time people could remember the meanings but not the exact forms in which particular sentences had been written. It should be noted that if people read texts with the intention of obtaining ideas or information, probably they have no need to commit the exact sentence forms to long-term memory since one of the very useful characteristics of language is that there are usually a number of different ways in which a particular idea can be expressed. There is indeed evidence that, when reading, people make inferences relating to the 'super-ordinate' goals of the passage, even though such goals are to some extent abstracted from the particular surface form of the text, which can express the same goal in various ways. For example, responses to individual words within a passage are faster if the words are consistent with the general 'super-ordinate' goals of the passage than if they fit with a more local, 'sub-ordinate' goal (e.g. local to the specific clause rather than the whole passage; see Long, Golding and Graesser, 1992). If long-term memory for passages is based in part on such predictions, the surface form of the text will not be well remembered. We should note, however, that this evidence for maintenance of the meaning but not the surface form of the text may reflect the use of procedures that 'tap' long-term memory; as we will show below, there is some evidence that it may be useful to maintain representations of the surface form of sentences in the shorter term.

Lexical ambiguities

Many words in English are lexically ambiguous; the same spelling can convey two different meanings (e.g. ring – as in something worn on the finger or the noise made by a telephone). Humorous sentences can be based on this, as in:

13. Why did the tap run? Because it saw the kitchen sink!

In some cases, the ambiguity operates at the level of the phrase rather than the single word, as in the eye-catching headline:

14. Blue murder in the Tories' heartlands!

Clearly here a blue murder is not literally a murder – the phrase conveys more than the meaning of the component words. Yet even the phrase blue murder is ambiguous, since it can refer either to a piece of skulduggery that someone might have got away with, or to (as in this case) a particularly disastrous by-election result for one British political party.

Much research has examined how sentential contexts constrain the processing of such ambiguous words and phrases: can a context be so biasing that only one meaning of ambiguous words or phrases plays a part in sentence analysis? Recent work on this topic suggests that contexts can bias the processing of words as they are read so that only the contextually appropriate meaning is active (e.g. Tabossi and Zardon, 1993). The second meaning of an ambiguous word or phrase may only become active after some time – if at all (e.g. if the meaning biased by the context is also much more common than the other meaning, then it is possible that only the frequent meaning is activated). Thus, when reading through a passage rapidly, ambiguities at the individual word level may go unnoticed, and may only be detected after an appropriate pause has been inserted. Comedy, as they say, is all in the timing!

Ideas in texts

What precisely is implied when we state that readers obtain ideas or information from texts? How is the content of a sentence or a longer piece of writing expressed by an author and recognized by a reader? Long texts usually contain many ideas, but even single sentences can have more than one. For example, sentence 15 conveys the information that the girls and the boys, as separate groups, played different games but did so simultaneously: at least three ideas.

15. The girls played cricket while the boys played rounders.

If we accept the argument that a particular idea can be expressed in more than one way, even using different words, it follows that we need some way of describing the ideas themselves that does not necessarily tie them to particular words. Contemporary researchers use the terms *proposition* to denote a basic unit of meaning that is expressed linguistically, with every proposition consisting of a *predicate* and one or more *arguments*. Generally, a predicate is identified with the verbal unit in a sentence and the arguments are the concepts related to it. Taking the first part of sentence 11, we can see that this is a statement about two characters, *Jacob* and a *cat* who are linked together in a particular relationship expressed by the verb *chase*. The term proposition then refers to the way in which those elements in the sentence are related to each other which can be expressed formally as:

P (chase, Jacob, cat)

The order of the three components signals that Jacob was the chaser. Predicates and arguments are abstract concepts and therefore not always synonymous with the actual words in a sentence. In this example, neither the tense of the verb nor the definite article is represented, so the proposition could represent: Jacob will, or might, chase a cat.

16. The horses in the stable ate their hay.

Sentence 16 expresses an idea about horses eating their hay, and also about where this happened. Thus there are two propositions, P1 and P2.

P1 (eat, horses, hay)
P2 (Location: in, horses, stable)

These two propositions could be expressed as: The horses ate their hay while they were in the stable.

Long sentences can consist of many propositions which are interrelated and further related to those in other sentences as in:

17. The horses in the stable ate their hay. When they had finished, the stable-boys took them into the yard.

P1 (eat, horses, hay)
P2 (Location: in, horses, stable)
P3 (finished, horses, hay)
P4 (take, stable-boys, horses)
P5 (Location: in, horses, yard)
P6 (When: P3, P4)

This process of analysing sentences according to their propositions provides an objective way of assessing the content. However, do readers use the propositions in a text; do propositions have psychological validity? If propositions that can be identified objectively do indeed coincide with the units of meaning perceived by a reader, then the more propositions there are in a text the longer it should take to read. Kintsch and Keenan (1973) devised sentences which contained equal numbers of words but varying numbers of propositions and found that relative reading times reflected the number of propositions that were recalled. In another study it was found that reading time was proportional to the number of arguments associated with each proposition. The greater the number of arguments the more conceptually complex are the propositions, and the greater the number of propositions the more complex is the text, so it is perhaps not surprising that reading time increases if people try to understand the text. Thus we have a useful means of identifying meaning and quantifying complexity in texts that also appear to have psychological validity.

Kintsch and Keenan suggested that propositions in a well-written text are organized in a network termed the *text base*, and that there is a hierarchical relationship between propositions based on the level of importance that each proposition has to the text as a whole. Within this hierarchical organization, high-level propositions can be retrieved more easily than low-level propositions (which are accessed only after traversing down the hierarchy). In sentence 18, P1 would be a level 1 proposition because it provides the principal theme for the brief piece of text. Research has shown that such a high-level proposition is recalled better than low-level propositions (Kintsch and Keenan, 1973; McKoon, 1977). From this it appears that readers are able to form a mental representation of a text base as sentences are read. From their pattern of recall it can be judged whether readers understood the text base in the way the author intended, and the extent of the misunderstanding can be assessed by comparing the propositions in the recalled accounts with those of the author.

Prior knowledge

At some time most of us will have had the experience of struggling, yet failing, to understand something we are reading, and then being unable to give an account of it, perhaps because the text seems confusing and lacking in coherence or because the words and concepts they represent are unfamiliar. As we saw in example 2, it is often necessary to have prior knowledge of the topic in order to understand what is written, which may be even more obvious in the following sentence:

18. Because gravity bends, or lenses, light (according to Einstein's theory of relativity), dark matter can be discarded when it distorts one's view of luminous matter. (*Scientific American*, 1992)

To understand sentence 18, we require more than an elementary knowledge of physics; we need to be able to be familiar with some of the theoretical concepts mentioned. However, even when there are no obvious references to highly specialized technical knowledge, readers may still report that they cannot understand a piece of prose, nor are they able to recall much of it, as Bransford and Johnson (1972) found in an experiment using a passage of which the following is an extract:

19. The procedure is actually quite simple. First you arrange things into different groups. Of course, one pile may be sufficient depending on how much there is to do. If you have to go somewhere else due to lack of facilities that is the next step, otherwise you are pretty well set. It is important not to overdo things. That is, it is better to do too few things at once than too many.

In contrast, another set of readers, given the same passage but with a title, 'washing clothes', signalling a familiar experience, found the material easy to understand and recall. They could assign specific meanings to words such as *pile* and *facilities* and recognize how the statements interrelate. Without the title, the theme is obscure and the passage seems both abstract and difficult to understand. So, for comprehension to occur, it is not sufficient that readers possess relevant knowledge, it is necessary for that knowledge to be activated to provide a semantic context. It seems that the semantic context has several consequences in reading, affecting overall comprehension as well as the time taken to read individual words (see earlier). The term *schema* is used to denote an organized knowledge (topic) structure, and the term *script* for the knowledge people have about culturally familiar events and situations, such as washing clothes, eating in a restaurant etc. Scripts and schema can provide the frames of reference for making sense of texts, and the presence of a title will stimulate the use of specific schemata through which the meanings of words and phrases will be determined. The use of inappropriate schemata may lead to misunderstanding, and an absence of relevant schemata (no knowledge) will result in an almost total lack of understanding.

When readers draw on their schemata they are able to elaborate and embellish for themselves an author's statements and the outcome can be seen in their accounts of material as they recall it. For example, in a now classic study, Bartlett (1932) showed that, where people did not have the appropriate schema for a passage, their recall was not only poor but it might contain details that were not in the original text.

Schemata also provoke readers to predict further sequences; for example, if we read:

20. Jim fell off the ladder and . . .

we would expect Jim to be hurt, perhaps seriously; we would not expect him to jump about, singing and dancing. Miller (1980) found that people's reading rate was fastest when their expectations of what they would read was confirmed. It seems that expectations based on schemata help to attribute meanings to words and make the text comprehensible. Using the concept of schemata enables us to explain how some readers with specialized knowledge (schemata) are able to understand and remember texts such as sentence 18 that other readers have great difficulty with.

Coherence in texts

Despite having relevant knowledge and being able to recognize the concepts in a text, the text may still be difficult to understand because it seems poorly organized and without clear links between the components. Haviland and Clark (1974) argued that a sentence is best understood in the context of the sentences that immediately precede it. Haviland and Clark used two pairs of sentences, such as:

21. John left the beer in the case. The beer was too warm to drink.

22. John left the picnic supplies in the car. The beer was too warm to drink.

In sentence 21 there is repetition of *the beer* so that the meaning of the second sentence is unambiguous whereas in 22 it is necessary to assume that *the beer* was among the *picnic supplies* and it was found that people took longer to register comprehension of the second pair than the first pair of sentences. Lesgold, Ruth and Curtis (1979) found that sentences are easier to integrate meaningfully when the sentences occur near or together and are not separated by irrelevant material. So 23 is easy to understand, 24 also, but 25 much less so.

23. A thick cloud of smoke hung over the forest. The forest was on fire.

24. A thick cloud of smoke hung over the forest. The smoke was thick and black, and began to fill the clear sky. Up ahead Carol could see a ranger directing traffic to slow down. The forest was on fire.

25. A thick cloud of smoke hung over the forest. Glancing to one side, Carol could see a bee flying around the back seat. Both of the kids were jumping around but made no attempt to free the insect. The forest was on fire.

Although the importance of possessing relevant knowledge for understanding a text has been stressed, the motive of many readers is to add to their existing knowledge, to gain more information or to be able to think about things in a fresh way. Research has shown that that endeavour is helped by strategies that give coherence to written texts thereby assisting readers to distinguish the old or given from the new information. Examine sentence 26:

26. It was her grandmother who brought Jane home.

We recognize two main elements: that Jane was brought home (the *given* information) and that the person who did so was her grandmother (the *new* information). The same given-new elements can be distinguished in other ways:

27. The person who brought Jane home was her grandmother.

28. Jane was brought home by her grandmother.

In sentence 16 a propositional analysis identified the linkages between the ideas in a text. Therefore linguistic processes that assist readers in sorting out the given from the new propositions are not only going to facilitate the reader's understanding of a text but are also going to help the integration of new and old information.

Inferences

In discussing the role of schemata in understanding it was suggested that readers elaborate or add to the information that is presented by the author by reference to stored schemata concerning particular events and actions. If we take example 22, a connection between the two sentences can be made if we know enough about picnics to be able to assume that it is possible that some people will take beer on picnics. Thus an unstated link becomes one that is made by the reader who is encouraged to do so by the close positioning of the two sentences. This type of link is known as an *inference* of which there are two principal types, logical and pragmatic.

Logical inferences depend on our knowledge of certain rules. For example:

29. When Ruth took six plates from the cupboard she dropped two.

We infer that Ruth continued to hold four plates and there is no other possibility.

Pragmatic inferences on the other hand rely on our general knowledge but have an element of probability. For example;

34. Ruth dropped two plates.

We might infer that one or both or neither broke, depending on what other information we might have about the circumstances. If the sentence was followed by

35. She fetched a brush to sweep up the plates.

we would infer that both plates broke despite the author not having stated it explicitly. Authors indeed assume that readers will engage in inferencing and therefore will write explicitly only what they believe to be essential to enable readers to understand the text. If it is important that readers obtain very specific information from a text then it must be written in a way that prompts only the correct inferences.

Types of text

In a literate culture, people read a wide variety of texts, including novels, newspapers, instruction manuals, research reports, textbooks and poetry, and they will have different reasons for reading each. Even a cursory examination of examples of the different types (genres) reveals variations in presentation and overall structure. Most research has focused on narrative stories which are written not merely for entertainment but often as vehicles for presenting information, such as in school textbooks and advertisements. Thorndyke (1977) demonstrated that events in narratives are organized into a structure that can be represented by a setting, a theme, a plot and a resolution, with the principal characters having goals to achieve. It is suggested that readers possess a schema for stories that guides them through and assists their understanding of the sequence of events, and that this schema operates in parallel with schemata for specific events and types of characters that help readers to understand particular incidents.

Researchers have also attempted to apply a schema analysis to non-narrative texts, often called expository because their objectives are to expose topics. Miller (1985) suggested that although such texts vary greatly, schemata for causes, plans and goals have wide relevance. Particular genres appear to have a common structure that assists people in reading them; research reports and instruction manuals are examples (Kintsch and van Dijk, 1978; Thorndyke, 1979).

On the maintenance of surface representations

We have noted that people are notoriously bad at remembering the exact surface form of passages over the longer term. However, we should not take such a finding to indicate that surface forms of sentences are never maintained. In particular, one use of surface representations may be to help the reader go back and re-process material that was difficult to interpret on 'first pass'. For example, people with poor ability to maintain verbal information over the short term (e.g. perhaps due to their having had a specific brain lesion) are often very impaired at interpreting long sentences in which the meaning of the sentence is dependent on the word order (e.g. see Vallar and Shallice, 1992). For example, in order to understand and carry out an action appropriate to a sentence such as:

36. With the pencil touch the pen

it is crucial that word order be taken into account – since the act of touching the pen with the pencil is reversible (i.e. it is possible to touch a pencil with a pen) it is not sufficient to base interpretation of the sentence on known likelihood of events in the world irrespective of the word order (note that this is possible with a non-reversible sentence such as 'with the pencil touch the building'). People with poor short-term verbal memories may often encounter problems with understanding such reversible sentences, particularly if the sentences are 'padded out' so that the number of words exceeds short-term memory capacity, as in 37.

37. With the long striped pencil that was bought in the shop around the corner gently touch the green fountain pen.

Results such as this suggest that a short-term memory representation may be useful for a form of mental re-check, either when a sentence may require re-analysing if the original interpretation turns out to be wrong or when it is important to maintain word order to interpret the sentence correctly. The short-term representation that seems to act as a 'back up' system for re-interpreting sentences also seems specifically to be verbal in nature. It can be extremely difficult to understand syntactically complex sentences when verbal short-term memory is occupied by a second task or by having to recite an irrelevant phrase (try to parse example 4 (b) whilst reciting the word 'the' over to yourself – a very difficult task!) (see Baddeley, 1986). This may also be one reason why sentences such as 38 are difficult to comprehend:

38. Willing swallows wallow willy-nilly in the wily willows.

Example 38 contains words that are phonologically similar to one another. It is well known that verbal short-term memory is poor for stimuli that are phonologically similar, presumably because such stimuli interfere with one another within the verbal short-term memory system (Baddeley, 1986). When phonologically similar words are used in a sentence, it may be difficult to 'backtrack' using a verbal short-term memory representation, making comprehension difficult.

Thus, though long-term memory representations appear to be based on the meaning or semantics of the passage, verbal short-term memory representations also appear to be used and they can help us disambiguate passages that we do not interpret perfectly first time through. Note that this verbal representation is used even though the words remain written on the page, suggesting that this aspect of reading at least remains close to the processes involved in interpreting spoken language; presumably dependence on a verbal short-term memory system is highly over-learned and involved in re-checking the meaning of spoken passages.

This brings us back to where we began in the recoding of single written words, that is the issue of the relations between spoken and written language processing. On that issue we earlier presented evidence that procedures specific to the processing of written forms of words develop and seem important for skilled reading (e.g. for the identification of words with irregular correspondences between their spellings and their sound, which must be recognized visually in order for the correct pronunciation to be retrieved). We close the chapter by remarking on one other visual ability that also seems important for reading, but one which may serve in helping the re-interpretation of sentences – the maintenance of a visual representation of the positions of words in the text. Kennedy and Murray (1987) reported that skilled readers were remarkably accurate at making 'regressive' saccades back to parts of a text that contain relevant information which may help resolve ambiguities in interpreting the meaning of words later in a passage, and that the accuracy of subsequent re-fixations did not vary as a function of the length of the regressive saccade. Such a result suggests that skilled reading depends on the maintenance of short-term visual as well as short-term verbal representations. The study of reading clearly illustrates the various forms of interaction that can exist between vision and language, and it is important for understanding both.

The theoretical studies of reading also indicate practical consequences concerning reading development in both normal readers and dyslexic children. For instance, we have already noted that it seems very important in the first stages of reading for children to develop good non-lexical reading procedures, since such procedures will both help them deal with new words and (apparently) help in the laying-down of the visual (lexical) reading process (Stuart and Coltheart, 1988). As far as dyslexic children are concerned, the work highlights the importance of establishing the type of problem they encounter in word reading (e.g. are there problems with a lexical or a non-lexical procedure?), since it is only following this that appropriate rehabilitation strategies can be initiated. Having a good theoretical account of how we process written language is vital for developing good teaching and remediation procedures.

Notes

1. It should be noted, however, that some surface dyslexics do understand the meaning of the word from the written form, even though they may mispronounce an irregular word, whilst others show impaired access both to word meaning and to lexically derived phonology. These different patterns can be understood in terms of there being lesions to different parts of the lexical reading process. For instance, impaired access to word meaning could result from a lesion affecting visual memories for words; good access to word meaning along with impaired access to lexical phonology could stem from a lesion affecting the process of going either from visual memories or the meaning of words to the associated names.

Further reading

ELLIS, A.W. (1993) *Reading, Writing and Dyslexia*, London, Erlbaum.

GOSWAMI, U. and BRYANT, P. (1990) *Phonological Skills and Learning to Read*, London, Erlbaum.

HUMPHREYS, G.W. and BRUCE, V. (1989) *Visual Cognition: Computational, Experimental and Neuropsychological Perspectives*, London, Erlbaum, Ch. 7.

SINGER, M. (1990) *Psychology of Language*, London, Erlbaum.

WILLOWS, D.M., KRUK, R.S. and CORCOS, E. (1993) *Visual Processes in Reading and Reading Disabilities*, London, Erlbaum.

References

BADDELEY, A.D. (1986) *Working Memory*, Oxford, Oxford University Press.

BARON, J. (1973) 'Phonemic stage not necessary for reading', *Quarterly Journal of Experimental Psychology, 25*, 241-6.

BARTLETT, F.C. (1932) *Remembering*, Cambridge, Cambridge University Press.

BESNER, D. and HILDEBRANDT, N. (1987) Orthographic and phonological codes in the oral reading of Japanese kana, *Journal of Experimental Psychology: Learning, Memory and Cognition, 13*, 335-43.

BRANSFORD, J.D. and JOHNSON, M.K. (1972) 'Contextual pre-requisites for understanding some investigations of comprehension and recall', *Journal of Verbal Learning and Verbal Behaviour, 11*, 717-26.

CASTLES, A. and COLTHEART, M. (1993) 'Varieties of developmental dyslexia', *Cognition, 47*, 149-80.

COLTHEART, M., MASTERSON, J., BYNG, S., PRIOR, M. and RIDDOCH, M.J. (1983) 'Surface dyslexia', *Quarterly Journal of Experimental Psychology, 37A*, 469-95.

DOCTOR, E. and COLTHEART, M. (1980) 'Children's use of phonological encoding when reading for meaning', *Memory and Cognition, 8*, 195-209.

FUNNELL, E. (1983) 'Phonological processes in reading: new evidence from acquired dyslexia', *British Journal of Psychology, 74*, 159-80.

GOSWAMI, U. and BRYANT, P. (1990) *Phonological Skills and Learning to Read*, London, Erlbaum.

HAVILAND, S.E. and CLARK, H.H. (1974) 'What's new? Acquiring new information as a process in comprehension', *Journal of Verbal Learning and Verbal Behavior, 13*, 512-21.

KENNEDY, A. and MURRAY, W.S. (1987) 'Spatial co-ordinates and reading: comments on Monk (1985)', *Quarterly Journal of Experimental Psychology, 39A*, 649-56.

KINTSCH, W. and KEENAN, J. (1973) 'Reading rate and retention as a function of the number of propositions in the base structure of sentences', *Cognitive Psychology, 5*, 257-74.

KINTSCH, W. and VAN DIJK, T. (1978) 'Toward a model of text comprehension and production', *Psychological Review, 85*, 363-94.

LESGOLD, A., ROTH, S.F. and CURTIS, M.E. (1979) 'Foregrounding effects in discourse comprehension', *Journal of Verbal Learning and Verbal Behavior*, **18**, 291–308.

LONG, D.L., GOLDING, J.M. and GRAESSER, A.C. (1992) 'A test of the on-line status of goal-related inferences', *Journal of Memory and Language*, **31**, 634–47.

McCANN, R.S. and BESNER, D. (1987) 'Reading pseudohomophones: implications for models of pronunciation assembly and the locus of word frequency effects in naming', *Journal of Experimental Psychology: Human Perception and Performance*, **11**, 777–87.

McCONKIE, G.W. and ZOLA, D. (1979) 'Is visual information integrated across successive fixations in reading?', *Perception & Psychophysics*, **17**, 578–86.

McKOON, G. (1977) 'Organization of information in text', *Journal of Verbal Learning and Verbal Behavior*, **16**, 247–60.

MEYER, D.E. and SCHVANEVELDT, R.W. (1971) 'Facilitation in recognizing pairs of words: evidence of a dependence between retrieval operations', *Journal of Experimental Psychology*, **90**, 227–34.

MILLER, J.R. (1980) Reported in SINGER, M. *Psychology of Language*, Hillsdale, NJ, Erlbaum.

MILLER, J.R. (1985) 'A knowledge-based model of prose comprehension: applications to expository texts', in BRITTON, B.K. and BLACK, J.B. (Eds) *Understanding Expository Text: A Theoretical and Practical Handbook for Analyzing Explanatory Text*, Hillsdale, NJ, Erlbaum.

NEELY, J.H. (1991) 'Semantic priming effects in visual word recognition: a selective review of current findings and theories', in BESNER, D. and HUMPHREYS, G.W. (Eds) *Basic Processes in Reading: Visual Word Recognition*, Hillsdale, NJ, Erlbaum.

PATTERSON, K.E., MARSHALL, J.C. and COLTHEART, M. (1985) *Surface Dyslexia: Neuropsychological and Cognitive Studies of Phonological Reading*, London, Erlbaum.

RAYNER, K. and POLLATSEK, A. (1987) 'Eye movements in reading: a tutorial review', in COLTHEART, M. (Ed.) *Attention and Performance XII*, London, Erlbaum.

SACHS, J.S. (1967) 'Recognition memory for syntactic and semantic aspects of connected discourse', *Perception & Psychophysics*, **2**, 437–42.

STANOVICH, K.E. and WEST, R.F. (1981) 'The effect of sentence context on ongoing word recognition: tests of a two-process theory', *Journal of Experimental Psychology: Human Perception and Performance*, **7**, 658–72.

STUART, M. and COLTHEART, M. (1988) 'Does reading develop in a sequence of stages?', *Cognition*, **30**, 139–81.

TABOSSI, P. and ZARDON, F. (1993) 'Processing ambiguous words in context', *Journal of Memory and Language*, **32**, 359–72.

THORNDYKE, P.W. (1977) 'Cognitive structures in comprehension and memory of narrative discourse', *Cognitive Psychology*, **9**, 77–110.

THORNDYKE, P.W. (1979) 'Knowledge acquisition from newspapers and stories', *Discourse Processes*, **2**, 95–112.

VALLAR, G. and SHALLICE, T. (1992) *Neuropsychological Impairments of Short-term Memory*, Cambridge, Cambridge University Press.

VAN ORDEN, G.C. (1987) 'A ROWS is a ROSE: spelling, sound and reading', *Memory and Cognition*, **15**, 181-98.

VAN ORDEN, G.C. (1991) 'Phonologic mediation is fundamental to reading', in BESNER, D. and HUMPHREYS, G.W. (Eds) *Basic Processes in Reading: Visual Word Recognition*, Hillsdale, NJ, Erlbaum.

WEST, R.F. and STANOVICH, K.E. (1978) 'Automatic contextual facilitation in readers of three ages', *Child Development*, **49**, 717-27.

WYDELL, T.N., PATTERSON, K.E. and HUMPHREYS, G.W. (1993) 'Phonologically mediated access to meaning for Kanji: is a ROWS still a ROSE in Japanese Kanji?', *Journal of Experimental Psychology: Learning, Memory and Cognition*, **19**, 491-514.

Chapter 3

Theories of Cognition: Conceptual Knowledge and Problem Solving

Koen Lamberts

Cognitive psychology covers a wide range of issues, which are all somehow related to the way in which people represent and process information. Cognitive psychologists study topics as diverse as memory and learning, visual object recognition, reasoning, decision making, problem solving and so on. Of course, it is impossible even to attempt to give an overview of such a broad discipline in a single chapter. Therefore, I shall focus only on two areas of cognitive psychology. The first area deals with the structure and organization of human knowledge, while the second addresses the way in which people solve problems. The choice of these two topics is not entirely arbitrary. They both have a long tradition, and they have recently witnessed remarkable theoretical developments. Therefore, I will present them as illustrations of cognitive psychologists' continuing attempts to provide scientific explanations of very complex mental phenomena.

The organization of knowledge: concepts and categories

One of the central topics in cognitive psychology concerns the structure and organization of human knowledge. Human beings have the ability to acquire, store and retrieve vast amounts of information. In order to do so, their cognitive system is equipped with a number of mechanisms for organizing and structuring the information that is processed. Among these, the mechanisms that underlie people's ability to form *concepts* are absolutely essential. Concepts are defined here as cognitive representations of categories. People are able to discover and employ a wide variety of patterns and regularities in the continuous flow of information they encounter. Many of these regularities are categorical. We tend to group things together, so we can treat them on the same basis for some purpose. If I know, for instance, that the object in front of me is a member of the *chair* category, I know that it is probably safe to attempt to sit on it. Concepts allow us to predict our environment, and to respond appropriately to new situations.

The study of concepts has a very long history. In western metaphysics and epistemology, issues related to the nature and status of categories and concepts have been studied for more than 25 centuries. It is remarkable, therefore, that research on concepts has only become truly important in psychology since the early 1950s. Probably, the dominance of the behaviourist paradigm in the psychology of the first half of this century is the cause of this relative indifference. A key assumption of behaviourism was that behaviour could be explained scientifically without reference to 'cognitive' constructs (such as knowledge or mental representation). Behaviourists studied the relations between observable stimuli and responses. Of course, research on concepts had no place in their programme.

In the early 1950s, a fundamental change took place with the advent of the information-processing paradigm. Behaviour was now considered as the result of an information-processing sequence, in which people build cognitive representations of their environment and manipulate these representations in order to produce actions. Consequently, the study of the mental processes that link stimuli and responses became essential, and cognitive psychologists soon took up the study of concepts.

Despite its relatively short history, the psychological study of concepts has gone through some major theoretical changes. Three thoroughly different views on the fundamental nature of concepts have dominated the field. These views can be called the Classical view, the Prototype view and the Exemplar view (cf. Eysenck and Keane, 1990; Medin and Smith, 1984; Smith and Medin, 1981).

The classical view

As the name suggests, the Classical view of concepts has a long tradition in psychology. According to this view, concepts are characterized by a list of defining attributes. For instance, the concept *BIRD* would consist of attributes like *has feathers*, *has wings*, *lays eggs* and so on. These attributes are considered as the true building blocks of concepts. When people have to verify category membership of an object (that is, when they have to decide whether the object belongs to a particular category), they will compare the object's attributes with those of the concept. If the object possesses all the defining attributes of the concept, it is assigned to the category represented by the concept; otherwise, the conclusion is that the object is not a member of the category.

This view has some important implications for the nature of concepts. First, it implies that the boundaries between categories are rigid and well defined. By applying the definition of a concept, it is possible to decide unambiguously whether an entity belongs to it or not. Second, the Classical view also implies that all members of a category are equally representative. There are no 'better' or 'worse' examples of a concept. Third, the Classical view naturally leads to the assumption that concepts are hierarchically structured. This means that the defining attributes of more general concepts (e.g. *ANIMAL*) are inherited by subordinate, more specific concepts (e.g. *DOG*). So, if an *ANIMAL can breathe* and *has a skin*, this is also true of a *DOG*. Finally, the Classical view has implications for the way in which people are assumed to acquire concepts. If concepts essentially consist of lists of defining characteristics, the central task in concept formation is finding these characteristics. In an important series of experiments, Bruner *et al.* (1956) studied the strategies that people use to discover defining attributes of artificial concepts. The stimuli in their study were a number of cards, such as the examples shown in Figure 3.1.

The cards differed on a number of dimensions, such as *shape* (circle, square or cross), *number* of objects on the card (one, two or three), and *colour* (green, red or black). On the basis of these dimensions, concepts were defined by the experimenter. These concepts had the form of a simple rule. Only the cards that corresponded to the rule were in the concept. Concept rules could be simple (*CIRCLE*), conjunctive (*BLACK AND SQUARE*) or disjunctive (*TWO OBJECTS OR CROSS*).

The subjects' task was to discover the rule the experimenter had in mind. Typically, the subjects were shown a series of cards, and were asked to indicate for each card whether they thought that card was in the concept or not. The experimenter immediately gave feedback about the correctness of their response. For this and similar tasks, Bruner *et al.* documented a number of strategies used by the subjects. One common strategy was called the 'wholist' strategy, and it is most easily explained by an example. Suppose the concept was *BLACK AND SQUARE*, and the first card shown was as depicted in Figure 3.2.

Because this was the first card, the subject could only guess whether or not it belonged to the concept. Assume the subject guessed 'Yes', and that the experimenter confirmed that this was a correct response. In the wholist strategy, the subject would now take all the features of this positive instance as a hypothesis about the concept. So, the subject's hypothesis at this point would be 'Two Black Squares'. The next card presented was as shown in Figure 3.3.

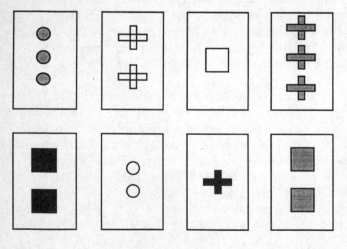

Figure 3.1 *Example of cards used in* **Bruner** et al.*'s (1956) experiments*

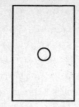

Figure 3.2 *The first card shown*

Figure 3.3 *The second card shown*

Figure 3.4 *The third card shown*

This card did not correspond to the hypothesis. The subject therefore responded 'No', which was also correct. There was no need to revise the hypothesis. The third card was as illustrated in Figure 3.4. Again, this card did not fit the hypothesis, so the response was 'No'. However, this response was wrong; the card was a member of the concept. The subject would now modify the hypothesis such that it would include only those elements that the old hypothesis and the last positive instance had in common, namely 'Black Square' (which happens to be the concept). This strategy is very easy to apply, because the subjects only need to remember the current hypothesis.

Despite its intuitive appeal, the Classical view of concepts has been severely criticized (see, for instance, Medin, 1989; Smith and Medin, 1981). First, the Classical view's core assumption, which states that concepts consist of defining features, is probably fundamentally wrong. For many concepts, it is virtually impossible to determine what the defining features might be. Try, for instance, to list defining features for *FURNITURE* or *VEGETABLE*. Wittgenstein (1958) gave the notorious example of 'game'. Probably, there is no single attribute or combination of attributes that all games have in common, and that would enable unambiguous distinction between games and non-games. However, the fact that defining attributes are hard to find for many concepts does not imply that people are completely unable to use concepts that have clear definitions. Indeed, Bruner *et al.*'s (1956) experiments demonstrate that such concepts are handled very well, and that people can apply efficient strategies to acquire them. The stimuli and the task in Bruner *et al.*'s experiments, however, are rather different from the natural settings in which concepts are formed. Many real-life concepts are acquired without immediate and perfectly reliable feedback. Moreover, it is not always obvious that a simple rule is there to be discovered in the first place. Therefore, the results from the Bruner *et al.* study may only apply to a very limited sub-set of concepts. Most concepts appear to have a structure that is fundamentally different from rule-like definitions.

A second problem with the Classical view is that the boundaries between categories are not always clear at all. This follows directly from the first problem. If there are no defining features, there is no simple rule that can be used to determine unequivocally whether an entity belongs to a given category or not. For instance, is a barstool a chair? A number of experimental results indicate that category representations are not as stable as the Classical view suggests. Subjects tend to disagree among each other about the category membership of certain entities. For instance, some but not all subjects classify bookends as furniture (McCloskey and Glucksberg, 1978). Moreover, people's category judgments are not stable over time, and can vary from one experimental session to another (cf. Barsalou, 1987; Barsalou and Medin, 1986). If defining attributes would underlie categorization, such instability should not occur.

Finally, the Classical view seems wrong in assuming that all concept members are equally representative. People can order the instances of many categories in terms of their 'typicality' or 'representativeness' (e.g. Mervis *et al.*, 1976). Moreover, these typicality judgments are usually quite stable, and agreement among subjects tends to be high. So, most people would rate an *apple* or a *pear* as more typical instances of the *FRUIT* category than a *coconut* or an *olive*. Such typicality differences are important, because they are related to the efficiency of categorization. Typical instances are categorized faster and more accurately, for instance (Smith *et al.*, 1974).

These shortcomings of the Classical view have led to the development of a number of alternative theories about the fundamental nature of concepts and categorization. As noted earlier, these alternative views can be divided roughly into two classes: prototype views and exemplar views.

The prototype view

In prototype theories, the idea that defining features form the basis of concepts is abandoned. Instead, it is assumed that concepts are organized around an abstract representation, which is called a prototype. The notion of a prototype has been defined in a number of different ways, but usually it corresponds to an abstract, summary representation of the central tendency of the category. The prototype for *BIRD*, for instance, would contain a number of attributes that are characteristic for birds, such as *has feathers*, *can sing*, *lays eggs* and so on. As such, a prototype summarizes attributes that tend to occur in the instances of the category. An important difference from the Classical view is that these attributes are no longer considered as defining. Instead, they are characteristic or representative only. So, although most birds will have at least some of the properties outlined above, it is not strictly necessary that they have all these properties. An *ostrich* or a *penguin*, for instance, is a member of the *BIRD* category, although it doesn't fly. The attributes of a prototype are therefore not used as the basis of clear-cut decision rules. In a prototype view, categorization is usually considered as a probabilistic process, in which the decision whether or not an instance belongs to a given category depends on the similarity of that instance to the prototype of the category.

The prototype view solves most problems encountered by the Classical view. In a prototype view, the boundaries between categories are fuzzy (Rosch,

1973) and not absolute. As a consequence, unclear cases are handled naturally. A *television* can well be considered as *FURNITURE*, because it has several attributes in common with the prototype of that category: it is usually found inside people's houses, can be decorative, and one can put a vase or a lamp on top. On the other hand, a *television* also differs from the prototypical *FURNI-TURE* on a number of other dimensions. It requires electricity to operate, it has buttons and switches, it usually doesn't stand on the floor, and so on. Whether or not a *television* is classified as *FURNITURE* will ultimately depend on the relative weight that is assigned to the different dimensions. If the focus is primarily on the fact that televisions are usually found in living rooms or bedrooms, the conclusion that a television is furniture is relatively straightforward. If more weight is assigned to other dimensions, a different conclusion may well be reached. In this manner, a prototype view allows for context dependency of categorizations, and can thus explain the instability of concepts between and within subjects. The prototype view also handles typicality effects very naturally. In most prototype theories, typicality is assumed to depend on the similarity of an instance to a category prototype. For instance, a *sparrow* (which is usually rated as a highly typical bird) will be more similar to the prototypical *BIRD* than a *penguin*.

The Prototype view leads to a perspective on concept acquisition that is thoroughly different from the Classical view. Instead of systematically searching for defining features, prototype theories assert that people form concepts through a process of abstraction. Through repeated encounters with instances of a category, the characteristic features of these instances will be retained in memory, and eventually form a prototype. Prototype theories differ in their assumptions about the nature of this abstraction process. Some argue that it involves an active search for characteristic features, while others claim that it is a fairly automatic side-product of repeated contact with category members.

The exemplar view

The third (and most recent) view on concepts is the exemplar view (Medin and Schaffer, 1978; Nosofsky, 1986). This view differs fundamentally from the Classical view and the Prototype view, because it relies on the assumption that concepts are not built on any sort of summary representation whatsoever. Instead, this view holds that a concept simply consists of a list of instances. For instance, the concept *BIRD* would be equated with a collection of exemplars, which would include (at least in principle) all birds that have been encountered so far. As such, the concept is not represented by defining attributes (as in the Classical view) or by characteristic attributes (as in the Prototype view).

A direct consequence of this view on concepts is that the process of categorization is assumed to involve comparisons between the instance that is to be categorized on the one hand, and the exemplars stored in memory on the other hand. In most exemplar theories, these comparisons involve computations of similarity between the instance and the stored exemplars. The probability that an instance is assigned to a given category depends on the summed similarity of that instance to all the category members.

As an illustration of the principles of exemplar models, let us assume that we are in a situation where we have to determine whether a given object is a *TABLE* or a *CHAIR*. Further assume that all the objects we consider have four dimensions only, and that all these dimensions are binary (which means that they can take only one of two values, which are coded here as 0 and 1). The first dimension refers to the material the object is made of. It can have the values wood (0) or metal (1). The second dimension is the shape of the top surface: round (0) or square (1). The third dimension is colour (white, 0, or black, 1), and the fourth dimension is weight (light, 0, or heavy, 1). Given these dimensions, an object can be represented by a string of 4 binary numbers. For instance, the code 0010 refers to a wooden object that is round, black and light. Now assume that a person has encountered eight objects, four of which were *TABLES* and four of which were *CHAIRS*. According to exemplar theories, these eight objects would be stored in memory. If we use the codes, the relevant part of that person's memory could be represented as shown in Table 3.1.

Now, assume that an object coded as *1000* is presented, and that the subject has to decide whether this object is a *TABLE* or a *CHAIR*. Before we can compare this object to the stored exemplars, we need to define what we understand by 'similarity'. A simple, but useful definition of similarity could be the following:

$$\text{Similarity} = \frac{\text{number of common features}}{\text{number of dimensions}}$$

According to this definition, the similarity of two objects depends on the number of dimensions on which the objects have the same value. For instance, *0011* and *0110* have two features in common, so their similarity will be 0.5. An exemplar model would compute the probability that an object x is classified as a *TABLE* as follows:

Table 3.1 *Example of exemplar memory: four tables and four chairs are stored in memory*

Tables				Chairs			
Material	Shape	Colour	Weight	Material	Shape	Colour	Weight
0	1	1	0	0	1	0	0
0	1	0	1	1	0	0	1
1	0	1	1	1	0	1	0
0	0	1	1	1	1	1	0

Note: The meaning of the binary codes is explained in the text.

$$\text{Prob}\,(x \text{ is a TABLE}) = \frac{\sum_{i}[\text{similarity}\,(x, \text{table}_i)]}{\sum_{i}[\text{similarity}\,(x, \text{table}_i)] + \sum_{j}[\text{similarity}\,(x, \text{chair}_j)]}$$

So, this probability corresponds to the summed similarity of object x to all exemplars of the *TABLE* category, divided by the summed similarity of x to all exemplars stored in memory. Applied to stimulus 1000, this formula yields

$$\frac{0.25 + 0.25 + 0.5 + 0.25}{(0.25 + 0.25 + 0.5 + 0.25) + (0.5 + 0.75 + 0.75 + 0.5)} = 0.333$$

The probability that *1000* will be categorized as a *TABLE* is therefore 0.333, or one in three. Two times out of three, the object will be classified as a *CHAIR*, because it is more similar, overall, to the *CHAIR* exemplars than to the *TABLE* exemplars.

Intuitively, exemplar models may seem rather implausible. We certainly don't have the experience that we remember every single object or event we encounter, and that we classify new objects or events by computing similarities to instances we know. However, such subjective impressions can be very misleading. The exemplar view does not imply, for instance, that people should be able to recall or retrieve every single instance in memory. It merely states that instances leave traces in memory, and that these traces are accessed in categorization; no claims are made about whether access to stored exemplars is a conscious process or not. Analogously, similarity computations might be carried out unconsciously, in a highly parallel and extremely fast manner.

Confronted with empirical data, exemplar theories of categorization have been remarkably successful. They can account accurately for people's classifications across a wide range of stimuli and tasks. The exemplar view can handle unclear cases and conceptual instability through its assumptions about the probabilistic nature of categorization. In addition, differential weighting of dimensions provides a mechanism by which classification becomes task or context dependent. Typicality effects are also easily accommodated. The most typical instances of a category will be those that are generally most similar to the category exemplars in memory. A *canary* is a more typical *BIRD* than a *penguin*, because it has more features in common with the *BIRD* exemplars in memory than a *penguin* does.

Much empirical research has been devoted to distinguishing between the prototype view and the exemplar view. This is not an easy task at all, because prototype and exemplar models can lead to very similar predictions. For various reasons, it might even be impossible in principle to determine which account is superior (Barsalou, 1990).

Recently, the prototype view and the exemplar view have been criticized, because they rely so heavily on the concept of similarity. Similarity is a rather problematic notion, because it so unconstrained (cf. Goodman, 1972). An apple and a dog, for instance, are similar in an infinite number of ways. They are both smaller than a car, they can't fly, they don't sing and so on; the list never ends. This implies that things can be made as similar to each other as one would like, or even that all things are equally similar to all other things. In order to evaluate similarity in a meaningful way, it is absolutely necessary to specify which dimensions are involved. Put differently, similarity can only be judged with respect to certain properties (cf. Medin *et al.*, 1993). It has been argued that one of the central issues in categorization has been overlooked by prototype and exemplar models, because they don't explain how the relevant dimensions for similarity judgments are selected. Several authors have proposed that this selection depends on people's background theories about the conceptual domain (e.g., Murphy and Medin, 1985). These theories can impose essential constraints on similarity, because they can provide a justification for the inclusion or exclusion of certain properties.

To conclude this discussion of concepts and categories, it is perhaps useful to note that theory development in this area has proceeded along a path that is not untypical for cognitive psychology in general. The earliest theories of concepts (based on the Classical view) were very close to our intuitive, pre-scientific ideas about the organization of knowledge. Careful empirical work has shown that these ideas were wrong, and has led to the development of theories that show little resemblance to common-sense explanations.

Problem solving

Problem solving is a central aspect of everyday life. Informally, one can say that a problem arises whenever somebody wants to achieve a certain goal, while it is not immediately obvious how this goal could be attained, or while direct access to the goal is somehow prevented or restricted. Problem solving is essentially the process of finding a way to reach a goal. Typically, solving a problem involves two successive stages. First, a mental representation of the problem needs to be constructed. Next, the cognitive operations that will yield the solution are carried out.

Although it may seem a rather trivial step, construction of an adequate problem representation is not always easy. Usually, the problem solver will have to isolate the relevant pieces of information, or translate aspects of the problem into a more suitable form. The importance of the representation of a problem is nicely illustrated by the so-called mutilated checkerboard problem (Wickelgren, 1974). Imagine that you receive a checkerboard (which has 64 squares) and 32 domino pieces. The size of each domino piece is exactly equal to the size of two adjacent squares on the board. As such, it is possible to cover the entire board with the 32 domino pieces. Now assume that two squares are cut off at opposite corners of the board, as shown in Figure 3.5. Do you think it is possible to cover the mutilated checkerboard with exactly 31 domino pieces?

If you try to solve this problem, you will discover soon that it is not easy at

Figure 3.5 *The mutilated checkerboard*

all. You will probably try various arrangements of the domino pieces on the board, but it is not likely that you will find the solution. The problem is so difficult, because the representation you have been using probably doesn't include a very important fact, namely that each domino piece necessarily covers a white square and a black square on the board. If you take this into account, it will become apparent that it is impossible to cover the mutilated board with 31 domino pieces, because the two squares that were cut off are both white, which implies that the mutilated board contains more black squares than white squares.

This simple illustration shows that the success of attempts to solve particular problems may depend to a large extent on the way in which the problems are represented. Many problems can be represented in a variety of ways, and these representations may differ widely in their usefulness. It is not surprising, therefore, that people who are experienced problem solvers in a particular area tend to use problem representations that are different from those constructed by novices.

A fairly straightforward way to gain insight into the way people represent problems is having them sort a number of different problems into meaningful groups or categories. From the groupings that are produced, inferences about problem representations can be made. Chi *et al.* (1981) asked beginners and experts in physics to categorize a number of standard textbook problems. Interestingly, novices and experts produced very different groupings. The experts tended to classify problems on the basis of fundamental, underlying physics principles. They would produce, for instance, a group of 'energy conservation' problems. Novices, on the other hand, classified problems primarily in terms of 'surface' features. Novices would group together all problems that involved a sliding block on an inclined plane, for example. Obviously, experts would apply their thorough understanding of the domain to create representations that were optimal for solving the problems (see also Hardiman, *et al.* 1989).

Once a problem has been represented, the problem solver can proceed towards a solution. In most cases, a solution cannot be generated in a single step. Problem solving often involves a series of actions. At each step, the solver has to decide which action to take next, in order to maximize the chance of reaching a solution. A very useful and informative way to think about this process is in terms of *search* of a *problem space*. These concepts were introduced by Newell and Simon, in their seminal work on the mechanisms of human problem solving (Newell and Simon, 1972). Newell and Simon (1972) proposed that problem solving involves the progression from an initial mental state to a goal state, through a sequence of cognitive actions. These actions are called *operators*, and their effect is a transformation of the current state of the solution process into a new state. For instance, suppose that I would like to attend a meeting in a city with which I am totally unfamiliar. I have just arrived at the airport (about 20 miles from the city), and all the information I have is an address of the university where I am going; I know only that it is somewhere in the city centre. The initial state of the problem that I face is that I am at the airport. The goal state is my arrival at the university where the meeting is scheduled. To get there, I have a number of operators available. Assume that there are five: walk, take a bus, take a train, rent a car and drive, get a taxi. These are the actions from which I can choose. Unfortunately, I have to take some constraints into account: I don't have much money, and I should get to the meeting within an hour. In Figure 3.6, an overview is given of some of these operators and their effects.

This tree-like representation is called a problem space. It provides an exhaustive overview of all possible action sequences (in Figure 3.6 only part of the total problem space is shown). Only a few sequences will eventually lead to the solution. Other sequences are simply impossible (I cannot start my journey by taking a train, because there is no train station at the airport), or they violate the constraints that apply (I can't take a taxi, because it's too expensive). According to Newell and Simon's conceptualization, problem solving is essentially the process of finding a path through a problem space that will take the problem solver from the initial state to the goal state. Finding such a path involves a search process. Mentally, the problem solver will have to try and

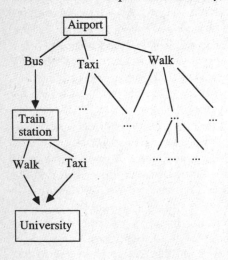

Figure 3.6 *Example of a problem space*

evaluate a number of different routes through the problem space, until a route is found that can produce the goal state.

For some problems (like the one in the example), the search process is relatively simple and straightforward. If a problem space is not too large, it can be searched in a very systematic manner. The problem solver can simply try different paths, until a path is found that leads to the solution. For many problems in daily life, however, the problem space can be immense. Suppose that the solution of a problem requires S steps, and that O operators are available at each step. The number of possible paths then equals O^s. For a problem situation with just 5 operators and 10 steps, the problem space will comprise 9, 765, 625 paths! Nevertheless, people can solve such problems. Obviously, they cannot perform an exhaustive search of such large problem spaces. Rather, they somehow manage to reduce the number of paths that need to be considered, by means of techniques called *heuristics*. Heuristics are rules of thumb, which can be used to find the most promising paths through a problem space. Many heuristics are applicable only in a narrow range of situations, because they rely on specific knowledge about a particular class of problems. For instance, in trying to get from the airport to the university, I could have decided to check the schedule of bus services first, because I know that buses are usually cheap and fast. However, Newell and Simon (1972) identified a number of so-called 'general-purpose' heuristics, which can be applied across a wide variety of different problems. One of these heuristics is means–ends analysis, which works as follows. First, the problem solver identifies the difference between the current state of the problem and the goal state. Next, an operator is selected which will reduce that difference. If the operator can be applied, the solver will do so. Otherwise, a sub-goal is created, to reach a state in which the operator can be applied. Means–ends analysis is then applied to this sub-goal, and so on. Consider the airport example again. The main difference between the initial state and the goal state is one of location. Consequently, an operator is selected that will reduce this difference. Assume that I select the operator 'take a train'. However, I cannot apply this operator, because there is no train station at the airport. Therefore, I would create the sub-goal 'get to a railway station' and apply means–ends analysis to that sub-goal. The difference between the current state and the sub-goal state can be reduced by taking a bus to the station, and because there is a bus at the airport, this operator can be applied. Once I get to the train station, I can apply the operator that I selected initially, and thus solve the problem.

Means–ends analysis can improve the efficiency of problem solving, because it replaces blind search of the problem space with guided search. Paths that will effectively reduce the difference between the current state and the goal state are considered first. For many problem types, this simple heuristic can lead to a considerable reduction in the number of paths that need to be considered. The sub-goal generation process in means–ends analysis also illustrates the use of problem decomposition. A large problem is reduced to a number of smaller problems that are easier to solve individually.

Although Newell and Simon's (1972) analysis of problem solving has had a tremendous impact on cognitive psychology, their framework has been criticized as well. It has been argued that the problem-space concept and the derived search methods can only be applied to well-defined problems, in which the initial state, the goal state and the operators are all clear from the start. In daily life, this is usually not the case. Quite often, much effort in problem solving is spent on trying to find a suitable problem representation or on finding the available operators. Many problems even require the discovery of new operators for their solution. The 'search-of-a-problem-space' metaphor contributes relatively little to our understanding of these aspects of problem solving.

Recent research on problem solving shows a movement away from the study of (relatively) simple puzzle-like problems, such as those studied by Newell and Simon (1972). Instead, more realistic problems have become the focus of attention. In solving such problems, people can use a wide variety of strategies. Among these are strategies based on *analogies* between problems. People have the ability to notice correspondences between problems, and to use this information in problem solving. As an illustration, consider Gick and Holyoak's (1980) experiments on analogical problem solving. Their subjects had to solve the notorious 'radiation problem'. A doctor wants to destroy a malignant tumour, using X-rays. The tumour is deeply embedded in healthy tissue. Destruction of the tumour will require high-intensity radiation, but high-intensity rays will also damage the healthy tissue. How can the doctor destroy the tumour, without affecting other tissue? When this problem was presented, only about 10% of the subjects were able to solve it. Perhaps you would like to try before you read on.

The best solution to the problem is the 'convergence solution'. Here, the doctor uses a number of low-intensity rays from different sources, which converge in the location of the tumour (see Figure 3.7). As a result, the radiation level in the tumour will be high enough to destroy it. The healthy tissue is not affected, though, because the intensity of the individual rays is not high enough to cause damage.

In Gick and Holyoak's (1980) study, subjects also heard a different story, about a general attacking a fortress. The general could not send his entire army directly onto the fortress, because the roads leading there were mined and would certainly not withstand the weight of a big army. Nevertheless, the

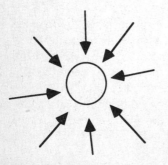

Figure 3.7 *Convergence solution for the radiation problem*

general managed to capture the fortress, because he divided his army into smaller divisions, which were not heavy enough to set off the mines. He sent these divisions across different roads, so that they converged in the location of the fortress. About 80% of the subjects who had heard this story first generated convergence solutions for the radiation problem. People could notice the fundamental structural correspondence between the two situations, and were able to transfer the solution from one domain (the general story) to another (the radiation problem). This ability is probably extremely important in everyday problem solving.

Conclusions

The brief discussion of two areas of research in cognitive psychology will have given you some idea about the nature of the issues this discipline deals with, and about the way in which theories about cognitive processes are constructed. Of course, it is impossible to give a comprehensive overview of the field. Accessible discussions of many other facets can be found in most textbooks on cognitive or experimental psychology.

Further reading

BARSALOU, L.W. and MEDIN, D.L. (1986) 'Concepts: static definitions or context-dependent representations?', *Cahiers de Psychologie Cognitive*, **6**, 187–202.

CHI, M.T.H., FELTOVICH, P.J. and GLASER, R. (1981) 'Categorization and representation of physics problems by experts and novices', *Cognitive Science*, **5**, 121–52.

EYSENCK, M.W. and KEANE, M.T. (1990) *Cognitive Psychology: A Student's Handbook*, Hillsdale, NJ, Lawrence Erlbaum.

GICK, M.L. and HOLYOAK, K.J. (1980) 'Analogical problem solving', *Cognitive Psychology*, **12**, 306–55.

SMITH, E.E. and MEDIN, D.L. (1981) *Categories and Concepts*, Harvard, MA, Harvard University Press.

References

BARSALOU, L.W. (1987) 'The instability of graded structure in concepts'. in NEISSER U. (Ed.) *Concepts and Conceptual Development: Ecological and Intellectual Factors in Categorization* New York, Cambridge University Press, 101–40.

BARSALOU, L.W. (1990) 'On the indistinguishability of exemplar memory and abstraction in category representation', in SRULL T.K. and WYER, S. (Eds) *Advances in Social Cognition*, Volume III: *Content and Process Specificity in the Effects of Prior Experiences* Hillsdale, NJ, Lawrence Erlbaum, 61–88.

Barsalou, L.W. and Medin, D.L. (1986) 'Concepts: static definitions or context-dependent representations?', *Cahiers de Psychologie Cognitive*, 6, 187–202.

Bruner, J.S., Goodnow, J.J. and Austin, G. A. (1956) *A Study of Thinking*, New York, Wiley.

Chi, M.T.H., Feltovich, P.J. and Glaser, R. (1981) 'Categorization and representation of physics problems by experts and novices', *Cognitive Science*, 5, 121–52.

Eysenck, M.W. and Keane, M.T. (1990) *Cognitive Psychology: A Student's Handbook*, Hillsdale, NJ, Lawrence Erlbaum.

Gick, M.L. and Holyoak, K.J. (1980) 'Analogical problem solving', *Cognitive Psychology*, 12, 306–55.

Goodman, N. (1972) *Problems and Projects*, Indianapolis, IN, Bobbs-Merrill.

Hardiman, P.T., Dufresne, R. and Mestre, J.P. (1989) 'The relation between problem categorization and problem solving among experts and novices', *Memory and Cognition*, 17, 627–38.

McCloskey, M.E. and Glucksberg, S. (1978) 'Natural categories: well-defined or fuzzy sets?', *Memory and Cognition*, 6, 462–72.

Medin, D.L. (1989) 'Concepts and conceptual structure', *American Psychologist*, 44, 1469–81.

Medin, D.L. and Schaffer, M.M. (1978) 'Context theory of classification learning', *Psychological Review*, 85, 207–38.

Medin, D.L. and Smith, E.E. (1984) 'Concepts and concept formation', *Annual Review of Psychology*, 35, 113–38.

Medin, D.L., Goldstone, R.L. and Gentner, D. (1993) 'Respects for similarity', *Psychological Review*, 100, 254–78.

Mervis, C.B., Catlin, J. and Rosch, E. (1976) 'Relationships among goodness-of-example, category norms, and word frequency', *Bulletin of the Psychonomic Society*, 7, 283–4.

Murphy, G.L. and Medin, D.L. (1985) 'The role of theories in conceptual coherence', *Psychological Review*, 92, 289–316.

Newell, A. and Simon, H.A. (1972) *Human Problem Solving*, Englewood Cliffs, NJ, Prentice-Hall.

Nosofsky, R.M. (1986) 'Attention, similarity, and the identification–categorization relationship', *Journal of Experimental Psychology: General*, 115, 39–57.

Rosch, E. (1973) 'Natural categories', *Cognitive Psychology*, 4, 328–50.

Smith, E.E. and Medin, D.L. (1981) *Categories and Concepts*, Harvard, MA, Harvard University Press.

Smith, E.E., Shoben, E.J. and Rips, L.J. (1974) 'Structure and process in semantic memory: a featural model for semantic decisions', *Psychological Review*, 81, 214–41.

Wickelgren, W.A. (1974) *How to Solve Problems*, San Francisco, CA, Freeman.

Wittgenstein, L. (1958) *Philosophical Investigations*, Oxford, UK, Blackwell.

Part II

Developmental Psychology

Chapter 4

Early Development

Gillian Harris

The study of infant development is one of the areas of developmental psychology in which there has been much recent research and interest. The proliferation of research studies in this area over the last five years or so is probably the result of recent advances in methods of data collection. It is far more difficult to get information from infants than it is from any other age-group within developmental psychology. There are also many topics which are of recent interest to 'infant' psychologists; this chapter covers just some of those topics, specifically those which have been of recent debate and contention.

A world of confusion?

Many psychologists and philosophers have wondered what the world might be like to a newborn infant. Is it a world of confusion, or is the neonate born equipped with innate abilities that allow it to impose meaning on the incoming information from the surrounding environment?

Much of what we do when interacting with our environment is to impose structure. We have 'frameworks' of knowledge or understanding within which we try to make sense of new information. In the absence of good or complete information we make hypotheses about what might be going on, and base these hypotheses on past experience. If we want to be more sure about our environment, then we might test out our hypotheses to see if they are accurate. If we had no such 'framework' to help us make sense of the world, then the world would be a very frightening and fragmented place. For example, our understanding of the visual world is based on past knowledge about objects and their possible relationship to one another. We see a cup even though that cup might be partly occluded by the saucer; we know that the cup shape continues out of sight and behind another object. Whichever way we look at the cup, whichever way we hold it, we still perceive it to be a cup. Our 'knowledge' of it as a cup does not change as the retinal image changes. We are therefore able to maintain a world full of 'things' with known properties rather than a world full of odd and disparate patches of colour and light. A world of continuity and predictability is far easier to live in than one in which we have to try and make sense, in every passing moment, of every new piece of information. But what, then, is the world like for a newborn infant? They certainly have no past experience to help them to interpret what is going on around them, but is there a possibility that they might have some form of 'framework' to help them with learning about the world. Even a set of preferences would be helpful, so that they might know which are the most important stimuli for them to attend to, out of all that surround them. Many studies have therefore been carried out to see just what sort of 'framework' the neonate, or newborn infant, might have to help it make sense of the world and, using this 'framework', how quickly it is able to learn about important aspects of the environment.

Studying neonates

We cannot, of course, ask infants about their experiences; we have to base our conclusions about their likes and dislikes on our observations of their behaviour. From these observations, certain assumptions have been made. We assume that if a neonate turns towards one object rather than towards another then this indicates a preference; we also assume that if a neonate looks for longer at one object rather than at another that this also denotes preference. We can also assume that certain facial expressions, easily recognizable as grimaces or smiles, can tell us something about the infant's experiences. The infant can also learn to modify the sucking response, or head-turning response, and as a reward for this change in behaviour can get to see or hear specific stimuli. We make the assumption here, too, that the infants are most likely to modify their own behaviour in order to see or hear something that they like. One problem with these methods of data collection is that after experiencing a stimulus for a lengthy period of time the infant habituates; that is, even if they initially prefer it, they eventually get bored with it. This means that they will turn away from the stimulus and attend to something else. However, even this behaviour can be used to elicit information about the infant's ability to discriminate between two stimuli, and therefore it gives us information about the development of perceptual skills. For example, the infant might be presented with a picture of a simple geometric shape and allowed to look at the picture until they habituate and start to look away. The infant is then shown two pictures, the one that they have already seen and a second, slighty different shape. If the infant then looks for a longer period of time at the second shape, we know that they can tell the difference between the two shapes (Slater and Morrison, 1985). For the infant, the second shape is a new shape, one that they have not seen before and therefore want to attend to for longer. In this way we can use the fact that infants habituate to the stimuli to which we might expose them, to tell us more about their perceptual abilities.

Neonatal abilities

When we think about what it is important for the infant to attend to in the environment, we have to remember that the human infant, unlike other mammals, is relatively helpless and requires much support and protection from older human beings. The neonate cannot walk or crawl, in fact the little motor control that it does have is restricted to head and mouth movements. It cannot reach and grasp, although hand and foot clenching reflexes are present from birth. The neonate cannot go and get food, neither can it avoid danger; it relies instead on others to provide food and protection. The most important aspects of the environment for the human infant must, then, be other humans. Any innate, pre-existing 'framework' to help the neonate make sense of the world would need to direct the infant's attention towards socially salient stimuli. The first thing that the neonate would have to learn about would be other people, and the neonate would need to be able to attract or elicit caregiving behaviour in others.

Learning a preference

Existence within a social group depends upon the ability to communicate with others. Such social exchange is regulated by both verbal and non-verbal communication. It is therefore most important that the infant attend to two things: the human face and the human voice. Infant learning does not, however, begin at birth. Research has shown that learning a preference for the human voice starts in the womb. The first studies in this area established the fact that infants of only a few days old would modify their sucking patterns in order to hear their mother's voice reading a story in preference to that of a stranger (DeCasper and Fifer, 1980). The infants, in the first few days of their life, could therefore learn very rapidly to attend to the voice that they heard most frequently; a voice that would most probably be that of the caregiver. However, most researchers are now of the opinion that this learning to attend to known stimuli starts before birth. In a subsequent study, mothers were asked to read a children's poem to their unborn infants twice a day for the last weeks of their pregnancy. After birth, again using the neonates' sucking response as a measure, the infants were tested to see whether they preferred to listen to the poem they had heard read to them in the womb, or another, slightly different, poem also read by their mothers but that they had not heard before. The infants modified their sucking pattern to hear the poem that they had heard before birth (DeCasper and Spence, 1986). The infants would not be able to hear external sounds very clearly whilst in the womb, so the sound of the familiar poem read after birth must have been different from the way it sounded when read before birth, but the rhythm of the poetry reading would have remained the same. Therefore the infants learned to attend to speech rhythms and speech intonations that they had heard before. A good rule for the 'framework' that guides learning for the neonate is, then, to attend to the stimuli that you encounter most frequently. This ensures that the person who is providing most care and protection for the infant, and therefore the most important person in the infant's life, is attended to optimally. Following this rule, infants also rapidly learn to orient towards the smell of their mother's breast milk rather than to that of a stranger (Cernoch and Porter, 1985). This learned preference takes place over the first few weeks of life; it is not present at birth. And of course the innate preference that neonates have for sweet tastes means that, once they have located it, they will prefer to take in breast milk rather than something like water. However, this innate taste preference can also be modified by very rapid learning after birth. Neonates can learn a preference during the weeks after birth for any other milk taste, even if the milk feed that they are given is quite bitter. Once again the neonates learn a preference for that which they most frequently experience within their environment.

Current research also supports the idea that neonates seem to show very rapid learning about salient visual stimuli. In a study by Bushnell *et al.* (1989), new-born infants, of approximately 2 days old, were positioned so that they could see the faces of two people. One face was that of the infant's mother, the other face was that of a female stranger. The female stranger had similar skin tone, colour and facial contours to that of the mother. It was found that the infants preferred to look, that is to say they looked for longer, at their mothers' faces rather than at the strangers' faces. This does not mean that there is an innate preference for the mother's face but that the infant learns very rapidly to identify faces that have been seen before.

Visual preferences

It is still true, however, that young infants show a preference for human faces, even if they have never seen them before. The neonate's smiles, present from birth but bestowed at first fairly indiscriminately on any moving object, gradually come to be reserved for and mainly directed at human faces. In order to become a social animal, the human neonate has to learn to identify and preferentially attend to faces, rather than to other less salient stimuli within the environment.

In recent debate, two mechanisms have been suggested to explain the rapid preference shown by the neonate for human faces; the first, that there is an inborn 'face detector', the second, that the neonate has evolved a set of visual preferences which 'add up' to a preference for face-type stimuli. The 'face detector' theory suggests that the human visual system is designed so that any stimuli that are face type in configuration are attended to in preference to stimuli that might be equal in other ways apart from face-type similarity. The second hypothesis depends upon the knowledge that neonates attend preferentially to specific types of visual stimuli. Neonates do not have very 'good' eyesight; their visual acuity is poor, so that visual stimuli more than two feet away from them are not seen clearly. However, there are still some visual stimuli which are more likely than others to attract the attention of new-born infants. Examples of such preferred stimuli are those which are moving, of high contrast, symmetrical, three-dimensional, with curved rather than straight contours and less than two feet away. If we assume that the neonate would prefer to look at a stimulus which has all of these properties, then we can see that the human face, or a face-type pattern, would be such a stimulus. Various studies have been carried out in an attempt to understand what determines an infant's obvious preference for faces. Unfortunately, because different methods and stimuli have been used with infants at different ages, no really coherent answer has yet been obtained to this question.

Studies of face preference

The youngest infants to be tested were neonates who were studied almost immediately after birth. This very early study used a tracking procedure to test the neonates' preference for face-type patterns (Goren *et al.*, 1975). The infant to be tested was placed on the experimenter's lap, looking upwards. The experimenter then moved a 'bat' slowly across the infant's visual field, from side to side. The stimulus was drawn on the underside of the 'bat', visible to the infant but not to the experimenter. The degree of head and eye movement made whilst tracking the stimulus was measured. In this and later studies (Johnson *et al.*, 1991), comparisons were made between the infants' responses to a schematic face, to symmetrical rearrangements of components of the schematic face, and a blank 'bat'. The face-type configuration elicited the greatest degree of head and eye turn in comparison with the scrambled and blank stimuli. The scrambled stimulus, however, elicited more head and eye turning than did the blank stimulus. From these data we can conclude that neonates prefer to look at face-type stimuli rather than at the scrambled components of the stimulus, but this does not by itself support the claim for an innate face detection mechanism. There could be other symmetrical configurations, with spacing and visual contrast equal to that of the facial configuration, which neonates find equally attractive.

Carrying out such experimental studies on neonates, however, is difficult and time consuming, and measuring preference fraught with difficulties, therefore the more sophisticated experiments have been carried out on older infants. In a study carried out by Maurer and Barrera (1981), infants of 1 month and older were tested using the preferential looking technique. Slides of schematic faces and scrambled but symmetrical faces were shown to groups of 1- and 2-month-old infants. The length of time that the infants looked at the stimuli, until they turned away, was noted. Surprisingly, the 1-month-old infants did not look for longer at the intact faces than they did at the scrambled faces, although a preference for intact faces was shown by the 2-month-old infants. When this experiment was repeated with a much older age-group of infants included in the study (Johnson and Morton, 1991), a similar pattern was found. The 1-month-old infants showed no preference for face-type patterns, the 2-month-old infants did show a preference, but the 5-month-old infants did not show a preference. How can these data be explained, given that the neonates tested on the tracking experiment seemed to show a preference for faces?

A 'U'-shaped curve?

One way of explaining these data is to accept that perhaps infant development is not linear, although the concept of linear development is one to which many developmental psychologists subscribe. If we assume linear development we would expect infants to start out at birth with certain limited skills which they then develop in a systematic way, with a gradual increase in complexity. An alternative suggestion, however, is that infant cognitive and perceptual development might follow a 'U'-shaped curve. The infant might start out with certain rudimentary skills which might give the impression of quite complex processing abilities, but these abilities might then disappear, to be replaced at a later stage with a higher level version of the neonatal skill. It could be that the disappearance and appearance of these cognitive abilities is determined by a change in control of function by different areas of the brain; a change from lower to higher level functioning. This idea of a 'U'-shaped curve in development could explain how we might observe a preference for face-type patterns in the neonate, which disappears at 1 month and reappears at 2 months. Other abilities seem to follow a similar pattern. New-born infants seem to be able to imitate some of the facial expressions of adults. It is, however, difficult to believe that this is true imitation, because the new-born infant cannot yet be aware of which motor movements will produce the facial expressions that map onto or mimic the facial expressions of another. This rudimentary imitative skill similarly disappears after the first few weeks of life, and true imitation seems to re-emerge at about 6 months. At this later time the infant shows imitative skills which seem to be based on an internal representation of another's behaviour which the infant tries to match with similar behaviour.

When putting forward the idea of a 'U'-shaped curve in development, we must also, however, entertain the hypothesis that the differences found in preference for specific visual stimuli could just be due to different methods of data collection. Remember that, when investigating the visual preferences of the neonate, the infant's degree of tracking was measured, whereas with older infants the measure used was of preferential looking time.

Of the two hypotheses, that there is a innate face detector, or that preference for faces is just to do with a preference for stimuli that make up faces, then the second is possibly better supported by the data. Studies by Kleiner (1987) and Kleiner and Banks (1987), have shown that when neonates are tested for their preference for faces or for abstract stimuli that have similar properties to faces, then the infants prefer to look at the abstract stimuli. At 2 months, however, the infants prefer to look at the faces rather than at the abstract superstimuli. It would seem, then, that neonates are attracted by the 'properties' of the face as a perceptual stimulus, whereas older infants have learnt that a face is likely to be associated with a far more interesting range of other behaviours. By this later age human faces have become more salient to the infant. Interestingly, also at this later age of 2 to 3 months, infants prefer to look at pictures of females who are rated as attractive by adults, rather than at pictures that are rated as non-attractive (Langlois *et al.*, 1987). This means that both adults and infants have a preference for the same facial symmetries and ratios between facial features. In fact, the face that is most likely to be found attractive is a 'baby-type' face, with large wide-set eyes, a small nose and features confined to the lower half of the face, rather like many cartoon animals that we might find appealing. The reason that such baby-type facial characteristics are found attractive is that, as has been pointed out before, human infants are relatively helpless and must rely on others to care for them. The infant must therefore have 'properties' that attract others of the species to them. That the human race finds baby-type features attractive is a good beginning and obviously part of an evolutionary mechanism; nearly all humans are attracted to baby-like features.

Neonatal evolution has also tapped into the human's liking for reciprocal communication. We feel that others are listening to us if they turn and look at us when we talk; we feel that others like us if they smile at us. Infants will turn towards their caregivers, attend when they talk, and smile at them in preference to other objects or people. The infant has no communicative intent when carrying out such behaviour, but it seems to the caregiver that it does have such intent. The caregiver feels that the infant is listening to the content of their speech, and that some affection lies behind the smile. In this way the caregiver is drawn into interaction with the infant. Just as the infant is born with a 'framework' that makes them attend to other known humans, so adults are predisposed to respond positively to such infant behaviour. The infant acts 'as if' it loves us, and the caregiver responds.

Social relationships

So far we have concentrated on a discussion of the cognitive development of the neonate, but we also need to consider how the neonate first begins to form relationships with others; how the neonate really becomes a social being. The infant's first relationship is usually formed with the biological parent, although this does not have to be so. One term often used to describe this first relationship is that of 'bonding'. In discussions about difficult children we might hear the question raised about whether or not the infant has 'bonded' with the mother. Incidentally, we also hear of men retreating to the wild to carry out 'male bonding' rituals. The term 'bonding' is therefore used to describe an almost mystical reciprocal relationship between two people; a relationship that is somehow intangible. When reference is made to an infant and mother 'bonding' after birth, the implication is also that the process is almost instantaneous: like falling in love at first sight. Mother and baby are meant to 'bond' together immediately after birth and if this bonding process does not take place then the consequences are often thought to be dire.

Imprinting and bonding

The concept of imprinting, or early neonatal bonding, comes from studies carried out on animals. Ethologists in the 1950s observed that some bird and animal species would imprint upon, and follow, the first object that they saw after birth (Lorenz, 1958). Furthermore, studies of other animal groups had found that it was difficult to get females of some herding animals to accept and feed another's new-born if their own offspring had died. Because of these observations it was therefore thought that, within some animal groups, there was evidence for two forms of early recognition: that of the offspring for the parent, and that of the parent for the offspring. These assumptions were supported by work carried out by Harlow, also in the 1950s, who studied the relationship between rhesus monkeys: mothers, offspring and peers. He found that if infant rhesus monkeys were separated from their mothers for the first six months of life, and reared in isolation, then the monkeys' subsequent behaviour when integrated into the monkey troop was abnormal (Harlow and Harlow, 1973). In fact many of the behaviours shown by the isolated monkeys were similar to those shown by humans who were suffering from some extreme forms of mental illness.

Freud had already suggested, at the turn of the century, that early childhood experience could have an effect on the subsequent mental health of the adult. This was an idea that was also promoted by Bowlby, again in the 1950s, who started his work at around about the same time that Harlow was carrying out his studies on monkeys. Bowlby felt that some of the problems experienced by the delinquent boys with whom he was working were due to the fact that the boys had been unable to form a continuous reciprocal relationship with their mothers (Bowlby, 1953). These findings, from different areas of study, seemed to give an insight into the nature and importance of early relationships. Animal studies showed that there seemed to be some form of rapid imprinting occurring between offspring and mother, and at the time this was thought to be irreversible. Detrimental effects on subsequent adult functioning were observed where the animal had been kept in isolation immediately after birth. These observations were coupled to a hypothesis formed retrospectively by those working with adults with mental health problems or adolescents with conduct disorders; that is, that the neonate needed to form a relationship of some kind with its mother for subsequent optimal functioning.

At this point in history, given that women's roles in society were mainly shaped by biological destiny, it would have been assumed automatically that the first relationship formed by an infant would have to be with the biological mother. If this relationship had to be with the mother then it could of course take place immediately after birth. In the 1970s Klaus and Kennel brought all these ideas together and suggested that it was likely that the human neonate rapidly formed a relationship, or 'bonded', to the mother immediately after birth (Klaus and Kennel, 1976). It was also thought that such a relationship, once formed, would be irreversible and would be a necessary basis for the optimal mother–child relationship. In accordance with observations made of animal imprinting, it was thought that 'bonding' would occur as a result of physical contact between mother and child. And although, if we follow the logic of animal studies, such early physical contact would only enable identification through perceptual cues, either of the mother by the infant or of the infant by the mother; 'bonding' was thought to have an emotional component.

Freud and Bowlby stressed the importance to the child of forming a relationship with the mother. No one has yet suggested that it is of any benefit to the mother's mental health to form a relationship with her child, although from a socio-biological perspective this might be thought to aid gene survival. Klaus and Kennel, however, although suggesting that the bonding process was important for the infant, did not use infant behaviour as a measure of bond formation; they used instead measures of maternal behaviour. In fact they tried to quantify 'good mothering' skills. There was, then, some confusion about who was 'bonding' to whom, and whose behaviour would be modified.

Using measures of mothering skill, such as the amount of time spent looking at, or touching the infant, Klaus and Kennel carried out a study to look at the effect of post-partum contact on the relationship between mother and infant (Klaus *et al.*, 1972). In their study, one group of mothers was allowed extra contact with their new-born infants and the other group had the usual brief contact periods commonly allowed in hospitals at the time. Klaus and Kennel did find some differences in mothering skills according to how much contact time the mother had with the infant. These differences were interpreted as an indication that 'bonding' between mother and child had occurred to a greater extent in the extra-contact group. This finding changed the way in which childbirth subsequently was managed; it was thought important that the mother should be with her child immediately after birth. It also introduced the concept of 'bonding' to the world. Many mothers felt worried and guilty if they weren't able, or didn't have the opportunity to 'bond' with their infants. In addition, many fathers must have felt excluded from this relationship, for the 'bonding' hypothesis was based on the assumption that the first and primary relationship must be between the child and the mother.

Klaus and Kennel's early experiments to test the bonding hypothesis were, however, methodologically flawed, because both the investigators and the mothers knew which mother–infant pairs were in the extra-contact group. This knowledge altered the way in which the mothers behaved towards their infants. Subsequent studies which have controlled more carefully for such effects have found no difference in mothering behaviour due to extra contact between mother and child in the neonatal period (Svedja *et al.*, 1980). Indeed, if we consider the studies carried out on neonatal perceptual and cognitive abilities, we might think it strange to expect the neonate to be able to form an attachment of any kind in the first weeks of life. What we do know is that neonates will display behaviour which shows that specific perceptual stimuli have been encountered before. To be able to form an attachment, which we might define as a desire to maintain proximity to another, we could say that we need to be aware that we and others exist as separate entities. This is probably not a state of awareness available to the neonate. Mothers also similarly report that they have no immediate feeling of affection for their infant at birth. In fact many would willingly swap the baby for a cup of tea. So perhaps 'bonding', an immediate mystical attachment that occurs shortly after birth, is not a viable concept. In which case, just how and when does the first relationship form between infant and caregiver, and just how important is this relationship?

Attachment formation

Attachments between people usually form gradually over a long period of time, and current research suggests that this is also true of the first relationship between infants and their caregivers. The caregiver might think, as has been suggested earlier, that because the neonate preferentially turns towards them or smiles at them that the infant really feels some affection for them; but this is unlikely to be true. The caregiver is more likely to care for and protect an infant who seems to show signs of recognition and preference, than for an infant who is indifferent to their presence. However, the attachment process, of infant to caregiver, probably doesn't even start until the infant is about 6 weeks old. At this age the infant's smile becomes more discriminate; they begin to look and smile preferentially at the human face. And gradually, if the caregiver is a continuous presence in their lives, the infant will begin to be able to predict simple behaviours that might occur.

Much recent research also seems to show that the infant's behaviour 'meshes' with that of the caregiver; if the caregiver talks they will attend, if the caregiver is silent then the infant will be active. By the middle of the first year, at 6 months or so, the infant is able to start to play simple games of give and take. Also, at around this time, we might observe the first signs of distress if the infant is left by the caregiver. Towards the end of the first year, at about 10 months, we are likely to see clearer signs of attachment to the caregiver; the infant will clearly show distress if left, will move towards the caregiver (if mobile) and will show fear or wariness of people with whom they are not familiar. At this stage we might say that an attachment has formed between the infant and the caregiver. In order that an attachment can form the infant must be able to recognize the caregiver. In order to recognize someone the infant must be able to maintain an internal representation of that person, even in their absence. We can say that the infant is able to recognize someone if they can show a discriminatory response, that is if they respond differently to someone they know than to someone that they don't know. Hence a positive response to the known caregiver, and a fear response to an unknown stranger.

Object permanence

Attainment of these stages of social development is reflected in the attainment of certain cognitive skills: specifically, the understanding of object permanence. For the very young infant it is usually true to say that out of sight is out of mind. The infant will not usually look for an object that has been hidden. This has been interpreted by some psychologists, in the past, as a lack of understanding of object permanence; that is, the infant does not have an enduring mental representation of an object, or person, that they can no longer see.

The way in which the attainment of object permanence was first measured was by search tasks: a toy, with which the child was playing, would be hidden underneath a cloth or a cup. Although the infant might have sufficient motor skills physically to retrieve the object, they are not likely to do so until they reach the age of 9 months or so, an age similar to the one at which an infant might first display fear of strangers. The two observations could be thought to be linked, in that it could be assumed that an attachment to another could not form until the infant is able to maintain the concept of the existence of 'other', which is separate from self and has an enduring existence not dependent upon perceptual 'availability'. Once the infant has reached this stage then distress at separation from the caregiver emerges; the infant becomes aware that the caregiver actually maintains an existence elsewhere and that the infant is alone (although still not having at this age sufficient cognitive skills to be able to predict the caregiver's return). The 'fear of strangers' response might be thought to indicate the infant's awareness of a 'mismatch' between the internal representation of the caregiver and the sight of the stranger. However, recent studies have shown that infants have a concept of object permanence at a much younger age than was previously thought possible (Hood and Willets, 1986). Some infants at only 5 months of age will reach for a toy which they have seen placed either to their right or to their left but which is no longer visible to them because the lights have been turned out. The toy, therefore, does continue to exist for the infant even though they can no longer see it. Other more complex studies have shown that 5-month-old babies seem surprised when one object seemed 'impossibly' to pass through another, solid object (Baillargeon *et al.*, 1985). This was true even when the infant could no longer see the solid object. The infants were therefore able to hold in mind the fact that the solid object continued to exist even when they could no longer see it, and that such a solid object should block the passage of another object. In the light of these studies it is probable that the search tasks at which infants of 10 months fail are not measuring an infant's understanding of object permanence. In fact, it has been shown that infants will not pick up a cup to look for an object which has been hidden even if the cup is transparent and they can still see the toy that they are meant to be retrieving (Butterworth, 1977).

Fear of strangers

It is now generally accepted that the age at which object permanence is attained is at about 6 months or so, and, in fact, infants do usually begin to show separation distress from the caregiver at around this age. The fear of strangers response which might be observed in the older infant, however, is probably due less to the attainment of object permanence than it is to other factors. It has been observed that the fear of strangers response is less marked when the 'stranger' is used to playing and talking to babies (Kaye, 1982). The response is also less strong if the caregiver behaves in a positive manner towards the stranger. It has been observed that by the age of 10 months infants have become far more aware of, and skilled at, complex interactions with the other people around them. They will play quite elaborate games and occasionally even show an understanding of the other's expectations of the game by suddenly changing their behaviour. For example, in the middle of a 'give and take' game, the infant might not let go of the toy as had been expected. A current area of debate within developmental psychology is whether or not we can call such behaviour a form of 'teasing'.

Such games and expectations within a relationship will differ from person to person, depending upon with whom the child is playing. There will be different games with mother, father and sister or brother. However, just as the infant becomes able to predict what will happen in one situation, so they also become aware that there are situations in which they cannot predict events. The most obvious example of these is when meeting a new person. The 'fear of strangers' response is not usually a real fear response, it is more likely to be a period of thorough and wary inspection, as if the infant were watching the stranger to see what their behaviour will be like. When the stranger looks similar to the caregiver and behaves in a similarly positive way the infant will usually, eventually, interact with them. If the stranger looks unusual or behaves negatively then the infant is more likely to show fearful behaviour. The 'fear of strangers' response is, therefore, more likely to be associated with the attainment of the stage at which infants can predict others' behaviour than with the stage of object permanence.

Attachment measures

When the infant is mobile, and has achieved the developmental stages outlined above, then presence and strength of attachment to the caregiver can be measured. The usual technique used for measuring attachment is that of Ainsworth's 'Strange Situation' (Ainsworth *et al.*, 1978). The behavioural measures used, which are thought to be indicative of attachment, are those of distress at separation from the caregiver and positive behaviour at reunion with the caregiver after separation. The child's behaviour towards the caregiver is also compared with the child's behaviour towards a stranger. This procedure comprises seven stages; the child and caregiver are observed, usually by means of a camera link, playing together in an observation room. The seven prescribed 'moves' follow, during which the caregiver leaves and re-enters the room, the child is left alone with the caregiver, alone with the stranger, totally alone, or in the observation room with both caregiver and stranger. The child's response to these situations is analysed and assigned to one of three main categories, two of which are seen as indicative of 'insecure' attachment, and one of 'secure' attachment to the caregiver.

We might ask why psychologists want to know whether or not an infant is securely attached to the caregiver. This is because many people are still inter- ested in Bowlby's hypothesis: that early relationship experiences affect later adult functioning. We therefore need a measure of the child's experience of the relationship to test the hypothesis. We need to know whether or not the child shows pleasure on reunion with the caregiver, or prefers the company of the caregiver to that of a stranger.

Most psychologists now agree that children who have a secure attachment to their caregiver are more confident and self-assured than those who have an insecure attachment (Waters *et al.*, 1979), and, if the behaviour of the caregiver is also observed, it is easy to see why this might be so. Those children who are deemed securely attached usually have a caregiver who is consistent and 'sensitively responsive' in their interactions with the child; that is, they react in an appropriate and empathic way to the child's behaviour. Caregivers of chil- dren who are deemed insecurely attached, however, are often observed to be either hostile, totally rejecting the child's approaches for affection and care, or inconsistent in their caring behaviour. The inconsistent caregiver might re- spond with affection to the child's approach on one occasion, but on another occasion with hostility or criticism.

The child with a caregiver who always rejects them, that is one who is always hostile or critical, will usually show an attachment pattern that is described as 'avoidant'. This means that in the 'Strange Situation' the child will show neither distress at separation, nor pleasure on reunion, with the caregiver. In fact, the behaviour shown towards the stranger will sometimes be more positive than that shown towards the caregiver. The child whose caregiver is described as inconsistent is likely to show more ambivalent behaviour towards the caregiver in the 'Strange Situation'. The child will show distress on separa- tion and in fact be quite 'clingy'. The child will also show proximity seeking on reunion with the caregiver, but is less likely to show pleasure at reunion than is the securely attached child; this child is in fact more likely to be hostile on reunion. The behaviour of the child during play also reflects the inconsistent behaviour of the caregiver, with the child showing alternate approach/avoid- ance behaviour. This child's attachment is usually described as 'anxious'.

Peer-group interaction

It is thought that the nature of the attachment to the primary caregiver may, to some extent, determine the way in which a child might interact with others in subsequent relationships. This might also be at the root of the observations that early emotional experience might determine subsequent adult functioning. It has certainly been shown that nursery-school age children's behaviour with their peer group differs according to the rating of attachment security with their primary caregivers. Children with secure attachments are usually more confident and self-assured than are children rated as having insecure attachments, and are more sensitive to the needs of other children (Waters *et al.*, 1979). There is a higher rate of peer-directed aggression amongst insecurely attached boys (Turner, 1991). It has also been observed that the relationship between two insecurely attached children is likely to be more problematic than the relationship between securely attached children (Troy and Sroufe, 1987). Pairs of insecurely attached children are more likely to adopt 'victim' and 'bully' roles than are securely attached children.

These findings could be explained in that the children maintain the specific interaction style of the first relationship and carry it over into subsequent relationships. On the other hand, it could be that having an early relationship with a caregiver who is consistently caring in itself gives the child sufficient self-assurance and self-reliance to maintain other healthy relationships. For, if a key relationship is such that we are able to predict another's behaviour or reaction to our own behaviour and where the 'other' shows empathic response and positive regard towards us, then we are likely to learn both that we are able to predict and act effectively upon the world and the people in it, and that we are worthy of love. Prediction and control of the environment and high self-esteem are both factors that are likely to be associated with good adult mental health.

In Ainsworth's original study approximately one-third of the children that she observed were rated as having an insecure attachment with their primary caregiver. Given the possible long-term effects of insecure attachment this might seem to mean that one-third of the population is likely to have problems in later life owing to an early primary attachment dysfunction. However, infants do not only form one attachment in their early lives, they can form an attachment to anyone with whom they have a consistent reciprocal relationship; and such attachment formation recurs throughout life. The child may, therefore, have an insecure attachment to the mother but a secure attachment to the father, or to a grandparent. In fact many infants do not have their closest emotional relationship with the person who does most to promote their physical care. They might be closest to any biological relative, including a brother or sister, or to any non-biological caregiver. There is nothing special about the attachment to the biological mother apart from the fact that the mother is still the most likely person to have full-time care of the infant, and the relationship with the mother is likely to be the first relationship experienced by the child. We have also suggested that the first relationship might set the pattern for subsequent relationships. If this is the case, then, if the mother is the first attachment figure for the infant, this relationship might disproportionately affect the child's later behaviour and expectations when interacting with others.

Predicting outcomes

Research studies are currently being carried out to see whether or not the incidence of specific maladaptive mental states such as borderline personality disorder, or the incidence and prognosis of some mental illnesses, is dependent upon early attachment classification. That is, does the nature of the first relationship contribute to adult mental health? Perhaps this is just a slightly different way of framing Bowlby's original hypothesis: it is not so much the absence or presence of the primary attachment relationship that is of concern, but the security the child feels within that relationship.

Attempts to predict outcome from early childhood measures have of course been made in other areas of developmental psychology, but so far seem to have failed. For example, there have been many attempts to quantify and define infant temperament (Prior, 1992). It has often been observed that, in many studies of infant interaction or ability, the infant has seemed to contribute something unique to the situation. To come back, then, to our starting point, it often seems that infants do not come into the world as 'a blank slate to be written on'. Not only might they have a 'framework' to help them to begin to make sense of the world, but infants also seem to have individual differences from birth, which affect the way in which they act upon the world. We may term this 'personality', but more usually we apply the term 'temperament' to infants. The term temperament describes a natural disposition to respond in a specific way to different stimuli or environments. Any parent who has more than one child will say that their children had different ways of responding, from birth. Some psychologists might say that this is because no two children, even in the same family, share the same 'environment'; that parents will treat subsequent children differently because of gender or family position, or current stresses or traumas within the family life. This of course places a great deal of responsibility upon the caregiver; if the child subsequently shows any deviance that cannot be traced back to organic factors, then the family socialization process must be to blame.

Some attempts, however, have been made to establish differences between infants, present from birth and due to genetic rather than to social factors. One such series of studies has been carried out by Thomas and Chess (1977), who found that the descriptors 'easy', 'difficult' and 'slow to warm up' could accurately describe two-thirds of the population of infants that they were studying. And certainly these do seem to be useful descriptors for the way in which many infants react to their environment. An 'easy' child is described as being generally positive in affect, regular in behaviour such as sleeping and feeding, and as accepting new experiences well. 'Difficult' infants are described as irritable and irregular, and are not adaptable to change; they dislike changes in routine. Infants who are 'slow to warm up' are slow to adapt to changes in the environment, but are less likely to respond negatively to such changes than are difficult infants. However, when assuming a genetic influence we also assume that the effect on the infant's reactions to the environment will be relatively stable over time, or at least be predictive of similar reactions to the environment at a later time. But no measure of temperament based on these constructs accurately predicts subsequent measures of temperament. One of the problems here is that temperament measures are usually based on parental report, and parental report is subjective. That is, if parents describe their infant's behaviour in certain situations, then these descriptions are likely to be biased by the parent's own expectations, or interpretations, of the infant's behaviour. Infant temperament measures therefore tell us as much about the infants' parents as they do about the infant.

Infant temperament is thought to be an important factor in directing the infant's response to the world, but it cannot, at the moment, be measured in a way that has any predictive value.

Similar problems are experienced when trying to measure intelligence. We know that scores on measures of intelligence are partly explained by genetic factors, that is, measured intelligence is, to some extent, inherited. However, as with measures of temperament, no one test in infancy accurately predicts outcome on later adult intelligence tests. Some current research studies within developmental psychology are attempting to find early measures that are predictive of later intelligence, such as speed of problem solving. Surprisingly, perhaps, one measure that might be predictive is the time that an infant takes to habituate to a new stimulus. The faster the infant is able to assimilate all the properties of a new perceptual stimulus, then the more intelligent the infant might be.

Much of the work carried out in early developmental psychology is concerned, then, not only with what the child can do, and when she or he can do it, but also with which aspects of learning are pre-determined and which are purely a function of environmental interaction. One of the the most important questions is still: what does the neonate come into the world equipped to do? Is it a world of confusion, or is it a world that has some meaning for the infant even from birth?

Further reading

FIELD, T. (1990) *Infancy*, Cambridge, MA, Harvard University Press.
RUTTER, M. (1991) *Maternal Deprivation Reassessed*, London, Penguin.
SCHAFFER, H.R. (1990) *Making Decisions about Children*, Oxford, Blackwell.
SLATER, A. and BREMNER, G. (Eds) (1989) *Infant Development*, Hove, LEA.
SLUCKIN, W., HERBERT, M. and SLUCKIN, A. (1984) *Maternal Bonding*, Oxford, Blackwell.

References

AINSWORTH, M.D.S., BLEHAR, M. and WATERS, E. (1978) *Patterns of Attachment*, Hillsdale, NJ, Erlbaum.

BAILLARGEON, R., SPELKE, E.S. and WASSERMAN, S. (1985) 'Object permanence in 5-month-old infants', *Cognition*, **20**, 191-208.

BOWLBY, J. (1953) *Child Care and the Growth of Love*, Harmondsworth, Penguin.

BUSHNELL, I.W.R., SAI, F. and MULLIN, J.T. (1989) 'Neonatal recognition of the mother's face', *British Journal of Developmental Psychology*, **7**, 3-15.

BUTTERWORTH, G.E. (1977) 'Object disappearance and error in Piaget's stage IV task', *Journal of Experimental Child Psychology*, **23**, 391-401.

CERNOCH, J.M. and PORTER, R.H. (1985) 'Recognition of maternal axillary odours by infants', *Child Development*, **56**, 1593-8.

DeCASPER, A.J. and FIFER, W. (1980) 'Of human bonding; newborns prefer their mothers' voices', *Science*, **208**, 1174-6.

DeCASPER, A.J. and SPENCE, M.J. (1986) 'Prenatal maternal speech influences newborns' perception of speech sounds', *Infant Behaviour and Development*, **9**, 133-50.

GOREN, C., SARTY, M. and WU, P. (1975) 'Visual following and pattern discrimination of face-like stimuli by newborn infants', *Pediatrics*, **56**, 544-9.

HARLOW, H.F. and HARLOW, M.K. (1973) 'Social deprivation in monkeys', in *Readings from Scientific American*, California, W.H.Freeman.

HOOD, B. and WILLETS, P. (1986) 'Reaching in the dark to an object's remembered position; evidence for object permanence in 5-month-old infants', *British Journal of Developmental Psychology*, **4**, 57-66.

JOHNSON, M.H. and MORTON, J. (1991) *Biology And Cognitive Development: The Case of Face Recognition*, Oxford, Blackwell.

JOHNSON, M.H., DZIURAWIEC, S., ELLIS, H. and MORTON, J. (1991) 'The tracking of face-type stimuli by newborn infants and its subsequent decline', *Cognition*, **40**, 1-21.

KAYE, K. (1982) *The Mental and Social Life of Babies*, London, Methuen.

KLAUS, M.H., JERAULD, R., KREGER, N., McALPINE, W., STEFFA, M. and KENNEL, J.H. (1972) 'Maternal attachment – importance of the first post-partum days', *New England Journal of Medicine*, **286**, 460-3.

KLAUS, M.H. and KENNEL, J.H. (1976) *Maternal-Infant Bonding*. St. Louis, MO, Mosby.

KLEINER, K.A. (1987) 'Amplitude and phase spectra as indices of infants' pattern preferences', *Infant Behaviour and Development*, **10**, 49-59.

KLEINER, K.A. and BANKS, M.S. (1987) 'Stimulus energy does not account for 2-month-olds' face preferences', *Journal of Experimental Psychology*, **13**, 594-600.

LANGLOIS, J.H., ROGGMAN, L.A., CASEY, R.J., RITTER, J.M., REISER-DANNER, L.A. and JENKINS, V.Y. (1987) 'Infant preferences for attractive faces: rudiments of a stereotype?', *Developmental Psychology*, **23**, 363-9.

LORENZ, K. (1958) 'The evolution of behaviour', *Scientific American*, **119**, 67-78.

MAURER, D. and BARRERA, M. (1981) 'Infants' perception of natural and distorted arrangements of a schematic face', *Child Development*, **52**, 196-202.

PRIOR, M. (1992) 'Childhood temperament', *Journal of Psychology and Psychiatry*, **33**, 249-79.

SLATER, A.M. and MORRISON, V. (1985) 'Shape constancy and slant perception at birth', *Perception*, **14**, 337-44.

SVEJDA, M.J., CAMPOS, J.J. and EMDE, R.N. (1980) 'Mother–infant "bonding": a failure to generalize', *Child Development*, **51**, 775-9.

THOMAS, A. and CHESS, S. (1977) *Temperament and Development*, New York, Bruner/Mazel.

TROY, M. and SROUFE, L.A. (1987) 'Victimization amongst pre-schoolers: role of attachment relationship history', *Journal of the American Academy of Child and Adolescent Psychiatry*, **26**, 166-72.

TURNER, P.J. (1991) 'Relations between attachment, gender and behaviour with peers in pre-school', *Child Development*, **62**, 1475-88.

WATERS, E., WIPPMAN, J. and SROUFE, L.A. (1979) 'Attachment, positive affect and competence in the peer group: two studies in construct validation', *Child Development*, **62**, 1475-88.

Chapter 5

Life-span Development

Kevin D. Browne and Clive R. Hollin

Traditionally, the study of developmental psychology involved investigations into childhood and adolescence and, as exemplified by theories of Freud and Piaget, covered only the first 16 years of the human life-span (Mussen *et al.*, 1990). During the past 30 years, however, an interest has emerged in developmental changes associated with adulthood and old age. Concepts and theories have been constructed that engage the individual's complete life from conception and birth to death (Santrock and Bartlett, 1986). Such work is usually referred to as the study of 'Life-span Human Development'.

What is a developmental theory?

Simply addressing childhood and adulthood does not make a theory a life-span developmental theory. It is essential that any developmental theory focuses on changes over time. The description of how a psychological concept, such as intelligence, changes over time facilitates our understanding of development, whereas just the description of the concept itself would not. Thus, developmental theories serve to describe, organize, integrate and give meaning to facts collected from research and practice that are shown to change over time. Theories, once constructed, then guide the implementation of further research and future practices.

The concept of ageing is generally used to describe changes that occur to an individual with time. The concept of ageing is a complex one, which can be defined in several ways by focusing on chronological age, biological changes, psychological development, changes in social activities and contacts and interests in life. Variations on these aspects of ageing do not necessarily occur in a synchronized way, so that at any one time an individual may be at a different stage of biological, psychological and social development, none of which might correlate with chronological age. Nevertheless, most people follow a similar sequence of significant events in their lives and Figure 5.1 gives a typical example of a human life-span, together with the percentage of the UK population currently involved in those particular life changes (Central Statistical Office, 1994).

Years		Life Span
	0 .	Conception and Birth
20.3 per cent (Under 16)	5 .	Begin school
	10 .	Puberty/sexual interest
	16 .	Social identity develops
	18 .	Leave school/vote
	20 .	Begin occupation Leave parental home
35.3 per cent (16–39)	30 .	Marriage/set up own home Parenthood
	.	Change job/promotion Move home
	.	Change in social contacts
	40 .	Extra-marital affairs
	.	Possible separation/divorce
28.6 per cent (40–64)	50 .	Menopause
	.	Children leave home
	60 .	Grand parenthood
	65 .	Retirement
	70 .	Serious health problems
12.1 per cent (65–79)	75 .	Spouse dies (male life expectancy)
	.	Great-grandparenthood
	80 .	Death (female life expectancy)
3.7 per cent (Over 80 yrs)		

Figure 5.1 *A typical human life-span, per cent UK population 1991 (total 57.8 million) (source: Central Statistical Office, 1994)*

Human development

As the previous chapter on Early Development has indicated, infants begin life knowing little about their environment. Through reflexes, senses and natural curiosity they quickly acquire knowledge about the world around them. They are preadapted to select and attend to certain kinds of sounds and visual features which speeds the development of motor skills and finely tunes the senses. By 1 year of age infants have already assimilated an immense amount of knowledge about objects, people and experiences, and have accommodated this information to enhance their communication to others. Thus, the basic first steps of human development involve both remarkable qualitative and quantitative changes. Nevertheless, adult help and environmental stimulation are needed for this development to occur.

During childhood, adult–child interaction enhances the child's physical, perceptual, social and linguistic development which in turn promotes the cognitive (intellectual) and moral abilities that are essential to thinking, learning, self-identity and actualization (full development of one's potential).

Hence, from responsive parental care comes the sense that:

I can elicit care. (Infant)
I can affect the environment. (Child)
I can cope with the stress of change and challenge the environment. (Adult)

Indeed, Maslow's (1968, 1970) influential writings *Toward a Psychology of Being* and *Motivation and Personality* both view self-actualization as the pinnacle of human development, such that a person feels self-fulfilled by making full use of their potential abilities and talents. However, more basic needs must be met at least partially, before an individual is motivated to develop their full potential. Maslow postulated that seven basic needs can be hierarchically placed in order of importance for human action (see Figure 5.2), whereby an unmet need will come to dominate a person's activity. The most important are: (1) physiological needs – hunger, thirst, sleep and so forth; followed by (2) the

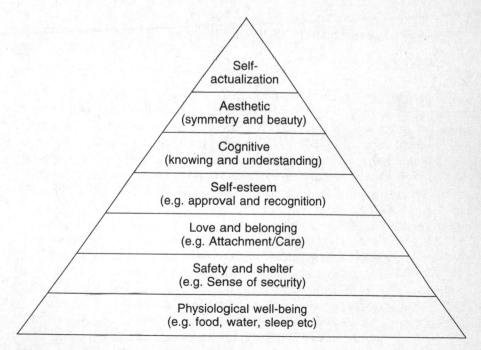

Figure 5.2 *Maslow's hierarchy of needs*

need for safety and shelter to give a sense of security. A sense of (3) love and belonging is the next most basic need, feeling attached to others and cared for. This is intrinsically linked to (4) self-esteem and the need to achieve in a competent way that gains approval and recognition, which in turn enhances (5) the need to know, understand and explore. With the first five basic needs met to some degree an individual requires (6) symmetry, order and beauty in their lives before feeling (7) self-fulfilled and content (self actualization).

Linked to the notion that certain basic needs have to be met before self-actualization, Allport (1961) describes the characteristics of the 'mature personality'. Again an adequate sense of self-worth was seen as fundamental to maturity. Thus, contemporary psychology holds the belief that a child must mature psychologically as well as physically for optimal adult development.

Besides Maslow's motivational model of development and behaviour and Allport's ideas on the mature personality, there have been many other attempts to describe changes that may or may not occur during a person's life-span. A number of different perspectives on human development have evolved. Some researchers emphasize a fixed number of developmental stages through which individuals progress (e.g. Freud, 1905; Piaget, 1954; Erikson, 1965; Kohlberg, 1976). Others prefer to see development in a more flexible way, placing emphasis on the gradual learning of skills and abilities (e.g. Bandura, 1973, 1977), while some authors claim there are critical periods in development, where significant transformations occur to each individual (e.g. Bowlby, 1969).

Contemporary views on the giants of developmental theory

Stage Theories

Sigmund Freud. The first comprehensive theory of child and adolescent development originated at the beginning of the twentieth century with Freud's psychoanalytical approach. Freud (1905) formulated a developmental theory of psychosexual stages (see Table 5.1) to explain how unconscious impulses arise and how they influence the behaviour of a developing child through emotional conflict. According to this theory, children have sexual interests and pleasures in the particular part of the body that is a predominant characteristic for their age. Hence, the first three years are characterized by desires (libido) of the mouth (oral stage), the anus (the anal stage), and the penis (the phallic stage).

At each stage the child is motivated by the desire to satisfy biological needs and obtain pleasure by the release of tension (the pleasure principle): for example, sucking, defaecation and masturbation respectively. It was Freud's notion that parent–child interaction during these stages determines the child's basic personality which becomes essentially fixed by the age of 6 years. A period of 'latency' follows until the child reaches adolescence and enters the final genital stage of pleasure and satisfaction through the opposite sex. Contemporary psychoanalysts (neo-Freudians) place less emphasis on the Id or pleasure principle and more emphasis on the Ego or Self (Colarusso, 1992). The Self can actively master the environment rather than just control drives to satisfy biological impulses.

The strengths of Freud's theory are that: first, he proposes that the first few years of life are critical for the development of personality; second, he claims that infants and children develop through an invariable sequence of (conflict) stages. Together, these notions form the backbone of psychodynamic developmental psychology and have heavily influenced research, clinical practice and therapy with both children and adults (Miller, 1993).

Erik Erikson. Erikson's contribution to developmental theory is based on Freud's ideas and is important in that he identifies social and cultural influences on development and the individual's search for identity. Even more important is the fact that Erikson was the first to provide a comprehensive developmental theory covering the whole life-span.

According to Erikson (1965), development occurs through a series of psychosocial conflicts throughout the whole life-span. Like Freud, Erikson is a stage-theorist who claims that feelings and social relationships have a critical role in a person's development. But, unlike Freud's notion of stage fixation in the absence of sufficient gratification in childhood, Erikson proposes a sequence of eight developmental stages that each involve an individual coping with a crisis that must be resolved in some way. He emphasizes the importance of culture and the balance of individual needs against the needs of the social environment. At each point in development, there is a psychosocial crisis with two possible extreme outcomes (see Table 5.1). Erikson agrees with the Freudian belief that problems arising in infancy can last a lifetime. The suspicious and pessimistic adult is viewed as an infant who failed to develop trust and achieve autonomy.

Overall, Erikson's contribution has strengthened the psychodynamic approach by expanding it to provide a broad perspective on development. However, his Psychosocial Theory lacks a description of mechanisms of change from one developmental stage to another or the dynamics of conflict resolution. Like most other psychodynamic theories its weakness is a lack of systematic research and factual evidence. As Miller (1993) states, the theory remains 'a loose connection of observations, empirical generalisations and abstract theoretical claims' (p. 171).

Jean Piaget. Piaget (1954), emphasized the biology of behaviour and thought. He formulated a sequence of stages for cognitive (intellectual) development, which shows how the child construes knowledge differently at each stage (see Table 5.1). However, as with all stage theories, children do not simply graduate from one stage to another. This is because the form of mental reasoning most recently mastered never entirely replaces earlier forms of reasoning. Thus, adults may often resort to child-like ways of thinking, especially when under stress or facing a new challenge.

88

Table 5.1 *Developmental stage theories*

Age	Psychodynamic				Cognitive	
	Freud		*Erikson*		*Piaget*	
	Stage	Psychosexual focus	Stage	Psychosocial focus	Stage	Intellectual focus
1st year Infancy	Oral	Oral pleasure	Basic trust vs mistrust (hope)*	Social support	*Sensori-motor 1-4	Differentiates self from objects
2nd year Infancy	Anal	Control of body	Autonomy vs doubt (will)*	Independence	*Sensori-Motor 5 and 6	Achieves object performance, shows intention
3–5 years Early childhood	Phallic-Oedipal	Sex-role identity	Initiative vs guilt (purpose)*	Self care skills	*Representational (pre-conceptual and intuitive)	Represents objects in images and words classifying object by single feature
6–11 years School age	Latency	Repression of sexuality	Industry vs inferiority (competence)*	Social skills	Concrete operations	Thinks logically about objects and events, conservation of number(s), mass(s), and weight(s); classifies object on several features

Stage	Genital		Definition of self	Formal operations
14–20 years Adolescence	Genital	Identity vs role confusion (fidelity)*		Thinking logically about abstract propositions; concerned with future and hypothetical problems
20–35 years Young adulthood		Intimacy vs isolation (love)*	Meaningful relationships	
35–65 years Middle adulthood		Generativity vs self-absorption (care)*	Caring for others	
65+ years Older adulthood		Integrity vs despair (wisdom)*	Self-fulfilment	

*Thinking Ego-centric.

Heterosexual interests

Note: ( )*Desired outcome of psychosocial crises.

More evidence is available for the Cognitive Theory of Piaget, as many of his ideas on the developmental stages of mental reasoning can be tested experimentally.

Many researchers have used Piaget's ideas and formulated stage theories for the development of self-recognition, moral reasoning etc. Some, such as Kohlberg (1976) have not limited the notion of development to specific age-groups, so that the various stages of moral reasoning may take a lifetime to achieve (if at all).

Behavioural theories

A more flexible approach to human development is provided by Behavioural Theories which are more concerned with the observable changes seen in person–environment interactions. Less emphasis is placed on internal emotional and mental processes, as they are not directly measurable, and emphasis is given to environmental conditions. According to behaviourists there are no developmental 'stages' in the way people learn. The mechanisms of learning are the same for all ages. These mechanisms occur during a person's interaction with his/her environment. The process of learning is based on the notion that behavioural responses to environmental cues that are followed by a desired outcome (i.e. reinforced) are more likely to be repeated in future. Conversely, responses that are followed by an undesired outcome (i.e. punished) are less likely to be repeated.

Albert Bandura. It was from this perspective that Albert Bandura (1977) developed the concept of a 'Social Learning Theory'. This theoretical approach began to bridge the gap between the behaviourist and psychodynamic ideas as, without denying the power of the environment, it recognized the importance of internal processes such as thoughts and feelings. Greater weight was given to cognitive processes as individuals in childhood and adulthood were seen to learn by observing and imitating others. In addition, Bandura introduced the concept of 'Social Reinforcers' where a behavioural response is followed by another person's positive or negative reaction, which in turn enhances or inhibits the chances of the same behavioural response happening again. Thus, behavioural theories regard development as a continuous process of learning across the entire life-span.

Critical period theories

John Bowlby. All the giants of human developmental theory have been influenced by Darwinian ideas of evolution, but only Bowlby has managed successfully to tie together the evolutionary focus on adaptation with the psychodynamic and behavioural importance of social relationships during infancy and childhood.

Bowlby (1969) argues that there is a critical period of learning in human development when infants are genetically predisposed to form close attachments to caring adults. He claims that the quality of infant-to-caregiver attachment is greatly determined by parental behaviour and the quality of care the infant receives. This idea of an interaction between nature (instinct) and nurture (learning) is supported by research evidence which shows that infant attachment is universal across varied cultures, but the 'security' of attachments varies greatly within each population studied.

As Erikson observed, some infants are confident and can trust that their parents will be available and responsive to them. According to Bowlby, these infants have secure social attachments. Erikson also observed the contrary: some infants are doubtful about their parents' availability and mistrust others. Bowlby claims these infants have insecure and anxious attachments.

Bowlby is regarded as a psychodynamic therapist but he adapts some ideas from cognitive and behavioural theories. He writes that infants begin to develop generalized social expectations of their caregiver's behaviour, so that by the end of their first year, infants have an 'internal working model' of their parents' accessibility, sensitivity, responsiveness and acceptance. In turn, the infant builds a reflective view of self as worthy or unworthy. Bowlby argues that this 'internal working model of self' heavily influences personality formation, especially the growth of autonomy, initiative and identity as described by Erikson (1965).

However, Bowlby contests Freud's ideas on the nature of the relationship between early experience and later problems. Psychological disorders in individuals are not always a result of sexual seduction or due to their fantasies and secret wishes. He argues that conflicts are the result of actual adverse experiences in the broadest sense, during the formation and maintenance of early social relationships.

Bowlby (1984) claims that insecurely and anxiously attached infants have a greater probability of psychological disorders in adulthood. He proposes that children who experience a rejection of their attachment behaviours can develop 'Affectionless' personality characteristics. This view is of considerable importance in relation to contemporary understanding of child abuse. The literature on child abuse contains numerous reports regarding the high number of abusive parents who were themselves victims of abuse as children (Browne and Herbert, 1995).

It is now widely accepted that the interactions between parent and child are fundamental to human development in general. Therefore, the infant, given the preadaptations for interactive development, requires the opportunity for interaction, and the importance of a turn-taking pattern of early parent–child interaction has been stressed by many researchers (Smith and Cowie, 1991). For, without a cyclic interpersonal process, both the establishment of a secure parent–child relationship and further cognitive and social growth of the child may be retarded (Herbert, 1991; Webster-Stratton and Herbert, 1994).

The notion of critical developmental periods has now been applied to the whole life-span (Levinson *et al.*, 1978; Gould, 1978). These critical periods are generally linked to times of transformation from one life-stage to another. Hence, learning and development is not seen as a continuous process but one that speeds up and slows down to meet the demands of rapid changes in the environment, during certain critical periods in a person's life-span (see Table 5.2). This process is seen in cognitive development of an individual's mental reasoning: the inquisitive mind of a child and adolescent adapts to an achieving mind of a young adult. In middle age a person's mind must think in responsible terms in relation to a career and to dependants. In old age the mind is concerned with reflection and reintegration of a life-span of activity (Kimmel, 1990).

Table 5.2 *Life-span developmental periods (adapted from Gould 1978 and Levinson, et al. 1978)*

Developmental task	Age	Critical periods	
		Late adulthood	
	65		
		Late adult transition (retirement)	
Acceptance of past, general mellowing of views	60	Culmination of middle adulthood	⎫
	55		⎪
Looking back on life achievement		Age 50 transition (reflection on life clock)	Middle adulthood
	50		⎬
Settling down: accepting one's life		Entering middle adulthood	⎪
	45		⎭
Period of urgency to attain life goals: awareness of time limitation; realignment of life's goals		Mid-life transition (reflection on career clock)	
	40		
		Settling down in relationships and career	⎫
	34		Early adulthood
Questioning self: role confusion, marriage and career		Transition age 30 (reflection on relationships)	⎬
	28		⎪
Develop independence, commitment to a career and/or to children		Entering the adult world	⎪
	22		⎪
Leave family, peer relationship orientation	18	Early adult transition	⎭
Desire to escape parental control		Adolescence	

Adolescence

Of all the stages of life, there is little doubt that adolescence is one of the most studied periods of human development. For that reason, we have selected adolescence for particular discussion in the present context.

The American child psychologist G. Stanley Hall stands as a major influence on contemporary thinking about adolescence. Hall (1904) argued that adolescence is a time of '*sturm und drang*', a period of 'storm and stress', characterized by emotional upheaval, suffering, passion and rebellion against adult authority. Most theorists have remained faithful to the idea of adolescence as a time of 'storm and stress', and although we might now prefer to use terms such as 'adolescent conflict' the modern-day spirit remains essentially the same. However, it is also true that a great many young people seem to get along quite nicely, enjoying life with little evidence of conflict throwing their life into turmoil.

If we take the stance that adolescents are a socially defined group – that is, a group which is given its identity by the society and culture in which it exists – then to understand adolescence we must look to two main areas. The first is the individual adolescent; the second is social and cultural factors of particular importance to the adolescent (Hollin, 1988).

Individual factors

During adolescence a number of individual changes are taking place. The most obvious changes, of course, are those brought about by the onset of puberty such as changes in the shape of the body, the development of secondary sexual characteristics, hormonal and biochemical changes, height and weight changes, and a change to mature sexual functioning.

Biological changes. The biological changes which take place during adolescence (Table 5.3) are often referred to as puberty: these changes have

Table 5.3 *Biological changes in adolescence*

Female	Male
Acne appears	Acne appears
Body hair appears	Body hair appears
Breasts develop	Facial hair appears
Body contours become rounded	Larynx enlarges
Uterus enlarges	(causing deeper voice)
Menstruation begins	Genitals enlarge
Weight gain	Weight gain
Height gain	Height gain

one main function, to allow the individual to be able to reproduce. The changes which are taking place are chemically complex, but can be summarized as being essentially changes in levels of hormonal activity. Hormones are chemical secretions from the glands which interact with different groups of cells in the body, causing the cells to change in both structure and function. In adolescence the sex hormones testosterone for males and oestrogen for females are of particular importance.

The age at which these changes take place varies both within and between the sexes. Some females show the first signs of puberty, usually breast development, as early as 9 years of age, while others will show no signs until they are about 14 years old: some females will begin to menstruate at 11 years old; others not until they reach the age of 16. In males puberty can begin as early as 10 years or as late as 16 years (Brooks-Gunn and Reiter, 1990).

While these changes are of great importance, we cannot really think of them as the best definition of adolescence. It must have been the case 100 years ago that young people went through the biological changes similar to those we witness today, yet no one then called this 'adolescence'. Therefore, while we cannot ignore the physical changes taking place, we must look to other personal changes in attempting to gain a full understanding of adolescence. It is here that we move to the altogether less obvious realms of psychological change.

Psychological changes. The number of developmental tasks involved in adolescence (see Table 5.4) places a lot of demands on the individual during this period of their life-span. This creates heavy psychological demands on the person and consequently a number of psychological changes take place.

The psychological changes taking place centre on the adolescent's need to revise their opinion of themselves: in other words, to construct a new self-concept to take account of the changes they are experiencing. The adolescent's change in self-concept may extend to a range of beliefs, attitudes and values: thus the adolescent may revise their opinion of how physically attractive they

Table 5.4 *Developmental tasks of adolescence* (after Havighurst, 1973)

1. Achieving new and more mature relations with age-mates of both sexes	5. Preparing for marriage and family life
2. Achieving a masculine or feminine social role	6. Preparing for an economic career
3. Accepting one's physique and using the body effectively	7. Acquiring a set of values and an ethical system as a guide to behaviour – developing an ideology
4. Achieving emotional independence from parents and other adults	8. Desiring and achieving socially responsible behaviour

judge themselves to be; may change their moral values; may develop a new sense of what they might be able to achieve in life; may reassess their views of what society, friends, parents seem to expect from them; and may restructure their view of themselves as a man or woman and what they expect from other men and women. In total the adolescent's view of themselves comes under close scrutiny and various changes, some major some minor, are made.

Most people have an 'ideal self', the person we would be if not for our various shortcomings, lack of skills and so on. This ideal self might be based on an actual person such as a friend, a parent or a celebrity; alternatively it might be a mixture of imagined and real ideals from a variety of sources. It is always interesting to try and work out your own ideal self: list the ideal values you would like to hold and the individuals you feel best exemplify these values. While our ideals change throughout our lives, during adolescence they change at a greater pace and are probably more prone to the influence of other people than is the case later in life.

The degree of similarity between an individual's self-concept and their ideal self can be crucially important: a good match leads to high self-esteem, a poor match produces low self-esteem. Self-esteem can be thought of as the emotional evaluation that we make about ourselves; an evaluation usually in terms of feelings of approval or disapproval with the way we see ourselves. With evaluation of the self undergoing various changes during adolescence, the adolescent's self-esteem can rise and fall over relatively short periods of time (Jensen, 1985).

Therefore, adolescents are in a period of self-questioning that comes from changes encompassing their rapid physical growth and sexual maturation at a time when they have just established their competence in formal operational mental reasoning, the way adults think (Piaget, 1954). The chief concerns of adolescents are to establish their identity and develop a commitment to a career path. However, adolescents may feel ambivalent about their identity and as a result may experience anxiety and feel incapable of making decisions or choosing roles. Erikson (1965) therefore describes the adolescent crisis in psychosocial development as 'identity versus role confusion'. To compensate for role confusion an adolescent may become completely committed to some fashionable hero or ideal. An adolescent may also become committed to a deviant peer group and may become dependent on drugs and alcohol (McMurran and Hollin, 1993). Another reaction is to seek temporary relief in young love, where the adolescent seeks to define his or her own identity through a close relationship with a peer. This manifests itself as another problem for society as a third of all illegitimate births involve teenage girls and a third of teenage brides are pregnant.

It should not, however, be thought that these changes occur in a vacuum. Psychological research has consistently shown that the level of self-esteem in children and adolescents is related to both the style of parenting and the parents' level of self-esteem. Stanley Coopersmith, one of the influential figures in this field of research, suggested that a style of parenting which minimizes punishment and avoids undue criticism and withdrawal of love leads to high self-esteem in children and adolescents (Coopersmith, 1967). Parents with low self-esteem display low self-esteem attitudes and behaviour, in turn imitated by children and leading to a low level of self-esteem for them also. The complicated interaction between biological change, psychological change and social factors is illustrated by research which has looked at the effects of early and late development. It was found that boys who mature early are at a distinct advantage: they are more popular with peers and with adults, seem more relaxed and self-confident, and are less dependent upon others (Jones, 1965). This finding has been linked to self-esteem in that boys who are stronger, quicker and so on will tend to do well in physical activities such as sport; this in turn leads to favourable comments from adults, high status with peers and therefore high self-esteem. The findings for females appear to be different from those for males (Peskin, 1973). The early-maturing female adolescent becomes self-conscious as the development of secondary sexual characteristics emphasizes the difference between her and other girls of her age. It appears that these differences between early and late maturers in adolescence disappear in adulthood.

The biological changes in adolescence can also influence the way that the adolescent sees their role in life as a member of either the male or female sex. The term 'sex role' is a double-edged one: it can be used to refer to one's view of oneself as 'masculine', 'feminine' or some combination of the two; or alternatively to refer to one's opinion of what role men and women should be playing in society. Adolescents typically show many of the traditional views of the appropriate roles for females and males (Hollin, 1986).

Social factors

The most obvious changes in social behaviour facing adolescents are their relationships with the opposite sex. The adolescent may experiment with all aspects of sexual behaviour including making and breaking relationships, intimacy and even marriage (Katchadourian, 1990). However, other social changes are taking place: the adolescent's role in his or her family may shift, relationships with parents are traditionally strained as the adolescent struggles for independence; the adolescent is called upon to make decisions relating to work and education which can have effects for years to come; and the adolescent's own circle of friends and acquaintances may change as like-minded young people are found who sympathize and agree with the changes taking place. With regard to the last point, it is paradoxical that, at a time of such personal change, adolescents are great conformers with the rules of their particular sub-culture.

The young person who is experiencing biological change and maturing psychologically may feel ready to assume a new, more responsible role in life; may, in short, want to be treated as an adult. The adult world, on the other hand, may not share the adolescent's view. The young person is seen as still having child-like qualities, still growing up and still needing to be treated like a child. The inevitable result of such differences is a struggle for control, a struggle between the adolescent who wishes, like other adults, to have control over their own actions; while the adult, often for all the best reasons, wants to control their child as they have always done. The classic adolescent rebellion is therefore usually against authority – authority that typically manifests itself in adult form (Epps and Hollin, 1993). This struggle for independence is most keenly felt within the family.

Families.   Some families experience their adolescent son or daughter as a problem during this time of their lives. In fact, 6 per cent of parents ring help lines to say that their adolescent children are severely maltreating them (Parentline, 1990). Indeed, recent research into family functioning has brought to prominence a previously neglected type of family violence, namely that where parents are physically abused by their adolescent children (Gelles and Cornell, 1990).

Prevalence rates of 'parent abuse' are still controversial and vary widely depending on the definition used and the method of collecting data. A comparison of the data on aggressive acts between children and their parents from the National Family Violence Resurvey (Straus and Gelles, 1988) reveals that the extent of violence by teenagers towards their parents was much lower than parent-to-teenager. Thirty-four per cent of teenagers (15–17 years) had been physically assaulted by a parent in some manner (i.e. parent threw something, pushed, grabbed, shoved or slapped), with 7 per cent suffering severely violent acts (i.e. hit with fist or object, kicked, beaten, threatened with knife or gun). In comparison with this, 10 per cent of teenagers (15–17 years) were violent to their parents, 3.5 per cent severely. Previously, prevalence rates for any act of violence against parents were estimated as 8 per cent to fathers and 6 per cent to mothers (Peek *et al.*, 1985), with later studies claiming the prevalence of severe 'parent abuse' as high as 5 per cent (Agnew and Huguley, 1989; Parentline, 1990).

It should be pointed out, however, that the parental victim of aggression from their adolescent child has not always been violent to the child in the past. Livingstone (1986) found that 29 per cent of single mothers in the USA are hit by their teenage children. He claimed that these violent sons and daughters may have learnt this aggressive control of their mother from their estranged violent father. Alternatively, he postulates that the violence to the mother may be a way of punishing the parent for the pain of the parent's divorce and family separation.

There are many potential causes of conflict between adolescents and their caregivers. The adolescent culture of the day may cause adult unease because of its clothes, hairstyles, music, friends, dating, sex, homosexuality, drugs etc. The stereotype is that all households with an adolescent are in a state of permanent uproar, as parents and adolescent clash on just about everything. Yet this is not the case; some young people have a remarkably happy adolescence, their relationship with their parents growing and developing to accommodate the changes taking place. The differences between families who struggle with adolescence and those who cope and thrive has been studied in detail (Herbert, 1987).

Studies of families have revealed three important aspects to parental behaviour: these are *affection, authority* and *anxiety* (Becker, 1964).

Affection in parenting can be thought of as the amount of support the parent or caregiver shows to the child. This is behaviour characterized by 'child-centred' attitudes and behaviour, such as accepting, approving of and understanding the child, together with praise for achievement and little or no use of physical punishment. Authority, as the term suggests, is related to the degree of power the parent elects to use. This is seen in the use of a great many restrictions on what the adolescent is permitted to do, and strict enforcement of rules and demands such as in household rituals, obedience, behaviour towards brothers and sisters, and household chores. Finally, anxiety is defined as unduly high levels of concern for the child, leading to excessive protectiveness and worry about the child's welfare. The calm parent is the exact opposite: able to balance their concern for the child's welfare against the need for the child to develop independence.

As in all things, some degree of moderation is usually the best course and this is what would be found in most families: some degree of give and take between the adolescent and their parents. However, too little or too much of anything can lead to difficulties, and certain patterns of parental behaviour have been found to be associated with particular types of adolescent difficulties (Smith, 1983).

Those parents who are low in support, power and anxiety set few boundaries and restrictions for their children. The adolescent is left to his or her own devices, without any control over what they do. Significant numbers of delinquent adolescents come from this type of family. At the other extreme, adolescents from overly hostile and restrictive families are liable to be aggressive themselves. Highly controlling families tend to be associated with adolescents who lack assertion and are seen as shy and anxious.

At the other end of the scale are those parents who are high in affection and support. It is often said the 'love is all', that if children and adolescents are loved then everything will be all right. However, love needs to be balanced with the right amounts of power and concern. The family styles which seem to have the most to offer are the 'democratic' and 'organized' types. Democratic parents are supportive of their children without excessive use of power, or too much emotional involvement to the detriment of close relationships. A characteristic of the democratic family is the 'family council' in which rules are set jointly by parents and adolescent on an equal basis. Unlike the indulgent parent who acts in fear and trepidation, the democratic parent expresses confidence in the adolescent's judgment. Adolescents from this type of family encounter new experiences without the need to rebel against adult restrictions.

Similarly, the organized type of family is highly supportive, but chooses to exercise greater parental authority. The authority is usually directed towards the adolescent's achievement and success in life. Adolescents from this type of family are generally compliant and respectful to authority, they may well be successful in life, although without the same sense of freedom and creativity as some of their peers.

In conclusion, it is the type of interaction between the adolescent and their parents which is crucial. While issues will arise which are potential sources of disquiet, the way in which they are resolved is the important thing. Contrary to the popular myth, families with adolescents can be happy families!

Finally, we should not forget the expectations and opportunities society holds for the adolescent: the education, recreational and employment openings provided by society, and the legislation, rules and procedures it has formed to contain and regulate adolescent behaviour. It should be remembered that adolescents are big business: the music, clothing and publishing industries in particular have a great deal invested in the 'teenage market'. Further, a great many specialists, such as psychologists, psychiatrists, youth workers and social workers, earn a living from adolescents, particularly adolescents with problems (Kazdin, 1993).

Conclusion

The recent recognition that biological, psychological and social development continues throughout an individual's life-span and does not culminate in adolescence is an important one. This is not to say that the developmental changes of childhood are not paramount for human development. Indeed, research has shown that early childhood experiences set the scene for favourable or unfavourable developmental changes during adolescence and adulthood. This chapter has presented in detail the developmental stage of adolescence, which can be seen as a transitionary period between childhood and adulthood, being influenced by the past and yet influencing the future development of every individual.

Further reading

HERBERT, M. (1987) *Living with Teenagers*, Oxford, Blackwell.

JENSEN, L.C. (1985) *Adolescence: Theories, Research, Applications*, St Paul, MN, West.

KIMMEL, D.C. (1990) *Adulthood and Ageing*, 3rd ed., Chichester, Wiley.

MUSSEN, P.H., CONGER, J.J., KAGAN, J. and HUSTON, C.A. (1990) *Childhood Development and Personality*, New York, Harper & Row.

SANTROCK, J.W. and BARTLETT, J.C. (1986) *Developmental Psychology: a Life-cycle Perspective*, 2nd ed., Iowa, W.C. Brown.

References

AGNEW, R. and HUGULEY, S. (1989) 'Adolescent violence towards parents', *Journal of Marriage and Family*, **51** (3), 699–711.

ALLPORT, G.W. (1961) *Patterns and Growth in Personality*, New York, Holt, Rinehart & Winston.

BANDURA, A. (1973) *Aggression: A Social Learning Analysis*, Englewood Cliffs, NJ, Prentice-Hall.

BANDURA, A. (1977) *Social Learning Theory*, Englewood Cliffs, NJ, Prentice-Hall.

BECKER, W.L. (1964) 'Consequences of different kinds of parental discipline', in M.L. HOFFMAN and L.W. HOFFMAN (Eds) *Review of Child Development*, Vol 1, New York, Russell Sage Foundation.

BOWLBY, J. (1969) *Attachment and loss*, Vol 1: *Attachment*, London, Hogarth.

BOWLBY, J. (1984) 'Violence in the family as a disorder of the attachment and caregiving systems', *American Journal of Psychoanalysis*, **44**, 9–31.

BROOKS-GUNN, J. and REITER, E.O. (1990) 'The role of pubertal processes', in S.S. FELDMAN and G.R. ELLIOTT (Eds) *At the Threshold: The Developing Adolescent*, Cambridge, MA, Harvard University Press.

BROWNE K.D. and HERBERT, M. (1995) *Preventing Family Violence*, Chichester, Wiley.

CENTRAL STATISTICAL OFFICE (1994) *Social Trends*, London, HMSO.

COLARUSSO, C.A. (1992) *Child and Adult Development: A Psychoanalytic Introduction for Clinicians*, New York, Plenum Press.

COOPERSMITH, S. (1967) *The Antecedents of Self-Esteem*, San Francisco, CA, Freeman.

EPPS, K. and HOLLIN, C.R. (1993) 'Authority and hatred', in V. VARMA (Ed.) *How and Why Children Hate: A Study of Conscious and Unconscious Sources*, London, Jessica Kingsley.

ERIKSON, E.H. (1965) *Childhood and Society*, revised ed., Harmondsworth, Penguin.

FREUD, S. (1905) *An Outline of Psychoanalysis* (1940), in J. STRACHEY (Ed. and Trans.) *The Standard Edition of the Complete Psychological Works of Sigmund Freud*, Vol 23, London, Hogarth Press.

GELLES, R.J. and CORNELL, C.P. (1990) *Intimate Violence in Families*, 2nd ed., Beverley Hills, CA, Sage.

GOULD, R.L. (1978) *Transformations*, New York, Simon & Schuster.

HALL, G.S. (1904) *Adolescence*, Englewood Cliffs, NJ, Prentice-Hall.

HAVIGHURST, R.J. (1973) 'History of developmental psychology: socialization and personality through the life-span', in P.B. BALTES and K.W. SCHAIE (Eds) *Lifespan Developmental Psychology*, New York, Academic Press.

HERBERT, M. (1987) *Living with Teenagers*, Oxford, Blackwell.

HERBERT, M. (1991) *Clinical Child Psychology*, Chichester, Wiley.

HOLLIN, C.R. (1986) 'Sex roles in adolescence', in D.J. HARGREAVES and A.M. COLLEY (Eds) *The Psychology of Sex Roles*, London, Harper & Row.

HOLLIN, C.R. (1988) *Just a Phase? Essays on Adolescence*, Leicester, Youth Clubs UK Publications.

JENSEN, L.C. (1985) *Adolescence: Theories, Research, Applications*, St Paul, MN, West.

JONES, M.C. (1965) 'Psychological correlates of somatic development', *Child Development*, **36**, 899–911.

KATCHADOURIAN, H. (1990) 'Sexuality', in S.S. FELDMAN and G.R. ELLIOTT (Eds) *At the Threshold: The Developing Adolescent*, Cambridge, MA, Harvard University Press.

KAZDIN, A.E. (1993) 'Adolescent mental health: prevention and treatment programs', *American Psychologist*, **48**, 127–41.

KIMMEL, D.C. (1990) *Adulthood and Ageing* 3rd ed., Chichester, Wiley.

KOHLBERG, K. (1976) 'Moral stages and moralization: the cognitive-developmental approach', in T. LICKONG (Ed.) *Moral Development and Behavior*, New York, Holt, Rinehart & Winston.

LEVINSON, D.J., DARROW, C., KLEIN, E.B., LEVINSON, M.H. and McKEE, B. (1978) *The Seasons of a Man's Life*, New York, Knopf.

LIVINGSTONE, L.R. (1986) 'Children's violence to single mothers', *Journal of Sociology and Social Welfare*, **13**, 920–33.

MASLOW, A.H. (1968) *Towards a Psychology of Being* 2nd ed., New York, Harper & Row.

MASLOW, A.H. (1970) *Motivation and Personality* 2nd ed., New York, Harper & Row.

McMURRAN, M. and HOLLIN, C.R. (1993) *Young Offenders and Alcohol Related Crime*, Chichester, Wiley.

MILLER, P.H. (1993) *Theories of Developmental Psychology*, 3rd ed., New York, Freeman.

MUSSEN, P.H., CONGER, J.J., KAGAN, J. and HUSTON, C.A. (1990) *Childhood Development and Personality*, New York, Harper & Row.

PARENTLINE (1990) *Annual Report*, Thundersley, Essex, OPUS – Organisation for Parents Under Stress.

PEEK, C., FISHER, J.L. and KIDWELL, J.S. (1985) 'Teenage violence towards parents: a neglected dimension of family violence', *Journal of Marriage and the Family*, **47** (4), 1051–8.

PESKIN, H. (1973) 'Influence of the developmental schedule of puberty and early development', *Journal of Youth and Adolescence*, **2**, 273–90.

PIAGET, J. (1954) *The Construction of Reality in the Child*, London, Routledge & Kegan Paul.

SANTROCK, J.W. and BARTLETT, J.C. (1986) *Developmental Psychology a Life-Cycle Perspective*, 2nd ed., Iowa, W.C. Brown.

SMITH P.K. and COWIE, H. (1991) *Understanding Children's Development*, 2nd ed., Oxford, Blackwell.

SMITH, T. (1983) 'Adolescent reactions to attempted parental control and influence techniques', *Journal of Marriage and the Family*, **2**, 533–41.

STRAUS, M.A. and GELLES, R.J. (1988) 'How violent are American families? Estimates from the National Family Violence Resurvey and other studies', in G. HOTALING, D. FINKELHOR, J. KIRKPATRICK and M. STRAUS (Eds) *Family Abuse and its Consequences: New Directions in Research*, Beverley Hills, Sage, Ch. 1, 14–37.

WEBSTER-STRATTON, C. and HERBERT, M. (1994) *Troubled Families and Troubled Children*, Chichester, Wiley.

Part III

Individual Differences and Learning

Chapter 6

Individual Differences

Patrick A. Tyler

Everybody is unique. There is nobody else in the world who is quite like you or me. We differ for biological reasons: our own particular arrangement of the DNA on our chromosomes is unique, so any characteristic which is even slightly influenced by our genes will contribute to our uniqueness. We also differ for environmental reasons: no two people can occupy the same environment at the same time throughout their lives. So any characteristic which is influenced by environment, experience and interaction with other people will contribute to our uniqueness.

The study of consistent individual differences in behaviour defines the psychology of personality. It should be noted that this textbook definition conflicts with the popular lay view of personality which corresponds to something like charisma and individual character: 'Betty has a wonderful personality'. By contrast and more prosaically, the personality psychologist might give Betty a personality test and conclude that she rates rather high on sociability, neuroticism and agreeableness, but low on conscientiousness and intellectual interests. She might be better advised to apply for jobs as a receptionist or a salesperson than as a librarian or police officer.

Theories of personality and individual differences

Historically the study of individual differences in behaviour has given rise to many different theories about their origins. Hall and Lindzey (1957), who wrote the leading textbook of theories of personality, discussed in detail about 20 different theories, a far from comprehensive selection. The reasons for such prolific theorizing on this subject seem to be twofold: (1) we all have our own views on human nature and human behaviour and this is indeed one of the ways in which we differ from everyone else; (2) the nature of the subject makes it difficult to generate and test hypotheses about personality differences, and therefore it is difficult to refute other people's theories and confirm our own.

Despite the profusion of theories about individual differences, it is sensible to identify four major themes or approaches underlying them. Psychoanalytic theories, following the teachings of Freud and his associates, emphasize the important role of unconscious processes and early traumatic experiences in the formation of personality. By contrast humanistic and cognitive theories propose that it is the operation of conscious processes and the striving for self-fulfilment which guides and gives consistency to our lives. Social learning theories mainly underline the role played by the environment, especially the social environment and social experience, in the development of our individuality. Finally, though historically first, the type and trait theories, while accepting the role played by all of these factors, emphasize the importance of understanding the particular combination of characteristics for the prediction of a person's success in life. An example of the trait approach can be seen in the description given above of Betty's personality and the use to which a personality psychologist might put such a description.

Psychoanalytic approaches

At the end of the nineteenth century, the first practitioners of the newly emerging discipline of psychology were dominated by the traditions of British philosophy and German physical science. The complexity of the human mind was thought to be decomposable (like white light and complex sounds) into simple components, and the method by which this analysis could be achieved was called introspection. A highly trained observer in the laboratories of Wilhelm Wundt in Leipzig, Germany or E.B. Titchener at Cornell University in the USA would look into his own mind and analyse the flow of thoughts, memories and feelings like a physical scientist objectively analysing a chemical compound. The assumption was that human beings are rational creatures, whose motivations, thoughts and emotions are available to consciousness, and that introspection is a viable method of gaining access to them.

One of the lasting contributions of Charles Darwin to psychology was to erode the distinction between instinctive animals and rational human beings. The theory of evolution, described first in the *Origin of Species* (1859), and especially its application to human evolution in the *Descent of Man* (1871), started his followers looking for evidence of rational behaviour in animals and instinctive motivations in people. The first of these two lines of enquiry led to the study of animal intelligence (for example by Thorndike, 1899) and subsequently to the explosion of laboratory studies of learning in animals in the middle of the twentieth century. The second consequence of Darwin's revolution was to implant the concept of 'instinct' in those who were searching for the basis of consistency in human personality. Almost immediately, a host of new instincts were suggested, to 'explain' every sort of behaviour. The observation that some children like to climb trees could be explained by a tree-climbing instinct; enjoyment of sports by a game-playing instinct. Any new behaviour could be covered by naming a new instinct. By the 1920s nearly a thousand instincts had been proposed. Obviously these instincts were merely being used as labels, and had no explanatory value at all.

At that time, Sigmund Freud was developing a theory of personality which many considered more promising. The essence of his early theory was that everyone has a reservoir of instinctual energy, the libido, which generates fantasies, wishes and desires. In principle, the expression of these desires is harmful because of the social sanctions which they would incur, so they are held in check by that part of the mind which has learned to stay in contact with reality. There is also part of us which feels guilty if we do something which would not be permitted by society. These three parts of the mind have been labelled the id (the part which always seeks immediate pleasure), the ego (the part which stays in contact with reality) and the superego (the conscience).

Because our unconscious desires and impulses constantly push for expression and gratification without considering the consequences, we become anxious when they come into conflict with our concept of reality and our moral conscience. We therefore develop characteristic ways of protecting ourselves against this anxiety. The most important way of protecting ourselves is to block or repress any deep-seated memory which might hurt us if it came to the surface. A cue which might be expected to elicit the memory through association may be ignored or may produce obviously inappropriate responses. For example, if you have had strained relationships with your mother which you are repressing, you may react in an inappropriate way when you meet the mother of your friend, ignoring her, or treating her as if she is someone else. Repression is one of several ego defence mechanisms; another is regression, or the tendency to revert to a way of acting which is characteristic of an earlier stage of development (such as crying to get your way when frustrated).

Freud and most of his followers were mainly concerned with understanding and treating the psychological problems of their patients in the clinic. Understandably, then, much of his theorizing focuses on neurotic symptoms and their origins and removal. There is one controversial part of his theory, however, which does make an attempt to explain individual differences in normal personality. This is the theory that every child has to pass through three major stages during early childhood. The first is the oral stage when the focus of sexual stimulation for the infant is the mother's breast and the pleasure obtained from sucking. The second is the anal stage when pleasure is obtained from control over retaining or expelling the bowel movements. Finally in the phallic stage erotic pleasure is obtained from stimulating and manipulating the genital region. In the phallic stage the little boy notices that he has a penis like his father and vies with his father for the love of his mother. Fearing that his love will end with his powerful rival removing his penis, which would make him just like his sisters who presumably lost theirs in this way, he diverts his energy into admiration for and identification with his powerful father and so resolves his conflict. This is the oedipal conflict and its desired resolution. Little girls go through a similar cycle of loving the father, mourning their lost penis, and ending up with identification with mother, known as the electra complex. People's personalities differ because we each may be frustrated at a different stage of development and become fixated at that stage; later in life in anxiety-evoking situations we regress to that stage and develop an appropriate set of character traits. Oral character traits include dependency, pessimism and passivity; anal characteristics are orderliness, stinginess and stubbornness; and phallic traits include vanity in males and ambitiousness in females.

Freud's great contributions to psychology were the emphasis on unconscious motivation and the importance of inner conflicts in the generation of anxiety and psychological problem behaviour, the emphasis on sexuality and his recognition of the importance of early traumatic experiences in the development of personality. However, his theory is heavily criticized by psychologists (following the philosopher, Karl Popper, 1963) for being too all-encompassing and virtually untestable; it is therefore unscientific. Psychoanalysis is often thought of as more like a religion or belief system that does not need verification if you are a believer. Freud's theory has come under increasingly vigorous attack from psychologists and philosophers of science in recent years. Two of the strongest critics are Jeffery Masson (1985) and A. Grünbaum (1984). Masson in particular started an interesting and current debate about the reality of childhood sexual abuse, arguing that Freud wrongly changed his views from an early belief that neurotic adults remembered real events to the later theory that such repressed memories represented childhood fantasies and desires. Current research on this subject has important legal consequences (Loftus, 1993).

Despite the scepticism of many academic psychologists, Freud's theory has continued to stimulate research on individual differences. Much of the recent research has focused on the defence mechanism of repression. For example, since the late 1960s Lloyd Silverman and his associates (Weinberger and Silverman, 1987) have carried out a long series of experimental studies, using a procedure which they call *subliminal psychodynamic activation (spa)*. Images designed to activate unconscious thoughts or wishes are presented to volunteers for a fraction of a second on a blank screen. The volunteers are unable to report what they saw, but they are found to behave in accordance with predictions from Freud's theory. For example, depressed people, who are thought to be turning their unconscious oral aggressive impulses inwards, became more depressed when presented with aggressive images (a stylized picture of a cannibal); stutterers, who are proposed to suffer from anal conflicts, were presented with an image of a dog defaecating which increased their stuttering; schizophrenics shown an image of a charging lion with bared teeth increased their pathological symptoms. Male homosexuals, proposed to have oedipal conflicts, were presented with a picture of an older woman embracing a younger man, superimposed with the words 'fuck mommy', and rated pictures of male nudes as more attractive than before the presentation. While these images exacerbated symptoms, many other studies suggested that 'subliminal' presentation of the comforting words 'Mommy and I are one' tended to relieve schizophrenic symptoms, decreased phobic behaviours, facilitated behaviour therapies and increased adherence to a diet.

Taken at face value, Silverman's studies provide convincing experimental evidence for Freud's theory, but there have been severe criticisms of his methodology (e.g. Balay and Shevrin, 1988; Brody, 1988). Perhaps the most

serious problem is that other investigators using the same techniq\~
Silverman have frequently been unable to find the same results. Other crit\~
include the dubious use of statistics, selective citing of supportive results while
non-supportive ones are ignored and occasionally changing the theory to fit the
data. The whole concept of subliminal presentation, which implies an old-
fashioned notion of a sensory threshold, is also under severe attack in psychology. That people, especially emotionally disturbed people, are unwilling to
report seeing an emotion-evoking stimulus, does not necessarily mean that they
are not conscious of it. There is also doubt as to whether these studies are a true
test of Freud's theory, since they do not attempt to elicit the inner conflicts
suffered by each individual.

Another line of research on individual differences in personality which
shows a distinct influence of psychoanalytic ideas started with the work of
Byrne (1961). Some people are found to deal with anxiety-arousing situations or
stimuli by avoiding information about them, while other people positively seek
out such information. Byrne labelled the two extremes *repressors* and
sensitizers and devised a questionnaire to measure individual differences along
this dimension. Subsequent research has shown that while sensitizers attend
more to their own negative qualities and report more distress in stressful
situations, they do better if they are given preparatory information (Cook,
1985). Repressors seem to be people who are especially sensitive to criticism
and threat and deal with it by ignoring it if they can do so, but if forced to do
so they will attend to and worry about the situation (Baumeister and Cairns,
1992). The difference, then, is not thought to be one of distorted memory (as
Freud might have suggested) but of the way we attend to events, so this
research too fails to add support to Freud's theory.

Types and traits

People have been classifying each other into personality types, probably since
we began to speak. For example, in 319 BC Theophrastus, a student of the great
Greek philosopher-scientist Aristotle, proposed 30 personality types including
the Miser, who only paid attention to profit and loss, the Boor, who displayed
his ignorance in a loud voice, and the Gossip, who revelled in fictitious sayings
for pleasure. Theophrastus was moved to wonder how such different types
could emerge in the rather homogeneous environment of the Greek state. More
recently, psychologists have attempted more limited classification into small
numbers of personality types. For example, in an attempt to explain the horrors
of the Nazi period and the persecution of Jews and other despised people by
the Third Reich, an Authoritarian personality type was described in detail and
said to apply to many in power at the time (Adorno *et al.*, 1950). The authoritarian person is characteristically sycophantic to superiors, ruthless to inferiors
and very rule bound: you may recognize the type. Another personality type,
known as *Type A*, was developed to describe the sort of person who is prone

to high blood pressure and heart disease (Friedman and Rosenman, 1974): such people are characteristically hard-driving, ambitious and assertive.

Except for these few quite limited examples, classifying people into simple personality types has generally not been a fruitful approach to understanding personality differences in psychology. Rather, most effort has gone into finding a number of basic *dimensions* of personality along which everyone can be placed. In this endeavour, personality theorists have been attempting to emulate the early successes achieved in the field of intelligence. In the early part of this century, Alfred Binet in France laid an important trail for others to follow when he developed an intelligence test for children. Later the American psychologists Terman in 1916 and Wechsler from 1938 (see Aiken, 1985) developed mental tests which could be used to measure people's mental ability on a single IQ scale, so that they could be compared on one dimension in the same way that we can compare their height in centimetres or their weight in grams. As well as furnishing an established and successful pattern for the dimensional approach, intelligence testing also provided a tentative theoretical rationale. Charles Spearman, the English statistician-psychologist, found that some people tend to do well at any sort of ability test, whether it deals with verbal, numerical or mechanical abilities, while others do badly. He therefore suggested that there is an underlying general ability (which he labelled G) with a number of different special abilities (Spearman, 1904). A person with a fairly high G might still have quite low special numerical skills and therefore perform poorly on various mathematics tests. By contrast, Thurstone (1938) believed that there were a small number (about nine) primary mental abilities, but no broad general ability.

The statistical technique developed by Spearman and Thurstone to study intellectual abilities is known as factor analysis. The tendency for some people to do well on two tests and for others to do poorly on both is indexed by a measure of association known as the correlation coefficient. Correlation coefficients can vary between +1, indicating a perfect positive association, and −1, indicating a perfect negative association, with 0 indicating no association. If you and your classmates are given three tests of verbal abilities (say vocabulary tests) in consecutive weeks, some people will tend to come out consistently on top, and some people consistently at the bottom each time; that is to say the tests are likely to have high positive correlations among them, e.g. about +0.7; the same is true if three tests of numerical ability are given – again the correlations will be about +0.7. However, different people do well (or poorly) on the maths tests from those who do well on the vocabulary tests. The correlation between verbal and numerical tests may be about +0.2 on average: the correlation is low but positive, because some people are quite good at any kind of test, while others are not. If you look at the set of correlation coefficients among all possible pairs of the six tests, you will see a pattern, with high positive correlations among the purely verbal tests, high positive correlations among the purely numerical tests, and low positive correlations between the two types of tests. Using the technique of factor analysis in the way Spearman did, we would find three factors: a general factor which could account for the positive correlations among all the tests, a verbal factor which accounts for the higher correlations among the verbal tests, and a numerical factor which accounts for the higher correlations among the numerical tests. Thurstone's method would give two primary factors (verbal and numerical), which have a low, positive correlation among themselves. For further discussion of the development of intelligence tests and the current state of work on the measurement of intelligence the interested reader is referred to Kline (1991).

The success of intelligence testing was soon applied to the study of individual differences in personality too, and the first modern personality tests were developed during and soon after the First World War. The first personality questionnaire was Woodworth's Personality Data Sheet, which was based on questions a psychiatrist might ask in an interview to assess whether potential soldiers have personality problems which might interfere with their efficient functioning. Many more questionnaires have been developed subsequently; all such questionnaires have in common that they ask you to respond on an answer sheet to a number of personal questions about yourself: your honesty, friendliness, anxiety, hostility, impulsiveness, etc. are probed in detail. Examples of items on a personality questionnaire might be 'I prefer quiet inactive pastimes to more active ones' or 'I tend to be somewhat emotional' with five permissible responses ranging from 'Hardly at all' to 'A lot' (Willerman, 1975). As with mental abilities, the associations among all these characteristics can be investigated using the statistical correlation techniques described previously. It has been of enormous interest to psychologists in this field to know how many 'primary' personality characteristics there are, and these psychologists have disagreed dramatically over the proposed number.

Two personality psychologists working at about the same time, and using rather similar techniques, were Raymond B. Cattell in the USA and Hans J. Eysenck in the UK. Both were trained in the factor-analytic traditions of Spearman and Thurstone before the Second World War, and both developed their own approaches to the analysis of personality immediately after the war. Eysenck has preferred to adopt an analytic technique similar to Spearman's, one which produces a very small number of uncorrelated major dimensions which are thought to account for much of the consistency in our behaviour. Most of Eysenck's early theorizing focused on the dimensions of extraversion–introversion and neuroticism–emotional stability. Many of the early personality theorists, including those in the psychoanalytic tradition, had emphasized the importance of one or both of these dimensions. For example, it was the psychoanalyst Carl Jung who introduced the dichotomous labelling of people as extraverts and introverts, and it was the early psychiatrists who introduced the concept of neurosis to describe people who suffer from a level of anxiety which produces disabling symptoms. In the late 1960s Eysenck added a third major dimension, known as psychoticism, to his scheme (Eysenck and Eysenck, 1976). The Eysenck Personality Questionnaire (EPQ) has been developed to measure his three dimensions, and is in very wide use today.

When Eysenck started his studies of personality, he already had a theoretical orientation and a historical perspective. His first studies were of neurotic soldiers in the psychological clinic, and his measures were behavioural observations and clinical case notes on these patients (Eysenck, 1944). It was no surprise that the first general dimension to emerge was neuroticism, nor, given his orientation, that this was closely followed by extraversion–introversion. By contrast, Cattell's approach was much more eclectic. His first studies were of small groups of college students who knew each other well, and who were asked to rate each other using descriptive words culled from the English dictionary and carefully chosen to be as comprehensive as possible (Cattell, 1946). Cattell rejected the simplicity of Eysenck's broad general dimensions, claiming that they lose too much detail, and preferred the descriptive utility of a larger number of smaller-scale traits. Some people love to organize activities for the group, some like to dominate a conversation, some are impulsive and uninhibited in their behaviour; they would all be rated as extraverts on Eysenck's dimensions, but this general description does not indicate the form of the extraverted behaviour they each display. Cattell would feel that for the description to be useful there should be three dimensions, with a low positive correlation between them. Such an approach resulted in about 12 to 20 traits being elicited in each of Cattell's studies. Cattell, like Eysenck, has produced a widely used personality questionnaire which is designed to measure 16 Personality Factors and is therefore known as the 16 PF.

Cattell and Eysenck may be seen to have disagreed more strongly over the level of generality which is most useful for personality description than over the actual number of personality dimensions that exist. Eysenck's theory has always proposed that there are a number of lower level traits (e.g. sociability, dominance, assertiveness, activity and liveliness) included within each of his dimensions (which he has often confusingly referred to as 'types'). With the exception of sociability and impulsivity, subsumed within extraversion in the early theory, he has not been especially interested in describing these traits. Cattell, moreover, believed that there were four higher level dimensions (extraversion–introversion, anxiety, toughness–sensitivity and dependence–independence) which could be derived by factor analysis from his 16 traits and that Eysenck was using these 'second-order' factors which were too general to be of much interest. Recent research, which uses the 'space-age' technology of the desktop computer and statistical software and therefore has an advantage over the early work of these two forerunners of psychometrics, calls into question the conclusions of both men. Cattell's 16 factors have proved impossible to replicate, even when his own questionnaire is administered, and they seem to have emerged from the crude techniques which he was forced to employ (Kline, 1993). The 16 PF questionnaire is widely used, especially by occupational psychologists for advising employers on the suitability of job applicants and promotion prospects, a crucial decision for an individual's career. Yet the test is known to be an unreliable instrument, as it is normally used, so how can its popularity be justified? There are three possible reasons for the apparent contradiction: (1) there is enough validity imparted by the higher order factors, which are reliable, to make the 16 primary factors usable; (2) there is rarely any evaluation of the success of psychometric measures used in job selection, so that even the highly unscientific method of handwriting analysis has achieved some popularity; (3) personality characteristics have little to do with success in most jobs, so it makes little difference what personality test is used (see Kline, 1993). There are probably elements of truth in the first two of these suggestions, but the last one is an extreme point of view.

By contrast, Eysenck's three dimensions are found to be very reliable and are found in recent studies to emerge from factor analysis of different personality questionnaires (Kline, 1993). However, they are argued to be insufficient to provide a full account of the structure of personality. Most modern trait theorists, such as McRae and Costa (1990), have come to the conclusion that there are five major dimensions underlying human personality. The work which led to this conclusion was performed initially by Norman (1963), using Cattell's rating scales, but methods of analysis similar to Eysenck's. The five major dimensions he found were labelled Extraversion, Agreeableness, Conscientiousness, Neuroticism and Culture. A number of more recent studies using a variety of different techniques and different subject populations have repeatedly revealed essentially the same set of five traits. The most vigorous proponents of this five-factor view of personality have been McRae and Costa (1990), John (1990) and Goldberg (1990), who called them the 'Big Five' personality dimensions. Costa and McRae (1985) have developed a personality questionnaire named the NEO-PI in which Norman's Culture factor is renamed Openness to Experience (NEO-PI stands for Neuroticism, Extraversion, Openness Personality Inventory). This questionnaire contains six narrow trait scales for each of the five broad dimensions. Table 6.1 shows for each dimension a list of adjectives which would describe a person who was high on that dimension, and the names of the NEO-PI scales which contribute to each dimension. In addition, because there is not complete agreement about the naming of the dimensions themselves, some of the alternative names for each dimension are shown.

What this research shows is that when we describe our own or other people's personality we tend to use a selection of words in the English language which have similar meanings. For example we might describe a friend as nice or pleasant or helpful or easygoing, etc. Someone we do not get on with we may describe as nasty, mean, hostile, etc. These are all terms which lie on the same personality dimension of agreeableness (though at opposite ends of it). Norman found quite early in his research that not only can we rate ourselves and people we know well along the five dimensions, but we can also rate the people we do not know at all, and the same dimensions appear in the descriptions we use. So perhaps the dimensions were more a characteristic of the language we use than of our personality; we all have simple stereotypes of the people we encounter and these are constrained by the language we have available to describe them. So is it possible that the five personality dimensions are really five dimensions of the meaning of words in the English language? It now seems that there is not a clear-cut answer to this question: the main

Table 6.1 *Examples of adjectives and questionnaire scales defining the five factors (after McRae & John, 1992)*

Factor	Also known as	Adjective	Scale
Extraversion	I	Active	Warmth
(E)	Social adaptability	Assertive	Gregariousness
	Surgency	Energetic	Assertiveness
	Assertiveness	Enthusiastic	Activity
	Sociability	Outgoing	Excitement seeking
		Talkative	Positive emotions
Agreeableness	II	Appreciative	Trust
(A)	Conformity	Forgiving	Straightforwardness
	Likeability	Generous	Altruism
	Friendly compliance	Kind	Compliance
		Sympathetic	Modesty
		Trusting	Tender-mindedness
Conscientiousness	III	Efficient	Competence
(C)	Will to achieve	Organized	Order
	Responsibility	Planful	Dutifulness
		Reliable	Achievement striving
		Responsible	Self-discipline
		Thorough	Deliberation
Neuroticism	IV	Anxious	Anxiety
(N)	Emotionality	Self-pitying	Hostility
	Emotional control	Tense	Depression
		Touchy	Self-consciousness
		Unstable	Impulsiveness
		Worrying	Vulnerability
Openness	V	Artistic	Fantasy
(O)	Inquiring intellect	Curious	Aesthetics
	Culture	Imaginative	Feelings
	Intelligence	Insightful	Actions
	Intellect	Original	Ideas
		Wide interests	Values

evidence that the five dimensions are 'real', rather than an artefact of our language, is that almost identical dimensions are found in people of other cultures, including Dutch, German and Japanese (McRae & John, 1992). In the Chinese, five similar dimensions are also found but they do not map exactly onto those found in Europeans, which gives some evidence of language or culture dependence. The cross-cultural and cross-linguistic equivalence of the five traits does suggest that there is something universally and characteristically human about them. Currently research on the 'big 5' personality dimensions is very active as investigators attempt to extend their applicability to different personality-measuring scales in a variety of populations (McRae & John, 1992).

Social learning approach

During the first half of this century, while the psychoanalysis and trait approaches to personality were being developed, experimental psychology as an academic discipline had progressed rapidly with very different emphases. It seemed logical to early theorists in the psychoanalytic and trait traditions that behavioural consistency should arise largely from factors within ourselves, and that when we respond to external events or cues, we do so in a characteristic and fairly predictable way. By contrast experimental psychologists were emphasizing the way in which behaviours are under the control of environmental stimuli, for example through the process of classical conditioning (see previous chapter). Many experiments showed that rats and pigeons learn to respond appropriately when a cue (light or tone) reliably predicts a food reward. In the late 1930s a group of experimental psychologists at Yale University, under the aegis of the influential learning theorist Clark Hull, developed the first social learning theory of personality. In their subsequent book *Social Learning and Imitation*, Miller & Dollard (1941) proposed that the main external stimuli influencing human behaviour are social rewards such as approval by friends and relatives and social cues. Imitation of the behaviour of others is the most important learned response to social cues and it provides the main mechanism by which we acquire our uniqueness. Characteristic individual differences in patterns of responding were said to come about through the history of social rewards encountered by the individual.

Experimental psychologists have not in general been very interested in explaining individual differences in personality and behaviour. In the late 1920s another group of psychologists at Yale University, under Hartshorne and May (1928), had carried out a vast array of behavioural tests on a large number of young schoolchildren. In all some 17 000 schoolchildren were tested using several hundred different sorts of tests of honesty and altruism in a massive Character Education Enquiry published in three volumes from 1928 to 1930. In general these investigators found that even tests of purportedly similar characteristics, such as tests of honesty or tests of altruism, had very low correlations among themselves. This was taken as meaning that there was not a consistently honest or dishonest character trait in children. Other experimental psychologists subsequently confirmed that one behavioural measure of a trait such as sociability, or self-restraint, is not a good predictor of another behavioural measure of the same trait (e.g. Epstein, 1983). In 1968 Walter Mischel reviewed a number of findings of this sort in his book *Personality and Assessment* before arriving at the conclusion that there is no individual consistency in behaviour.

The publication of *Personality and Assessment* had a lasting and numbing effect on the study of individual differences in personality during the subsequent decade. While theorists such as Block and Epstein disputed both the facts and methodology which led Mischel to his negative conclusion, young psychologists were no longer recruited to this area, major books were not published, and university departments stopped teaching courses on individual differences. In the end, after a long and fascinating debate in the psychological journals, a generally accepted compromise has been reached. It is generally agreed that, as Mischel insisted, it is difficult to predict individual acts of behaviour either from other behaviours or from personality questionnaires. However, this is mainly because single behavioural acts are very unreliable reflectors of stable personality traits. If I place you in a room containing strangers, I cannot predict reliably whether you will approach and integrate with these people just by knowing how sociably you are rated by yourself or others. However, if we aggregate behaviours over a number of different times and situations, the average amount of social interaction will correspond quite well to the ratings. Individual acts of behaviour are too closely controlled by immediate situational cues to be predicted accurately: apparently trivial things such as the size of the room, the seating arrangements, the age and gender of the participants may be more important than your overall sociability rating. It would appear that stable and consistent individual differences in personality are a guide, a personal philosophy or a broad strategy which we use to help us cope with specific situations. They are not a prescription or blueprint telling us exactly what to do.

Cognitive-behavioural approaches

The concept of a personal philosophy or broad strategy guiding behaviour has been adopted from cognitive psychology, the fourth of our themes underlying theories of individual differences. Early cognitive theorists such as Kurt Lewin, George Kelly and the Gestalt psychologists, like the learning theorists, did not place much emphasis on explaining individual differences in behaviour. They did, however, introduce a number of important concepts taken up by more recent theories. One was the notion that the internal factors central to psychodynamic and trait theories and the external factors emphasized by the social learning theories were equally important; these interact with each other and with the behaviour itself in the determination of our actions. A second concept is the idea that our actions are largely governed by certain thought processes which interpret information coming from both internal (fear, excitement etc.) and external sources. A third idea common to many of the cognitive theories is that of plans, intentions and goals. We all set ourselves goals – either small immediate goals like going shopping for the next meal, or large goals like getting a degree or getting married. We make plans to achieve these goals and it is the achievement of these plans that motivates most of our behaviour.

Another idea which has been largely reintroduced to psychology recently is the self-concept. The clinical psychologist Carl Rogers has been particularly influential in this area. The way we see ourselves and the way we think other people see us acts as a sort of selective filter through which we process all our incoming information. Rogers and others have made a distinction between the actual self (how we think we are) and the ideal self (how we would like to be). There is always a discrepancy between the two, which in turn sets goals and motivates plans for self-improvement. The self-concept has been adopted and forms a central part of the social cognitive theories of Walter Mischel and Albert Bandura. Mischel (1990) has mainly emphasized the dimension of self-control, especially the rules and strategies children use to delay the pleasure of a desired object like a toy. Bandura (1986) has placed a lot of attention on the development of competencies and abilities to cope with particular problems and situations. The way we judge our self-efficacy in a situation will influence what we do, how much effort we expend, whether we persist in a task, how frustrated, angry or upset we get and our future beliefs about our competence in similar situations.

The computer modelling approach, which is the focus of much recent experimental psychology, has also made an impact on the area of individual differences in personality. Central to this approach is the idea that we form mental representations or images, often known as schemas, which help us interpret and organize information and behaviour. Schemas help us make sense of our experiences, especially when there is insufficient information available. For example we may form schemas of categories of individuals (as teachers, students, car drivers, parents, etc.) which are quite adaptive in that they help us behave appropriately because we know what to expect in any situation. Some theorists believe there are hierarchies of schemas of increasing generality: for example, the schema 'school teacher' encompasses lower level schemas such as secondary school English teacher and is encompassed by higher level schemas such as 'educator'. In general, middle-level schemas are thought to be most useful. The largest and most complex schemas are self-schemas. Markus (1977) has shown that people with a particular self-schema, such as 'I am an independent person', process supporting information quickly, resist information which contradicts the self-schema and remember relevant events and actions. Research on the self-concept, primarily from a cognitive-behavioural standpoint, is currently one of the most productive and interesting areas of investigation into personality and individual differences.

Research on personality and individual differences

Recent research on individual differences in personality and behaviour has been influenced by the four approaches described, but is much more orientated towards the solution of particular problems than towards theory testing. As a result it is beginning to demonstrate the ways in which different theoretical approaches may be integrated in the explanation of psychological phenomena. Two of the most active areas of research which have contributed to our understanding of this topic are behavioural genetic studies and studies on stress and coping strategies.

Research on the genetics of behaviour

An understanding of the genetic basis of behavioural differences is fundamental to any explanation of individual differences. Research in this area is now converging on a number of conclusions which have quite profound consequences for theories of individual differences. The main methods used by behaviour geneticists are the comparison of different sorts of twins, monozygotic (one-egg or identical) and dizygotic (two-egg or fraternal), and the natural experiment that is available when children are adopted. Very large numbers of twins and adopted children have now been subjected to measures of personality and abilities with interesting conclusions. First, the contribution of genetic factors to individual differences in personality and abilities is substantial. For global characteristics like extraversion and IQ, about 40 per cent of the differences between individuals is attributable to differences in the genes. Today the statistical techniques available for estimating the relative importance of genetic factors are very sophisticated and accurate. There are, however, a number of surprises in the data. The first is that the estimates of the relative importance of genes in various traits, such as extraversion and neuroticism, are similar for most traits measured. There are minor differences, of course, but the similarity of the correlation coefficients is quite striking. Second, it is found that members of the same family are alike for genetic reasons alone; there is no similarity among their personalities for non-genetic reasons such as interaction with parents, living in the same house, going to the same school. Third, odd results are sometimes found with identical twins who often resemble each other more than they should as predicted from their genetic relationship.

These recent findings (Plomin *et al.,* 1990) seem first of all to provide very strong support for a trait approach to personality. Clearly individual differences do exist in various personality traits, and these differences do have a biological basis. It is slightly disturbing perhaps that the strength of the genetic contribution does not seem to depend on whether the trait is one of the basic five robust traits or almost any other that can be measured reliably. The undiscriminating and unselective nature of the genetic contribution seems to suggest that biologically there is a smaller number of more primitive dimensions underlying the various personality dimensions, and that these then become differentiated and more distinguishable during development. There is in fact evidence that from the very earliest days of life infants differ in temperament on two dimensions. Some children are always more active than others, and some are temperamentally more unstable than others (Buss and Plomin, 1975, 1984). While these temperamental differences resemble later differences in extraversion and neuroticism, it seems possible that the dimensions of agreeableness and conscientiousness and all the minor personality characteristics are derived during development from the primitive temperaments. There is possibly also an even more basic temperamental difference of positive and negative affect (ranging from babies who are always happy and content to those who are often miserable). If there are just one or two original dimensions of infant temperament, which are strongly influenced by the genes and which then differentiate into the major personality dimensions, some of the puzzles described in the last paragraph would be resolved.

While genetic influences on personality are important, it should not be forgotten that environmental ones are even more important (they account for about 60 per cent of individual differences in personality). It is therefore astonishing that virtually all of this environmental contribution is found to be caused by factors which are not shared by other members of a family (Plomin and Daniels, 1987). This finding rules out the possibility that parental treatment, school, the type of neighbourhood, social or physical deprivation, family income, the number of books or bathrooms in the home have any influence on personality development. Perhaps this should not be surprising; after all, the same full range of personality characteristics is found in poor neighbourhoods as in wealthy ones. But past psychological and sociological theorists have placed considerable emphasis on the importance of these influences.

What are the environmental factors that do influence personality? Little success has yet been achieved in discovering the answer to this question, despite considerable efforts to do so. There may be a clue, however, in the greater than expected similarity of identical twins when they are raised together. These individuals are known to copy each other's tastes in clothes, music, friends etc. They probably often mould their own self-concept on the reflection of it that they see in their twin. They may well answer a personality questionnaire by trying to second-guess what their twin would say, almost as if they were being tested for the reliability of their answers. Of course they will often be wrong, one reason why the twin correlation is usually only 0.5 not 1.0. These data suggest that our self-concept is moulded during development as an adaptation of our unique genetic predispositions to our social environment. The nature of our characteristic interactions with those close to us, such as parents, siblings and especially close friends, is probably the most important environmental influence on personality development.

Research on stress and coping

Research on stress and coping strategies has its roots both in the biological and the social areas of psychology. It has been known since the beginning of the century that the experience of stress can have quite serious effects on health. It may be recalled that Freud's observation of the possible psychological origins for physical symptoms was instrumental in the development of his psychodynamic theory of personality. Walter Cannon (1932), the distinguished

American physiologist, shortly afterwards discussed the bodily reactions involved in the response to stressful stimuli as part of the body's adjustment to dangerous situations. Later, Hans Selye (1956) described in detail the stages of physical preparedness which the nervous and hormonal systems pass through during an alarm reaction. If the stressful stimuli persist, the body adapts to a state of constant preparedness for fight or flight (the General Adaptation Syndrome); however, this strain takes its toll in terms of a heightened propensity for cardiovascular disease and susceptibility to other diseases. According to this view, whatever the source of stress, its persistence will have the same general effects on the body and the health of the individual. While the physiologists were emphasizing stress outcomes in terms of physical health and bodily reactions, social psychologists were looking for the major causes of stress in the situation. For many years, the most important and identifiable causes were thought to lie in the major life events which we all experience: the death of a close relative, moving house, marriage, divorce, having children are stressful life events. These were all given a stress tally, and if you totted up too high a score in the course of a year you were thought to be very susceptible to various stress-related diseases (Holmes and Rahe, 1967).

In practice life is more complicated than either of these two approaches implies. Stress-related disease is not easily predictable from objective measures of environmental stressors. Some people seem to succumb easily with very little apparent pressure, while others withstand everything life throws at them and emerge unscathed. We would all like to know their secret! Various attempts have been made to relate these differences in stress response to personality. The largest amount of research on this topic has focused on the Type A behaviour pattern. In the 1950s two American cardiologists, Friedman and Rosenman, first described this behaviour pattern, which involves extreme competitiveness, impatience, hostility and direct, explosive speech (see Friedman and Rosenman, 1974). Subsequently many studies have confirmed the presence of a relationship between Type A behaviour and susceptibility to coronary heart disease. Two very large studies, the Western Collaborative Group Study (WCGS; Rosenman *et al.,* 1964) and the Framingham Heart Study (Haynes *et al.,* 1978) found Type A to be a predictor of coronary heart disease in initially healthy men and women. Such individuals seem to respond to stress, particularly uncontrollable stress, by increasing their work rate and becoming more competitive and hostile. The aspects of Type A that are most associated with coronary risk are hostility and the tendency not to express anger. Type A individuals react more strongly to stress with increases in heart rate and blood pressure and elevated levels of adrenal cortical hormones. Recent research has muddied the picture, however, and caused considerable controversy. A long-term follow-up of heart attack survivors from the WCGS found that post heart-attack victims who were Type A actually survived longer than others. In some way being Type A seems to protect against further fatal heart attacks, although it is not known whether this protection has a biomedical basis, or whether Type As take care of themselves better following a scare. There is evidence that individuals can learn to reduce the risky behaviours and thereby reduce the chance of subsequent heart attacks.

Type A behaviour (increasing work-rate and competitiveness, etc.) could be thought of as a characteristic strategy for coping with stress. A more widely accepted cognitive approach to stress and coping has been proposed by the clinical psychologist Richard Lazarus. In modern life, stressors come in a variety of guises: illness or death of a relative, too much work or no work, conflict with teachers, supervisors or relatives, role conflict (e.g. between being a good husband or wife and a good employee) or physical stressors like heat, poor lighting, natural disasters, and so on. How stressful we find these depends on their personal significance to us. Lazarus and Folkman (1984) suggested that we initially appraise the situation as being potentially harmful or threatening (primary appraisal), then we appraise our own coping resources available for dealing with the problem (secondary appraisal). Coping strategies fall into two major categories, problem-focused (planning ways of removing the stress by actively dealing with the problem) and emotion-focused (attempting to remove the stress by ignoring it or attending to something else). According to Lazarus and Folkman, which of these coping strategies is most effective will depend on the situation. However, our own research (Tyler and Cushway, 1992; Cushway and Tyler, 1994) has found that using emotion-focused strategies, such as avoidance coping, has relatively poor effects on mental health outcomes such as anxiety and depression.

Much recent research has been directed at finding personality dimensions which influence these cognitive appraisals of stress and the person's ability to cope. For example, some people seem to display helplessness in the face of stress, a feeling which seems to be conducive to the onset of illness and even death. Psychoanalytic theorists (Engel, 1968) have described a 'giving-up, given-up' complex which is associated with a lower sense of worth, a loss of gratification or relationships with others, confusion about past, present and future and reactivating of past episodes of giving up. This complex is very similar to the learned helplessness concept described by recent learning theorists (Seligman, 1975) as a basis for depression. When animals or people are put in a situation where they cannot control the onset of an unpleasant or stressful experience, they give up trying to escape and fatalistically endure it. The difficulty with helplessness considered as a general personality dimension is that people are quite discriminating and display helplessness in some situations but not others.

A more cognitive approach to helplessness in coping focuses on the explanatory style which people adopt when they are attributing causes to events (Peterson and Seligman, 1987). A pessimistic explanatory style is one which attributes unpleasant events to personal, long-lasting and pervasive causes: 'it's my fault, everything I do is wrong, it affects all my work'. There is good evidence which links a pessimistic explanatory style to lower performance in academic work, in sporting events and in the workplace and even to illness and death up to 35 years later (Peterson *et al.*, 1988). While the helplessness and pessimism research focuses on personality characteristics of people who are affected by stress, other research is concentrating on people who are resistant to stress. For example, Antonovsky (1987) believes that stress-resistant people have a sense of coherence, or a feeling that the world is comprehensible, manageable and meaningful. For them, stresses are challenges which they understand and feel that they have the resources to meet. Bandura (1982) would argue that they have a strong sense of self-efficacy or enduring belief that they can undertake an activity and eventually achieve a desired goal. People who have high efficacy expectations are more willing to take on a challenge, and more persistent when their efforts are frustrated. Scheier and Carver (1987) have also discussed the role of generalized expectancies about outcomes; optimists have generally favourable expectations about the future (regardless of whether they can personally influence it or not) while pessimists have unfavourable ones. Optimists are less likely to withdraw from stressful situations, experience less distress and engage in more active, problem-focused coping.

Summary

Research in the areas of behaviour genetics and stress and coping illustrates the extent to which contemporary psychologists are breaking away from the constraints of the traditional explanations of the origins of individual differences and combining forces to improve understanding. Even social-cognitive theorists, such as Mischel, once highly critical of the trait theorists for their emphasis on individual consistency (the essence of a traditional view of personality), are finding that they cannot sensibly describe individual differences in the cognitive systems which they believe to govern behaviour without considering personality dimensions. Meanwhile behaviour geneticists, while confirming the importance of inherited differences, are also providing the evidence for an even larger contribution from social-cognitive influences in individual differences in behaviour. The contribution of psychoanalytic theory, once shunned by respectable academic psychology, is gradually being recognized again, especially in the area of stress and coping. So far this convergence of ideas has not led to an integrated theory, and there are still disagreements among the theorists, not least over the amount of emphasis that should be given to the characteristics of the situation compared with those of the individual. So it may be optimistic to suggest that the problems of human individual differences will soon be solved, but I am an optimist.

Further reading

KLINE, P. (1993) *Personality: The Psychometric View*, London, Routledge.
MISCHEL, W. (1993) *Introduction to Personality*, 5th ed., Orlando, FL, Harcourt, Brace, Jovanovich.
PERVIN, L.A. (1993) *Personality: Theory and Research*, 6th ed., Chichester, Wiley.

References

ADORNO, T.W., FRENKEL-BRUNSWIK, E., LEVINSON, D.J. and SANFORD, R.N. (1950) *The Authoritarian Personality*, New York, Harper.

AIKEN, L.R. (1985) *Psychological Testing and Assessment*, 5th ed., Newton, MA, Allyn & Bacon.

ANTONOVSKY, A. (1987) *Unravelling the Mystery of Health*, San Francisco, Jossey-Bass.

BALAY, J. and SHEVRIN, H. (1988) 'The subliminal psychodynamic activation method', *American Psychologist, 43*, 161-74.

BANDURA, A. (1982) 'Self-efficacy mechanism in human agency', *American Psychologist, 37*, 122-47.

BANDURA, A. (1986) *Social Foundations of Thought and Action: A Social Cognitive Theory*, Englewood Cliffs, NJ, Prentice-Hall.

BAUMEISTER, R.F. and CAIRNS, K.H. (1992) 'Repression and self-presentation: when audiences interfere with self-deceptive strategies', *Journal of Personality and Social Psychology, 62*, 851-62.

BRODY, N. (1988) *Personality: In Search of Individuality*, London, Academic Press.

BUSS, A.H. and PLOMIN, R. (1975) *A Temperament Theory of Personality Development*, New York, Wiley.

BUSS, A.H. and PLOMIN, R. (1984) *Temperament: Early Developing Personality Traits*, Hillsdale, NJ, Erlbaum.

BYRNE, D. (1961) 'The repression–sensitization scale: Rationale, reliability and validity', *Journal of Personality, 29*, 334-49.

CANNON, W.B. (1932) *The Wisdom of the Body*, New York, Norton.

CATTELL, R.B. (1946) *Description and Measurement of Personality*, London, George Harrap.

COOK, J.R. (1985) 'Repression–sensitization and approach–avoidance as predictors of response to a laboratory stressor', *Journal of Personality and Social Psychology, 49*, 759-73.

COSTA, P.T., Jr. and MCRAE, R.R. (1985) *The NEO Personality Inventory Manual*, Odessa, FL, Psychological Assessment Resources.

CUSHWAY, D. and TYLER, P.A. (1994) 'Stress and coping in clinical psychologists', *Stress Medicine, 10*, 35-42.

ENGEL, G.L. (1968) 'A life setting conducive to illness: the giving up–given up complex', *Bulletin of the Menninger Clinic, 32*, 355-65.

EPSTEIN, S. (1983) 'Aggregation and beyond: some basic issues on the prediction of behavior', *Journal of Personality, 51*, 360-92.

EYSENCK, H.J. (1944) 'Types of personality - a factorial study of 700 neurotic soldiers', *Journal of Mental Science, 90*, 851-61.

EYSENCK, H.J. and EYSENCK, S.B.G. (1976) *Psychoticism as a Dimension of Personality*, New York, Crane, Russak.

FRIEDMAN, M. and ROSENMAN, R.F. (1974) *Type A Behavior and your Heart*, New York, Knopf.

GOLDBERG, L.R. (1990) 'An alternative "description of personality": the big-five factor structure', *Journal of Personality and Social Psychology*, **59**, 1216–29.

GRUNBAUM, A. (1984) *Foundations of Psychoanalysis: A Philosophical Critique*, Berkeley, University of California Press.

HALL, C.S. and LINDZEY, G. (1957) *Theories of Personality*, New York, Wiley.

HARTSHORNE, H. and MAY, M.A. (1928) *Studies in the Nature of Character*, I: *Studies in Deceit*, New York, Macmillan.

HAYNES, S.G., LEVINE, S., SCOTCH, N., FEINLEIB, M. and KANNEL, W. (1978) 'The relationship of psychosocial factors to coronary heart disease in the Framingham study', *American Journal of Epidemiology*, **107**, 362–83.

HOLMES, T.H. and RAHE, R.H. (1967) 'The social readjustment rating scale', *Journal of Psychosomatic Research*, **11**, 213–18.

JOHN, O.P. (1990) 'The "Big Five" factor taxonomy: dimensions of personality in the natural language and in questionnaires,' in L.A PERVIN (Ed.) *Handbook of Personality: Theory and Research* New York, Guilford, 66–100.

KLINE, P. (1991) *Intelligence: The Psychometric View*, London, Routledge.

KLINE, P. (1993) *Personality: The Psychometric View*, London, Routledge.

LAZARUS, R.S. and FOLKMAN, S. (1984) *Stress, Appraisal, and Coping*, New York, Springer.

LOFTUS, E.F. (1993) 'The reality of repressed memories', *American Psychologist*, **48**, 518–37.

MARKUS, H. (1977) 'Self-schemata and processing information about the self', *Journal of Personality and Social Psychology*, **35**, 63–78.

MASSON, J.M. (1985) *The Assault on Truth: Freud's Suppression of the Seduction Theory*, New York, Penguin.

McRAE, R.R. and COSTA, P.T., Jr. (1990) *Personality in Adulthood*, New York, Guilford Press.

McRAE, R.R. and JOHN, O.P. (1992) 'An introduction to the five factor model and its application', *Journal of Personality*, **60**, 175–215.

MILLER, N.E. and DOLLARD, J. (1941) *Social Learning and Imitation*. New Haven, Yale University Press.

MISCHEL, W. (1968) *Personality and Assessment*, New York, Wiley.

MISCHEL, W. (1990) 'Personality dispositions revised and revisited: a view after three decades', in L.A. PERVIN (Ed.) *Handbook of Personality: Theory and Research*, New York, Guilford, 111–34.

NORMAN, W.T. (1963) 'Toward an adequate taxonomy of personality attributes: replicated factor structure in peer nomination personality ratings', *Journal of Abnormal Social Psychology*, **66**, 574–88.

PETERSON, C. and SELIGMAN, M.E.P. (1987) 'Explanatory style and illness', *Journal of Personality,* **55**, 237–65.

PETERSON, C., SELIGMAN, M.E.P. and VAILLANT, G.E. (1988) 'Pessimistic explanatory style is a risk factor for physical illness: a thirty-five year longitudinal study', *Journal of Personality and Social Psychology*, **55**, 23–7.

PLOMIN, R. and DANIELS, D. (1987) 'Why are children in the same family so different from each other?', *Behavioral and Brain Sciences*, **10**, 1-16.

PLOMIN, R., CHIPUER, H.M. and LOEHLIN, J.C. (1990) 'Behavioral genetics and personality', in L.A. PERVIN (Ed.) *Handbook of Personality: Theory and Research*, New York, Guilford, 225-43.

POPPER, K. (1963) *Conjectures and Refutations: The Growth of Scientific Knowledge*, New York, Harper.

ROSENMAN, R.H., FRIEDMAN, M., STRAUS, R. WURM, M., KOSITCHEK, R., HAAN, W. and WERTHESSEN, N.T. (1964) 'A predictive study of coronary heart disease: the Western Collaborative Group Study', *Journal of the American Medical Association*, **189**, 15-22.

SCHEIER, M.F. and CARVER, C.S. (1987) 'Dispositional and physical well-being: the influence of generalized expectancies on health', *Journal of Personality*, **55**, 169-210.

SELIGMAN, M.P.E. (1975) *Helplessness: On Depression, Development, and Death*, San Francisco, Freeman.

SELYE, H. (1956) *The Stress of Life*, New York, McGraw-Hill.

SPEARMAN, C. (1904) 'General intelligence, objectively determined and measured', *American Journal of Psychology*, **15**, 201-93.

THURSTONE, L.L. (1938) *Primary Mental Abilities*, Chicago University Press.

TYLER, P.A. and CUSHWAY, D. (1992) 'Stress, coping and mental well-being in hospital nurses', *Stress Medicine*, **8**, 91-8.

WEINBERGER, J. and SILVERMAN, L.H. (1987) 'Subliminal psychodynamic activation: a method for studying psychoanalytic dynamic propositions', in R. HOGAN and W. JONES (Eds) *Perspectives in Personality: Theory, Measurement, and Interpersonal Dynamics*, Greenwich, CN, JAI Press, 251-87.

WILLERMAN, L. (1975) *Individual and Group Differences.* New York, Harper's College Press.

Chapter 7

Learning Theory

Glyn V. Thomas

Learning takes many forms and is involved in almost everything we do or say. It is essential for survival to be able to adapt to a changing environment, and learning is our principal means for doing this. It follows that understanding how and why people behave in a particular way will often involve learning. Of course, other factors are important too, such as heredity. Indeed, to be able to learn from experience at all is itself an ability which we have inherited. As we shall see below, heredity and experience interact in shaping how we behave.

Of the various forms of learning, I have selected just one for discussion in depth. This is *associative learning*, and I have selected it because of its importance in a great variety of behaviours and because theories of associative learning are central to psychology. It is also important as the basis for many clinical and educational procedures for helping people.

In this chapter I will first describe examples of associative learning and explain something of contemporary learning theories; second, I will discuss methods of studying learning; and third, I will select some recent developments for detailed discussion.

Examples and theories

One form of associative learning may already be familiar to you as Pavlovian (classical) conditioning. The popular image of Pavlovian conditioning is of a dog learning to salivate to the sound of a bell which has been paired with food. This may seem neither interesting in itself nor relevant to understanding much of human behaviour. Both impressions are mistaken. Associative learning is both highly relevant to everyday human behaviour and is a much more complex process than that suggested by the simple reflex described by Pavlov (1927).

The first example of conditioning that I wish to present is a case study described by Joseph Wolpe, a South African psychiatrist who pioneered many applications of conditioning principles in clinical psychology. The case concerns a middle-aged woman who for three years had been afraid to be alone in her house. Her fear had started one night when she was pregnant, her husband was away from home on business, and being on her own she had gone to bed early. After about one hour she noticed a warm sensation around her thighs, pulled back the bed clothes and discovered that the sheets were soaked in blood. She was terrified but managed to phone a doctor, who had her admitted at once to hospital. From then on she was frightened of being alone even though she realized that she had nothing to fear when she was no longer pregnant (Wolpe, 1981). This kind of irrational fear is an example of a phobia and is relatively common. Agras *et al.*, (1969) found that on average 77 people in every 1000 have experienced phobias, although many are relatively mild and not as disabling as that of Wolpe's patient.

Wolpe suggests that we can understand the origins of his patient's anxiety in terms of Pavlovian conditioning. Her miscarriage can be considered as an unconditioned stimulus (US), an event which in itself is naturally frightening. The circumstance of the miscarriage – being alone in the house – did not evoke any fear until it was associated with the miscarriage. Such an initially neutral stimulus which acquires significance through conditioning is known as a conditioned stimulus (CS). The fear elicited by the miscarriage (US) is termed an unconditioned response (UR), and the fear conditioned to the CS of being alone is termed a conditioned response (CR) (see Figure 7.1). Wolpe proposed that we consider the irrational fear of being alone simply as a conditioned response, a product of learning to associate the miscarriage with the situation in which it occurred.

A consequence of this view is that conditioning procedures might be effective in treating this woman's fear, and in fact this proved to be the case. What Wolpe did was apply a procedure which is now often called systematic desensitization (Wolpe, 1958). In this procedure he first interviews his client to discover what situations or stimuli evoke anxiety, and these stimuli are then rank ordered into an 'anxiety hierarchy'. The next step is to train the client to relax using a technique for producing deep muscle relaxation (Jacobson, 1938). The significance of deep muscle relaxation is that it is incompatible with strong emotions of any kind, including fear. The client is then exposed to fear stimuli of progressively increasing severity while maintaining deep muscle relaxation. The exposure to the conditioned fear stimuli can be imaginal (covert) or *in vivo*. The underlying rationale is that the relaxation will become associated with the conditioned stimuli and inhibit the conditioned fear they have come to

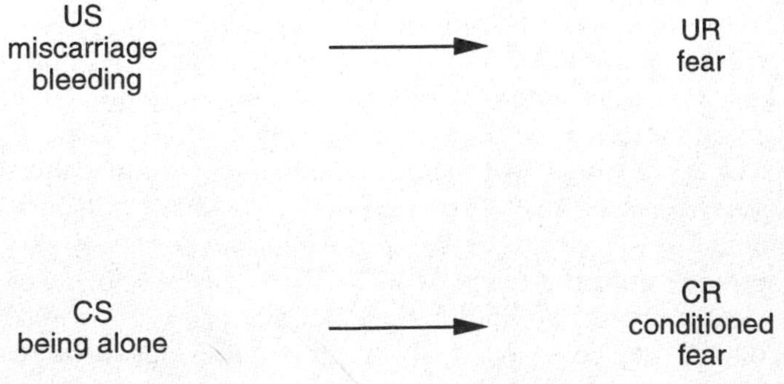

US
miscarriage
bleeding
$\longrightarrow$
UR
fear

CS
being alone
$\longrightarrow$
CR
conditioned
fear

Figure 7.1
Conditioning of a fear of being alone

elicit, a process which is sometimes referred to as counterconditioning or reciprocal inhibition.

Treatment normally begins by counterconditioning the conditioned stimuli lowest on the hierarchy which elicit the least fear, and then progresses to stimuli higher up the hierarchy only when fear to the lower stimuli has been successfully counterconditioned. In the case we have been discussing, Wolpe treated his client by counterconditioning periods of being alone with deep relaxation. This treatment completely eliminated her fear in 11 sessions, and she was still fully recovered at a three-year follow-up.

Hopefully the usefulness of this application of Pavlovian conditioning will persuade you that it might be worth understanding more about the processes underlying conditioning, if only so that we can devise even more effective interventions based on its principles.

Traditionally, Pavlovian conditioning has been regarded as a simple matter of transferring a reflex response from one stimulus to another by pairing. This view dates back to the beginning of the twentieth century and is perpetuated in the many textbooks which still present conditioning very much as a mechanical low-level process (see Rescorla, 1988). The trouble with this account is that it obscures the complexity and importance of the associative learning of which Pavlovian conditioning is but one example. Contemporary accounts of conditioning describe it instead as a process by which organisms learn from experience about the relations between events in the environment, and through it build up a representation of the structure of their world (Dickinson, 1980).

I want next to present this contemporary view of associative learning with reference to three issues: the conditions which produce learning, what is learned and how learning is translated into behaviour.

Conditions producing learning

The traditional view of conditioning is that the pairing, or contiguity, of two events is all that is necessary for them to become associated. Contiguity is undoubtedly important, but it is clearly neither a necessary nor a sufficient condition for learning to occur. As we shall see, research has shown that two events can occur together repeatedly and fail to become associated, and that associative learning can occur without pairing events together.

One of the clearest demonstrations that contiguity can fail to produce learning is provided by results reported by Rescorla (1966). In this study Rescorla was investigating the circumstances in which fear in dogs could be conditioned to a tone by associating it with shock. (The extent of fear conditioned to the tone was assessed subsequently by presenting the tone to the dogs while they were responding on an avoidance task – moving from one end of the box to the other to pre-empt the occurrence of a shock. On this task the dogs received a brief shock every few seconds if they remained stationary, but if they kept moving back and forth they could avoid all the shocks. Previous research had established that stimuli associated with shocks increase the rate of this kind of avoidance responding whereas neutral stimuli have little effect.)

The experiment compared three different ways for attempting to condition an association between the tone and shock. In all conditions, dogs were periodically exposed to a 2-minute presentation of a tone and a brief mildly painful electric shock delivered through the grid floor of the box in which they were tested. In the first condition, there was no correlation between the occurrence of the tone and the occurrence of the shocks (see upper portion of Figure 7.3). Consequently, the occurrence of the tone provided no information about the occurrence of shock, which was equally likely to occur in the presence and the absence of the tone. Consider now the sequence of events in the second condition, described in the middle portion of Figure 7.2. The shocks occurring during the tone exactly match those shown in the upper portion of the figure, so that the contiguity of tone and shock is exactly the same in each arrangement. In the arrangement shown in the middle portion of Figure 7.2, however, there are no shocks scheduled to occur in the absence of the tone, so that the tone is informative and predicts that shocks are likely to occur. Comparing the results from these two conditions suggests that it is the predictiveness of the tone, not its contiguity with shock, that determines whether or not conditioning will occur. In Rescorla's study no fear at all was conditioned to the tone in the uncorrelated condition. In contrast, in the second condition – in which the contiguity of shock and tone was exactly the same as the first – fear was strongly conditioned to the tone.

Turn now to the lower portion of Figure 7.2. This describes the third condition, an arrangement in which shocks in the absence of the tone match those shown in the upper portion of the figure, but no shocks are presented during the tone. Again the tone is informative – it predicts when shocks will not occur – but note that it is not itself paired with any other event. When tones

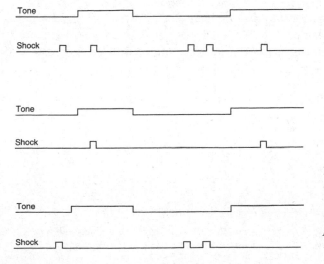

Figure 7.2 *Occurrences of shock (US) and tone (CS) in three conditions of a fear-conditioning procedure examined by Rescorla (1966)*

conditioned in this way were presented during avoidance they produced a *decrease* in responding, a result which suggests that the tone had been conditioned to reduce fear. This effect is normally described as conditioned inhibition. It is a form of associative learning which has been widely reported, but it cannot readily be accommodated by an account of conditioning based largely on contiguity.

By now your head may be spinning as you try to keep track of the complex procedures in Rescorla's experiment. The results, however, are easy to capture in the notion that organisms learn about predictive relations between events in their environment. Often when events are contiguous then you can predict the occurrence of one from the other, but not always. Rescorla's experiment shows that it is the predictiveness of one event from another, not simply their contiguity, which determines whether or not they will be associated.

Dickinson (1980) has expressed the idea that conditioning involves learning predictive relationships particularly clearly. He suggested that for most animals (including human ones) it is an advantage to be able to predict the occurrence of biologically important events. Simple examples are learning that some stimuli lead to food, and others warn you of danger. In consequence, most animals have evolved mechanisms for learning these relationships between events in their environment. One implication of this view is that animals will not learn associations involving events that are not usefully predictive. This suggestion is supported by a study of what is now known as the 'blocking' effect (Kamin, 1969). In this investigation, Kamin was seeking to condition fear in rats to stimuli such as lights and tones. In one experiment, rats were given 16 pairings of a light with shock, followed by eight pairings of a compound CS of light and tone followed by a similar shock US to that used in the first 16 trials. In a control condition, other rats received just the eight trials of the light–tone compound followed by shock, without pre-training with the light and shock. Following this training (see Figure 7.3), all the rats were tested to assess the extent of their fear conditioned to the tone component of the light and tone compound. The control rats showed significant fear of the tone, but the rats pre-trained with light–shock pairings had completely failed to acquire any fear at all to the tone. Notice that for both groups the tone had been paired with

	Pretraining 16 Trials	Training 8 Trials	Testing
Blocking group	L Shock	L T Shock	T?
Control group		L T Shock	T?

Figure 7.3 *Arrangements of shock (US) and tone and light in an experiment to demonstrate blocking of conditioning (Kamin, 1969)*

shock exactly eight times, but only in the control condition had any condition-ing to the tone occurred. The prior pairing of light and shock had blocked conditioning to the tone when it was subsequently paired with shock as part of a light and tone compound.

Kamin's explanation was that by the time the tone was introduced into the procedure, animals who had received the light–shock pre-training had already learnt to predict the occurrence of the shock from the occurrence of the light. Consequently, for them the tone was redundant because it gave no new infor-mation, and they failed to associate it with shock despite eight pairings. For the control animals the shock was initially unpredicted when the tone first oc-curred, and remained so until they had learned the relation between the light–tone compound and shock. These subjects, therefore, associated both the tone and the light with shock. (I should point out that Kamin's experiments included additional controls to rule out alternative explanations of his results. I have omitted these details here for the sake of clarity.)

Kamin argued from these results that a subject has to be *surprised* by an event to learn about it. When a surprising (unpredicted) shock occurs, Kamin argued, the subject searches recent memory for possible causes or predictors. The results of such a search are the formation of an association (a representa-tion of the relation between the shock and its predictors). If, however, a shock which is already well predicted occurs then the subject has no need to seek further predictors, there will be no memory search and thus no new learning.

The general idea expressed in Kamin's proposal is that learning occurs only when there is a mismatch between events in the real world and subjects' representations of them. It follows from this that learning is essentially a process which keeps a subject's representation of the world matched to reality. These ideas have proved extremely powerful and have been incorporated in somewhat different ways into several very successful theories of learning and attention (Mackintosh, 1975; Pearce and Hall, 1980; Rescorla and Wagner, 1972).

Let us consider now whether there are implications from these accounts of the circumstances producing learning for our analyses of real-life conditioning episodes such as that involving Wolpe's anxious client described above. Pre-sumably, her miscarriage would not have conditioned an association with anything had the woman had some basis on which to predict it. Predictiveness theories of learning suggest that it was because the miscarriage was *unexpected* that it became associated with the situation of being alone. In other words, contemporary theories about the circumstances of learning suggest that a frightening event might produce conditioned fear depending on whether or not it was already predicted.

In fact, a longstanding problem for conditioning explanations of the origins of fear is that for many people frightening episodes occur without apparently producing conditioned fear of the accompanying situation. Rachman (1977, 1990), for example, has pointed out that the blitz of major European cities during the Second World War was undoubtedly terrifying for those involved, but resulted in far fewer phobic neuroses than would be expected from a simple contiguity account of fear conditioning. The absence of fear conditioning in these circumstances is, however, relatively easily accommodated by the predictiveness theories we have been discussing on the basis that for most people there were prior warnings before the bombs started to fall in an air raid. These anticipated air raids would not, therefore, be as likely to condition fear arbitrarily to accompanying situations and incidental stimuli in the way that a totally unexpected explosion might.

What is learned?

Think back to Wolpe's client who developed a fear of being alone from the co-occurrence of her miscarriage with the circumstance of being on her own. It is perhaps natural to assume that this learning comprised the formation of an association between the antecedent stimulus (being alone) and the miscarriage, a CS–US association in the terminology of conditioning. There is, however, at least one other logical possibility, and that is that the CS of being alone became attached not to the US of the miscarriage but to the fear response it produced. We could characterize this possibility as a CS–UR association.

In the first case, CS–US learning, we could say that the woman was reminded of her miscarriage every time she was left alone, and became fearful because the thought of a miscarriage was so frightening. In the second case, CS–UR learning, we could say that when the woman was on her own after conditioning then the associated fear response was reactivated directly, without any mediating representation of the miscarriage.

These two possibilities have rather different implications for the prognosis and treatment of her fear. In the case of fear based on CS–US learning, the fear of being alone depends crucially on continued mediation by the fear of miscarriage. One rational approach to treatment would be to eliminate the association of being alone with miscarriage. An alternative would be to try to eliminate the anxiety elicited by thoughts of miscarriage of pregnancy. Counterconditioning to the woman's anxieties about miscarriage might be a way to implement this approach to treatment, but might not be practicable.

In fact, we know that Wolpe's patient acknowledged that her fear was irrational and it is not likely that she expected to start bleeding again every time she was left on her own. These considerations make it more likely that in this case her fear was based on CS–UR learning. A number of theorists have argued that this kind of response expectancy learning could play a crucial role in many human fears (Goldstein and Chambless, 1978; Kirsch, 1985; Reiss, 1980). The experience of intense fear is extremely unpleasant, and many people will go to great lengths to avoid situations in which they expect to experience fear. This 'fear of fear' can of course become a self-fulfilling prophecy, and it has been suggested that in some circumstances fears of this kind become self-perpetuating (see, for example, Eysenck, 1979). A rational approach to treating this kind of fear expectancy would be directly to countercondition with relaxation any fear elicited by the CS of being alone. This is in fact the treatment that Wolpe carried out successfully with this patient.

Translating learning into behaviour

In traditional formulations, Pavlovian conditioning is viewed very much as a matter of transferring a reflex response from one stimulus to another. Thus, in the case of Wolpe's patient with her miscarriage, the fear evoked by a miscarriage was simply transferred to the situation of being alone either by a CS–US association or by a CS–UR association.

There are some circumstances in which this account is adequate, and the CR appears to be a replica of some aspect of the UR. When Pavlovian conditioning involves signals for desirable events such as food, for example, then it is common to find that the conditioned response to the CS is some part of the subject's normal response to that US. Jenkins and Moore (1973), for example, reported that pigeons try to 'drink' a light that is paired with water, and try to 'eat' a light that is paired with food.

These results, and many others, can be explained by the notion that the subject learns to treat the CS as a substitute for the US. Some other findings, however, suggest that it may be more accurate to say that subjects' responses to a CS are made in anticipation of the US. Some results using a drug as a US show this particularly clearly, because here the anticipatory response is the opposite of the UR, rather than resembling it. The drugs in question are all of a kind which disturbs the body's internal equilibrium (homeostasis). In these cases, it seems as if the CR acts to compensate for an anticipated disturbance to homeostasis resulting from the UR. In one experiment, for example, Siegel (1972) gave rats repeated injections of insulin, a drug which acts to lower the level of sugar in the blood. We can think of these injections as a series of conditioning trials in which the external stimuli of the injection predicted an impending drop in blood sugar. Siegel tested for any conditioning by measuring blood sugar in the rats following a test injection of saline solution, which provided the external injection cues but without the drug. The conditioned response to the saline injection was a rise in blood sugar. (A saline injection in untrained rats has no significant effect on blood sugar levels.)

Conditioned responses which anticipate disturbances to homeostasis are easy to reconcile with the idea that conditioning is concerned with the learning of predictive relations between events. In this case, a preparatory physiological response becomes conditioned to a predictor of a drug. The occurrence of this kind of conditioned preparatory response may explain some of the effects of opiates such as morphine and heroin. It is a general feature of these drugs that habitual users develop tolerance to their effects, so that progressively increased doses have to be taken to produce the original euphoric or analgesic effects. Siegel (1978) has argued that tolerance develops because circumstances and stimuli associated with drug taking have come to predict the drug and consequently develop the capacity to elicit a conditioned preparatory response which counteracts the effects of the drug. It follows from this argument that tolerance to opiates should be context dependent, and there is evidence to suggest that this is the case. In animals it has been shown that tolerance to morphine's pain-killing effects can be conditioned to the room in which the drug injections are given: tolerance is reduced if the rats are tested in a different room. Similarly, human heroin addicts are more likely to suffer an overdose if they take the drug in an unfamiliar setting to which there are no conditioned tolerance reactions to counteract the effects of the heroin (Siegel, 1984).

Studying learning

From its earliest beginnings, the study of associative learning has included investigations of non-human animals (see Pavlov, 1927; Thorndike, 1898). The special emphasis given to studying learning in species such as the rat has undoubtedly influenced the kinds of theories of learning which have been developed, so it is worth considering some of the issues raised by this use of animals.

While animal behaviour can be interesting in its own right, the main aim of this kind of research has been to discover general principles of learning which apply to all animals including human ones. The decision to study learning in non-human animals has often been influenced by practical considerations. Rats and pigeons are generally simpler in terms of the organization of their behaviour than are human animals so that principles of learning may be easier to identify. It is also often easier to control the learning situation more precisely with non-human animals so that it is easier to determine the factors influencing learning (see examples above).

Sometimes, non-human animals have been chosen for study because it is easier to investigate with them procedures such as fear conditioning which it would be impossible or unethical to investigate in human subjects. This is an issue which arouses strong feelings, but allows of no easy answers. It is undoubtedly desirable to minimize suffering in animals, especially ones in our care; but it is also desirable to search for new treatments which may reduce human suffering. Many people adopt a compromise position, considering it acceptable to expose subjects to some discomfort if the likely benefits of the research appear substantial (see Thomas, 1991, for a more extended discussion of this difficult issue).

The study of a variety of species in the hope of finding general laws of learning does, of course, depend on there being important similarities in associative learning across different species and across stimuli and responses. Over time there has accumulated a considerable body of evidence that this is the case, but there are some important species-specific factors too (Seligman, 1970). Frequently, these species-specific factors seem to be more important at the stage of translating learning into behaviour than at the level of learning itself. It seems likely that different animals will learn about a signal predicting food in much the same way, but the translation of that learning into behaviour can be different. Each species may have specific inherited patterns of responding to food objects which an appropriate signal may come to elicit. Thus pigeons may peck at the signal, rats may lick and sniff at it.

There are also species-specific propensities that make it possible for animals to learn to associate some events fairly readily, but to associate others only with difficulty. Garcia and Koelling (1966) have provided the classic demonstration of inherited influences on learning. In this study rats were given sweet-tasting drinks accompanied by lights and noise. Subsequently the rats were either given an electric shock or made ill. Tests for learning showed that the rats had learned to associate the taste with illness but not with shock, and had associated the lights and noise with shock but not with illness. This pattern of learning can be explained as a reflection of rats' inherited capacities to learn relations which are likely to aid survival. Specifically, foraging rats need to learn quickly to avoid harmful substances, and the ability easily to associate distinctive tastes with subsequent illness would seem to be advantageous. In contrast, there seems little likelihood that external stimuli in nature will be informative about the toxicity or otherwise of accompanying foods, and so rats have evolved little capacity to associate lights and noise with illness. It is of interest that human subjects also seem to have a propensity to associate tastes with illness. Human cancer patients receiving therapies which produce nausea as a side-effect often report the emergence of food aversions which appear to be the result of this kind of conditioning.

Other important features of research into associative learning include the use of experimental methods and objective rather than subjective measures of behaviour and learning. As a result, research into learning has sometimes been accused of being too simplistic and concerned with artificially simple situations which have been selected for their amenity to experimental control rather than their relevance to real life. While it is true that rats pressing levers and responding to tones seems contrived, it is important to remember that research of this kind has led to important and practically useful conclusions about human learning and behaviour.

In a meta-analysis considering a range of therapies, Wolpe's procedure for systematic desensitization was found to have few equals for the treatment of specific anxieties (Smith and Glass, 1977). What is more, the evidence for its effectiveness is often more reliable than that available for many alternative therapies. Evaluations of learning-based treatments have traditionally been carried out using carefully controlled experimental comparisons of treatments whose effects have been measured objectively against well-defined criteria.

The importance of experimental evaluations of treatment effectiveness is well illustrated by the long-running controversy over the effectiveness of psychotherapy, particularly that based on psychoanalysis. In 1952, Eysenck challenged the psychoanalytic establishment by arguing that success rates claimed for traditional forms of psychotherapy were not significantly better than the rate of spontaneous improvement found in untreated patients. While Eysenck's analyses of his data have subsequently been questioned (see Bergin, 1971), there can be no doubt that properly controlled experimental evaluations of treatment effects are preferable to *ad hoc* comparisons of success rates. Treatments based on learning principles have long been associated with this kind of experimental orientation to evaluation research.

In one of the first well-controlled evaluations of Wolpe's systematic desensitization, for example, Paul (1966) compared three treatments for subjects with fear of public speaking. The first group received systematic desensitization in which stimuli associated with public speaking were counterconditioned with relaxation. The second group received psychotherapy aimed at giving them insight into the cause of their anxieties. The third group received a placebo treatment, a dummy 'tranquillizer' pill and tape recordings which were described as useful for reducing stress, but which actually should have had no specific effect on anxiety apart from creating an expectation of improvement. These comparisons, therefore, allowed systematic desensitization to be compared with a credible alternative treatment and a placebo control for patient's expectations of improvement. All the treatments were administered by insight therapists, so that any effect of their expectations would be in favour of insight therapy. Anxiety was measured in three ways: overt behaviour, physiological responses and self-report measures. The results showed that subjects in all three groups improved, but that subjects receiving systematic desensitization improved significantly more than did the subjects in the other groups. The superiority of systematic desensitization was still evident at a follow-up test two years later (Paul, 1967).

Note that in Paul's study, the effects of treatments were assessed using objective as well as subjective measures. The use of objective behavioural measures has long been a feature of learning research and also of the application of learning principles in clinical psychology. The advantages of this behavioural orientation and the dangers of over-reliance on subjective estimates are dramatically illustrated in a study of a long-term counselling and psychotherapy programme for delinquent teenage boys (McCord, 1978). Boys receiving this programme were generally enthusiastic about its benefits, and their counsellors too were convinced that the programme had delivered significant help to the teenagers who had participated. Objective measures, however, told a completely different story.

McCord found some 30 years later that, on a number of objective measures, men from the group who had participated in the programme were significantly worse off than members of the matched control group. Amongst other things, members of the treated group were significantly more likely than the control group to (1) have convictions for repeated criminal behaviour, (2) show signs of stress-related illness and alcoholism, (3) report low job satisfaction and low occupational status, and (4) die younger. These unexpected side-effects of a treatment designed to provide psychological help may have been due to several different factors. It is possible, for example, that receiving help from a counsellor unintentionally undermined the boys' self-reliance and rendered them less able to cope with problems and decisions in adult life after they had left the programme and their counsellor was no longer available. Whatever the reason, it is striking that subjective impressions completely failed to reflect these problems. While the objective measures used in learning research may sometimes seem to miss something of the richness of subjective data, their reliability is an important advantage that we cannot afford to ignore.

Recent developments

Some of the most exciting recent developments in learning theory have their roots in the 'surprise' hypothesis of conditioning which was presented above. The way in which the 'surprise' idea has been developed and reinterpreted is important for understanding the more recent developments. Consequently, our consideration of current theories will begin a little way back in the past.

Remember that learning can be considered as a process whereby organisms create representations of the relations between events in their environment. According to the 'surprise' hypothesis, organisms learn when there is a mismatch between their representation of the world – their expectations – and what actually occurs. This principle is embodied formally in one of the most important models of learning to date (Rescorla and Wagner, 1972). The distinctive feature of this model is that the notion of 'surprise' is itself expressed in terms of the strength of already existing learned connections between CSs and a following US. An unexpected or surprising US, according to this model, is one which occurs without being preceded by a CS with which it has a previously learned connection. Learning consists of changing the strength of the connections between CSs and a US. Pairing a CS and a US normally tends to increase the strength of the connection between them, but to a degree that depends on the pre-existing connections of that US with all the CSs present on that occasion. The greater the strength of the pre-existing connections, the less surprising the US will be when it occurs and the smaller the degree of strengthening that will result.

The Rescorla–Wagner proposals can be illustrated with a simple learning experiment in which a bell is paired with food. At the start of training the bell signifies little to the subject and its connection with food is zero. When the bell is first sounded and then followed by food, the hungry subject is (pleasantly) surprised. There was no prior reason to expect food and the result is a large increase from zero in the connection between bell and food in the subject's mind. On trial 2 the sounding of the bell activates this food connection so that the subject to some degree expects food to follow. When food does follow again, then the bell–food connection is again strengthened, but by a smaller amount than on trial 1. With each successive pairing the connection between bell and food gets stronger, thus increasing the expectation of food. As the expectation of food increases from trial to trial so the size of the increase in the bell–food connection conditioned on each trial gets progressively smaller. Eventually the strength of the bell–food connection reaches the point where the expectation of the food following the bell is so strong that no further strengthening of the connection occurs. Learning is then said to have reached *asymptote*. The resulting learning curve is shown in Figure 7.4. This type of negatively accelerated learning curve in fact corresponds closely to the learning curves that have been found empirically for a wide variety of species and learning situations (Mackintosh, 1974).

This is not the place for a full account of the Rescorla–Wagner model. Suffice it to say that it does a remarkably good job of explaining a range of learning effects (see above), and makes some very counter-intuitive predictions which have proved to be correct. Although the model does have limitations it is impressive in that it provides an account of seemingly complex learning based on surprise and predictiveness in terms of a few basic associative processes.

Essentially the same idea, that complex achievements can emerge from an interaction of simple associative processes, is a feature of a new kind of theory in psychology which is currently attracting considerable interest. These theories have been called variously neural network models, parallel distributed processing (PDP) models or connectionist models.

These PDP models, as I shall call them, attempt to explain many psychological phenomena in terms of a large number of parallel connections between stimulus input and response output. The distinctive character of this approach can be seen more easily if we take a specific example. How do you think the brain represents the idea of something, say your grandmother? One possibility is that somewhere in your head there is a specific area – perhaps one unique nerve cell – which is activated whenever the stimulus input corresponds to your grandmother. The alternative proposed by PDP models is that the neural

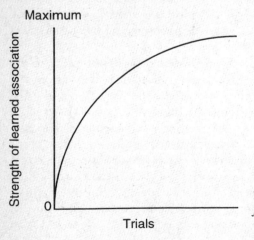

Figure 7.4 *A typical learning curve for the acquisition of a conditioned response*

representation of your grandmother (or any other idea) is distributed across a network of nerve cells. Specifically, the information corresponding to your grandmother is said to reside in a pattern of connections between a great many cells. The pattern of connections representing your grandmother is distributed across the network, hence the name for this kind of model. The same nerve cells can represent a great many different ideas as well as that of your grandmother. Each idea is represented by a different pattern of connections.

At the heart of all PDP models is the idea that the connections in a network can be modified by experience. Let us consider a neural network learning to produce the name 'duck' whenever an animal of the right category is presented. For our purposes, a duck can be considered to have a number of essential features (two legs, wings, tail, quacks and so forth) and a number of incidental features (colour, size). The network can be trained by presenting a set of animals (including some ducks) and is 'asked' of each whether or not it is a duck. The stimulus input consists of a set of features pertaining to the animal concerned, and the response output is the statement of whether it is a duck or not. The connections in the network activated by each stimulus input are strengthened or weakened depending on whether or not the response is correct. At first, all connections are equal and the network responds at chance. Whenever the network responds correctly, the connections that were activated on that trial are strengthened; whenever it is incorrect the connections activated on that trial are weakened. Eventually, after enough trials the network responds correctly to every animal in the training set. Furthermore, computer simulations of networks which have been 'trained' in this way have been found to respond correctly when tested on new stimuli not included in the training set.

To date, PDP models have shown surprising promise in explaining a number of seemingly complex accomplishments such as category learning and speech perception and production. The trained network in our example in some sense 'knows' what ducks are; and the knowledge is contained in the pattern of connections of different strengths established by the training. The interesting idea is that complex knowledge can be made up of simple associations of various strengths. What is more, one of the learning rules proposed for specifying how the connection strengths in a network are changed depending on the outcome of a training trial is the so-called delta rule. This rule turns out to be essentially the same as the learning principle in the Rescorla–Wagner model (Sutton and Barto, 1981).

To conclude, in this chapter I have tried to convey something of the contemporary importance of just one form of associative learning; namely, Pavlovian conditioning. As we have seen, theories of Pavlovian conditioning have led to important clinical interventions for a variety of problems such as phobias, and can help us understand the physiological and behavioural effects of drugs. The ideas embodied in contemporary theories of Pavlovian conditioning are also proving to be important in a great many areas of psychology, providing the basis for associative accounts of some surprisingly complex phenomena. The same theoretical principles discussed above can also help us understand learning about rewarding and punishing consequences of our own behaviour (Dickinson 1980), but that is beyond the scope of the present chapter.

Further reading

LIEBERMAN, D.A. (1993) *Learning: Behavior and Cognition*, 2nd ed., Pacific Grove, CA, Brooks/Cole.

THORPE, G.L. and OLSON, S.L. (1990) *Behavior Therapy: Concepts, Procedures, and Applications*, Needham Heights, MA, Allyn & Bacon.

References

AGRAS, W.S., SYLVESTER, D. and OLIVEAU, D.C. (1969) 'The epidemiology of common fears and phobias', *Comprehensive Psychiatry*, **10**, 151-6.

BERGIN, A.E. (1971) 'The evaluation of therapeutic outcomes', in BERGIN, A.E. and GARFIELD, S.L. (Eds) *Handbook of Psychotherapy and Behavior Change*, New York, Wiley, 217-70.

DICKINSON, A. (1980) *Contemporary Animal Learning Theory*, Cambridge, Cambridge University Press.

EYSENCK, H.J. (1952) 'The effects of psychotherapy: an evaluation', *Journal of Consulting Psychology*, **16**, 319-24.

EYSENCK, H.J. (1979) 'The conditioning model of neurosis', *The Behavioral and Brain Sciences*, **2**, 155-99.

GARCIA, J. and KOELLING, R.A. (1966) 'Relation of cue to consequence in avoidance learning', *Psychonomic Science*, **4**, 123-4.

GOLDSTEIN, A.J. and CHAMBLESS, D.L. (1978) 'A reanalysis of agoraphobia', *Behavior Therapy*, **9**, 47-59.

JACOBSON, E. (1938) *Progressive Relaxation*, Chicago, University of Chicago Press.

JENKINS, H.M. and MOORE, B.R. (1973) 'The form of the autoshaped response with or without water reinforcers', *Journal of the Experimental Analysis of Behavior*, **20**, 163-81.

KAMIN, L.J. (1969) 'Predictability, surprise, attention, and conditioning', in CAMPBELL, B.A. and CHURCH, R.M. (Eds) *Punishment and Aversive Behavior*, New York, Appleton-Century-Crofts, 279-96.

KIRSCH, I. (1985) 'Response expectancy as a determinant of experience and behavior', *American Psychologist*, **40**, 1189-1202.

MACKINTOSH, N.J. (1974) *The Psychology of Animal Learning*, New York, Academic Press.

MACKINTOSH, N.J. (1975) 'A theory of attention: variations in the associability of stimuli with reinforcement', *Psychological Review*, **82**, 276-98.

McCord, J. (1978) 'A thirty-year follow-up of treatment effects', *American Psychologist*, **33**, 284–9.

Paul, G.L. (1966) *Insight versus Desensitization in Psychotherapy: An Experiment in Anxiety Reduction*, Stanford, Stanford University Press.

Paul, G.L. (1967) 'Insight versus desensitization in psychotherapy two years after termination', *Journal of Consulting Psychology*, **31**, 333–48.

Pavlov, I.P. (1927) *Conditioned Reflexes: An Investigation of the Physiological Activity of the Cerebral Cortex*, G.V. Anrep, Trans., London, Oxford University Press.

Pearce, J.M. and Hall, G. (1980) 'A model for Pavlovian learning: variations in the effectiveness of conditioned but not of unconditioned stimuli', *Psychological Review*, **87**, 532–52.

Rachman, S. (1977) 'The conditioning theory of fear acquisition: a critical examination', *Behaviour Research and Therapy*, **15**, 375–87.

Rachman, S. (1990) 'The determinants and treatment of simple phobias', *Advances in Behaviour Research and Therapy*, **12**, 1–30.

Reiss, S. (1980) 'Pavlovian conditioning and human fear: an expectancy model', *Behavior Therapy*, **11**, 380–96.

Rescorla, R.A. (1966) 'Predictability and number of pairings in Pavlovian fear conditioning', *Psychonomic Science*, **4**, 383–4.

Rescorla, R.A. (1988) 'Pavlovian conditioning: it's not what you think it is', *American Psychologist*, **43**, 151–60.

Rescorla, R.A. and Wagner, A.R. (1972) 'A theory of Pavlovian conditioning: variations in the effectiveness of reinforcement and nonreinforcement', in Black, A.H. and Prokasy, W.F. (Eds) *Classical Conditioning II: Current Research and Theory*, New York, Appleton-Century-Crofts, 64–99.

Seligman, M.E.P. (1970) 'On the generality of the laws of learning', *Psychological Review*, **77**, 406–18.

Siegel, S. (1972) 'Conditioning of insulin-induced glycemia', *Journal of Comparative and Physiological Psychology*, **78**, 233–41.

Siegel, S. (1978) 'A Pavlovian conditioning analysis of morphine tolerance', in Krasnegor, N.A. (Ed.) *Behavioral Tolerance: Research and Treatment Implications*, NIDA Research Monograph No. 18, Washington, DC, US Government Printing Office, 27–53.

Siegel, S. (1984) 'Pavlovian conditioning and heroin overdose: reports by overdose victims', *Bulletin of the Psychonomic Society*, **22**, 428–30.

Smith, M.L. and Glass, G.V. (1977) 'Meta-analysis of psychotherapy outcome studies', *American Psychologist*, **32**, 752–60.

Sutton, R.S. and Barto, A.G. (1981) 'Toward a modern theory of adaptive networks: expectation and prediction', *Psychological Review*, **88**, 135–70.

Thomas, G.V. (1991) 'Animal experiments in psychology', in Cochrane, R. and Carroll, D. (Eds) *Psychology and Social Issues* Brighton, Falmer Press, 117–26.

Thorndike, E.L. (1898) 'Animal intelligence: an experimental study of the associative processes in animals', *Psychological Monographs*, **2** (4, Whole No. 8).

WOLPE, J. (1958) *Psychotherapy by Reciprocal Inhibition*, Stanford, CA, Stanford University Press.

WOLPE, J. (1981) 'The dichotomy between directly conditioned and cognitively learned anxiety', *Journal of Behavior Therapy and Experimental Psychiatry*, **12**, 35–42.

Part IV

Physiological Psychology

Chapter 8

Psychobiology

Philip Terry

Introduction

Studies of the ways in which biological processes regulate behaviour are cross-disciplinary: they draw extensively from developments in physiology, neuroanatomy, genetics and pharmacology, as well as from developments in psychology. Because of this cross-disciplinary nature, psychobiology encompasses a large and diverse range of research activities. However, common to most of these activities is a focus on the nervous system as the primary biological structure of interest. Of course, the nervous system presents a major challenge to our understanding; to compound this challenge, behaviour is also a notoriously difficult process to characterize and analyse, even in its outwardly most simple forms. These problems of diversity and complexity have encouraged a degree of specialization which makes it impossible to present a short overview covering all of today's most active areas of research; consequently, the present review is very selective. There is no single unifying theory or approach to psychobiology, so the main focus here will be on the methods used by psychobiologists to address a variety of research questions. However, before describing current methods and their applications in selected areas, some basic background material is necessary.

Brain and behaviour: basics

Levels of analysis: the nervous system

Any understanding of psychobiology requires some understanding of brain structure and function at different levels of analysis. The lowest level of analysis may be taken to be the individual nerve cell, or neuron. However, as we shall see, more basic levels can be identified, namely at sub-cellular or molecular levels. Nevertheless, using the neuron as our basic building block, we shall first 'move downwards' in scale, considering ever-smaller component parts and their functions, and then 'move upwards' in scale, looking at how aggregations of neurons combine to form functional systems and, ultimately, the brain as a whole. As we shall see in the next section, 'Methods in Psychobiology', experimental manipulations have been directed at each of these levels in attempting to understand the relationship between brain function and behaviour.

The neuron   There are many different kinds of nerve cell, or *neuron*, but each has several critical features in common. Neurons are cells, and carry out many of the same metabolic processes as other cells in the body. They are unique, however, in being specialized for the reception and transmission of electrochemical signals. Radiating outwards from a neuron's cell body are numerous filamentary processes (see Figure 8.1). Some of these, called *dendrites*, are specialized for the reception of impulses from other neurons. The integrated activity of signals received from other neurons either at these dendrites or at a neuron's cell body determines whether or not this particular

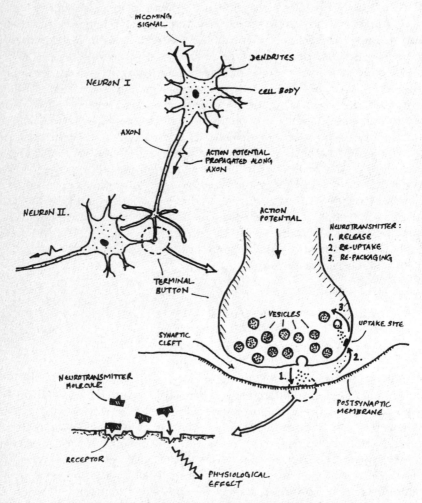

Figure 8.1 *The neuron, the synapse, neurotransmitters and receptors*

neuron will itself emit an electrochemical impulse. This impulse, or *action potential*, is an all-or-none electrochemical wave of fixed amplitude. For each neuron, one particular tendril, called an *axon*, serves to carry the action potential away from the cell body and towards a junction or junctions with other neurons. The axon terminals do not generally impinge directly onto the target neuron (or muscle), but instead end in nodules (called *terminal buttons*) with a narrow gap intervening between the terminal buttons and the target membrane. This target membrane is a localized region of either the cell body, dendrites or (less commonly) the axon of another neuron. The junction between the two neurons, i.e. between axon terminal button and target membrane, is called a *synapse* (Figure 8.1).

The synapse The synapse comprises three components: the terminal button of one neuron (sometimes referred to as the presynaptic terminal); a gap or cleft (the synapse proper); and the membrane of a second neuron (sometimes called the postsynaptic membrane). Signal transduction across the synaptic cleft is by passive diffusion of chemicals released from the presynaptic terminal. These chemicals, called *neurotransmitters*, are normally stored in sacs, or *vesicles*, within the terminal button. The arrival of an action potential at the terminal causes vesicles to fuse with the terminal membrane and to discharge their contents of neurotransmitter molecules into the cleft; the molecules diffuse across the cleft to the postsynaptic membrane (Figure 8.1). There, they interact, or bind, to specific sites on the membrane: these sites are called *receptors*.

Neurotransmitters, receptors and transporters The nervous system makes use of many different types of neurotransmitter; the various neurotransmitters differ in terms of their molecular structure. Examples of important neurotransmitters, implicated in the regulation of diverse behaviours and much studied by biological psychologists, include: dopamine, serotonin, norepinephrine, acetylcholine, gamma amino butyric acid (GABA) and glutamate. Typically, a given neuron will only manufacture and release a single type of neurotransmitter. All neurotransmitters affect a target tissue by binding to receptors, and a given neurotransmitter will only bind to a particular type of receptor. Even though a neuron may only release a single kind of neurotransmitter, it may have receptors for a number of different kinds. The binding of a neurotransmitter to its receptor changes the probability that the postsynaptic neuron will emit an action potential, a change which is effected by one of two mechanisms. (1) *Ion channels*: the interaction of the neurotransmitter with its receptor increases or decreases (depending on the neurotransmitter) the probability that a pore will open in the target membrane; this in turn leads to a change in the movement of charged molecules into and out of the neuron, so altering its likelihood of producing an action potential. GABA acts in this way: when it binds to a receptor (a GABA receptor), it makes the opening of an associated membrane pore more likely; when the pore opens, charged molecules move into the neuron and make it less liable to emit an action potential. (2) *Second messengers*: alternatively, the binding of a neurotransmitter to a receptor may change the likelihood of neural firing through the mediation of other biochemical events in the target tissue. Thus, for example, the binding of dopamine to certain types of dopamine receptors causes an increase in the activity of certain enzymes inside the target cell. The increased activity can, through complex biochemical chains of effect, alter the likelihood of an action potential, or even stimulate long-term changes in the cell which may affect its future responsiveness.

After binding to a receptor, the neurotransmitter returns to the synaptic cleft, where it may be either inactivated by an enzyme in the cleft (as is the case, for example, with acetylcholine), or taken back up into the terminal button from which it was released (as is the case, for example, with dopamine, serotonin and norepinephrine). Neurotransmitter uptake is an active process achieved by proteins called transporters located on the presynaptic membrane. The transporters move released neurotransmitter from outside the neuron, in the cleft, back into the terminal button. When back inside, the neuro-transmitters are re-packaged in vesicles for future re-use.

Brain nuclei and pathways We now move from the level of the neuron to larger-scale structure within the brain. The brain is not a homogeneous mass of neurons. Instead, it is organized into discrete sub-structures. Aggregations of neuron cell bodies are called brain *nuclei*, and bundles of axons traversing the brain, perhaps from one nucleus to another, are called *pathways*. Large, complex structures within the brain may themselves comprise several nuclei and numerous axon pathways. Such structures will often have a number of pathways entering them from other parts of the brain (*afferent* pathways) and various output pathways by means of which they communicate with other parts of the brain (*efferent* pathways).

Brain systems Thus the brain is a complex organization of interacting sub-structures. Each structure may subserve a particular function, or more commonly will interact with other structures in the brain to regulate function. A series of interacting structures, defined according to anatomical, neuro-transmitter or functional criteria, may be regarded as a *brain system*. Thus, for example, neurons utilizing dopamine as their neurotransmitter form discrete systems within the brain; one such system, called the *nigrostriatal dopamine system*, comprises: (1) a nucleus of dopamine neuron cell bodies called the substantia nigra, located towards the back of the brain; (2) an axon pathway, called the nigrostriatal bundle, projecting from the substantia nigra to more forward regions of the brain; (3) an area in which the axon terminals of the nigrostriatal bundle form synapses with another structure, in this case the *striatum*, itself comprising various sub-structures. This system is easily characterized in two of the three ways mentioned: by anatomical relationship (discrete structures and an interconnecting pathway); and by neurotransmitter type (dopamine neurons projecting to a structure rich in dopamine receptors). The system can also be defined functionally, since damage at any point causes a similar outcome – disruption in the control of voluntary movements. Indeed, degeneration of the nigrostriatal pathway is associated with Parkinson's disease, a chronic neurological condition characterized by impaired control of movement. However, in the control of complex behaviours, the neural systems involved are typically much more difficult to elucidate.

The brain   It is beyond the scope of this book to provide a detailed description of brain structure. Such a description, with accounts of the roles of various component parts in behavioural function, can be found in several comprehensive textbooks of physiological psychology (e.g. Carlson, 1994). Only a crude overview will be given, in order to provide the minimum background for the following two sections.

The brain is commonly partitioned into three components: the hindbrain, midbrain and forebrain (see Figure 8.2). Each component comprises a number of discrete structures. The major structures of the *hindbrain*, moving from posterior to anterior loci, include the *medulla*, *pons* and *cerebellum*. These structures are important for the control of certain critical physiological processes, such as respiration and maintenance of muscle tone (medulla), the regulation of arousal (pons), and motor coordination (cerebellum).

The *midbrain* is usually taken to comprise the *superior* and *inferior colliculi*, integral components of the visual and auditory sensory systems, respectively, and also numerous other nuclei residing just posterior to the

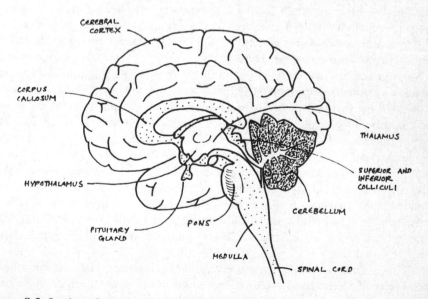

Figure 8.2 *Section through the midline of the human brain, showing the right hemisphere*

colliculi. At present, mention will only be made of the *substantia nigra*, a nucleus referred to above as being important to motor control. Anterior to the midbrain is the *forebrain*, itself comprising several complex structures. The *thalamus*, just anterior to the midbrain, is a cluster of nuclei which receive sensory and motor input from other brain structures and send efferent fibres to more anterior structures of the brain, in particular the *cerebral cortex*. The cerebral cortex is a layer of tissue overlying the two large lobes of the cerebral hemispheres; as such the cortex represents most of the visible surface of the brain. Much of the cortex comprises neuron cell bodies and dendrites; these neurons send axons down to more posterior brain regions, and receive axons from other parts of the brain, primarily via the thalamus. The cortex is not homogeneous in terms of functional organization, but may be partitioned topographically according to differential involvement with various sensorimotor processes. Thus, for example, input from the visual system, relayed primarily via the thalamus, terminates in a discrete region of the cerebral cortex located at the very back of the cerebral hemispheres. Similarly well-defined areas, located elsewhere on the cortical surface, are dedicated to the processing of information from other sensory modalities, and specific fields are also given over to the control of motor functions. Outside those areas of cortex specifically involved in sensorimotor analysis and control are regions with no such obvious function. These areas are commonly referred to as the *association cortex*. In fact, much of the association cortex is involved with the higher-order processing of the information handled by adjacent sensory or motor cortical areas. Because of this identification with higher-order cognitive function these regions have been of particular interest to cognitive neuropsychologists.

Finally, other forebrain regions of particular significance in the control of behaviour include the limbic system, the basal ganglia and the hypothalamus. The *limbic system* is a series of interconnected structures arranged around the inner rim of the cerebral hemispheres. One component structure, the *hippocampus*, has been intensively studied as a possible substrate for memory processes; other component structures, such as the *amygdala*, have been associated with emotionality and motivation. *Basal ganglia* is a collective term for a number of discrete nuclei, one of the most important (from the perspective of behavioural control) being the *striatum*. The striatum was mentioned above as a significant mediator of motor control. Lastly, the *hypothalamus* is a tiny but complex forebrain structure, located directly below the thalamus, with very important regulatory functions. It exercises some control over the release of various hormones into the bloodstream via its interrelationship with the *pituitary gland*, and it is critically involved in such diverse but biologically fundamental processes as sexuality, food and fluid intake and the regulation of body temperature.

This account of brain structure has already incorporated the findings of many years of research in psychobiology: thus component structures have been described more in terms of functions than in terms of anatomy. However, this brief account should not be taken to imply that individual structures possess individual functions – no single structure acts in isolation. Instead, various structures communicate to exercise control of behaviour.

Overview We have completed a very simplified tour of the nervous system, from the level of enzymes (e.g. second messengers) to the level of the whole brain, identifying various significant structures and processes along the way. Psychobiologists study the relationship between brain and behaviour at each of these different levels, as will become apparent.

Finally, it should be noted that not all psychobiologists approach the subject in terms of relating brain processes directly to behavioural output. Behavioural geneticists, for example, may attempt to determine whether psychological processes have an innate physical cause by looking for heritability of particular psychological or behavioural traits. Recent developments in molecular biology now permit behavioural geneticists to identify the gene or genes associated with such traits, at least in cases where the behavioural traits are easily defined and demonstrably inherited. Given that all behaviour is ultimately the product of the nervous system, these genes are presumed to exercise control of behaviour through their role in determining the way in which specific parts of the nervous system are constructed. Thus psychobiology is coming to encompass the full breadth of biology, ultimately moving towards explanations which integrate genetics, brain processes and behaviour.

Levels of analysis: behaviour

Although our understanding of the brain may be limited, arguably it still exceeds our understanding of behaviour. Behaviour is notoriously difficult to quantify meaningfully: the units of behaviour are not always apparent (see 'Measuring Behaviour'). This problem is compounded by the use of non-human animals in many studies, as is inevitable given the kinds of physiological intervention required by many experiments. Since non-human animals cannot report their experiences verbally, their behaviour must be studied directly. Such behaviour may be observed and recorded as it occurs, with no assumptions made concerning its relationship to unseen or psychological processes (e.g. recording movements), or the animal may be tested in a particular environment and from its pattern of responses inferences may be drawn concerning intrinsically unobservable psychological processes (e.g. tests of attention, decision making, problem solving, or internal states such as anxiety).

Behaviour as a variable has been used in different ways by psychobiologists. We have already seen that behavioural effects can be used to help clarify the nature of brain systems. It is sometimes assumed that this is the only reason for studying relationships between brain and behaviour. However, different approaches can be identified, the most common of which are described below.

(1) Trying to understand how biological systems control, modulate or determine particular features of behaviour. The preferred approach is interactive: behaviour informs biology, as well as vice versa. Physiological manipulations (see next section) may be employed not just to investigate behaviour itself (as in [2] below), but to understand how such behaviour is mediated by the nervous system. Often it is assumed that this kind of research always adopts the same format: the independent variable is the physiological manipulation, and the dependent variable is the behavioural outcome. However, there is a long tradition of research which adopts the opposite approach: monitoring biological changes associated with particular kinds of behaviour – in other words, behaviour is treated as the independent variable, and a specific feature of biological activity becomes the dependent variable.

(2) Physiological interventions may be used to study the structure and organization of normal behaviour. As an example, experimental brain damage may be imposed and the consequences for the organization of behaviour observed. Such a method may help define the relevant parameters underlying normal behaviour or psychological function. This approach has made significant contributions, for example, to our understanding of the organization of memory: looking at how different types of memory deficit emerge with different kinds of neural damage has been useful in developing theories of how memory processes are normally organized. Such an approach is particularly useful in psychology because of the difficulties inherent in trying to define 'natural units' of behaviour.

Methods in psychobiology

It should be apparent from the discussion of different approaches to the study of brain–behaviour relationships that physiological techniques fall into two main categories: direct manipulations of the nervous system, and methods of recording activity or changes in the nervous system. Few introductory texts discuss methods for studying behaviour, but it should be apparent (as noted earlier) that methods of behaviour analysis also fall into different categories.

The lesion method

Perhaps the mainstay of early physiological psychology, the lesion method is arguably the most direct method for examining brain–behaviour relationships. Nevertheless, there are problems particular to it. The lesion method involves the controlled destruction of specific structures or pathways in the brain. The behavioural correlates of brain damage are observed, and conclusions drawn concerning the role of the damaged tissue in the control of the observed behaviour. It is not difficult to see why this method became popular. Human

brain damage often has behavioural consequences which are not readily characterized; in addition, the site of damage may not be known precisely, or may
not be localized to a single structure or pathway. The lesion method offers the
promise of controlling for these factors, since the use of animals allows lesions
to be directed to circumscribed regions of the brain.

Lesions can be produced in various ways. *Aspiration lesions* are made by
inserting a fine glass capillary tube into the brain, and applying negative pressure to suck out the target tissue. Clearly this is best suited to structures located
near to the exposed surface of the brain, notably the cortex. *Radiothermal
lesions* are made by passing high-frequency alternating current through a fine
wire; the wire is insulated except for its tip, and the heat generated at the tip
kills neurons in its immediate vicinity. This method is better suited to small,
localized lesions deep within the brain. More recently, these methods have
been largely replaced by the use of *neurotoxic chemical lesions*; lesions are
produced by injecting chemicals with neurotoxic properties directly into the
target area. The chemicals are delivered via hollow metal tubes, or cannulae,
positioned such that their tips lie at or within the target area. One advantage of
this method is that chemicals with differing kinds of toxicity are available.
For example, ibotenic acid destroys neurons by killing cell bodies specifically;
thus any axon pathways in the vicinity of the lesion are spared. Thus, lesions
can be directed specifically to brain nuclei, and the potential for unintentional
damage to other brain structures is reduced. Specificity is important, since one
of the main problems with the lesion method is being certain that loss of the
intended target structure alone is responsible for any changes in behaviour. For
example, the discovery that rats overeat following damage to a particular
nucleus within the hypothalamus – the ventromedial hypothalamus (VMH) –
led to the suggestion that the VMH plays a role in the termination of feeding
(Hetherington and Ranson, 1942). However, it was later found that lesions to
the VMH commonly destroyed an axon pathway which runs from the VMH and
the paraventricular nucleus of the hypothalamus to structures of the hindbrain.
It appears likely that disruption of this pathway (and consequently of the
structures with which it communicates) is more important in generating the
observed behavioural syndrome (Kirchgessner and Sclafani, 1988).

There are several other reasons for caution in interpreting results from
lesion studies. One of the most famous criticisms is attributable to Gregory
(1961), who suggested that a similar approach to understanding the functional
properties of a machine could lead to some absurd conclusions: for example, if
the removal of a series of transistors from a television set resulted in a continuous howling noise, one might conclude that the function of the transistors was
to act as 'howl suppressors', obviously an inappropriate conclusion. In other
words, the dysfunction caused by ablating specific brain structures might be
uninterpretable in terms of normal brain function. This argument demonstrates
that the method should not be used in isolation, but (like other methods) needs
to be applied in the light of theory, and should generate results which may be
corroborated by other techniques. Also, it is important that the appropriate

behavioural measures be taken to assess the nature of the behavioural change associated with brain damage. For example, damage to a rat's frontal cortex might lead to marked impairments in its ability to perform a complex learned behaviour, not because the lesioned areas are critical to memory but because their loss impairs the animal's ability to coordinate its movements effectively.

On the other hand, it may be that a change in behaviour is revealed only under very specific conditions. For example, although the hippocampus has long been considered a brain structure of particular importance to the formation of memories, early lesion studies with animals failed to reveal profound learning deficits following hippocampal lesions. It now appears that these early studies tested rats on tasks which are readily learned even after drastic reductions of brain mass: simple tasks requiring the association of a single response with a single stimulus (e.g. Schmaltz and Theios, 1972). When tested on learning tasks which required information to be integrated within a spatial or temporal context (e.g. learning a specific location in relation to visual cues distributed around the test environment), the rats with damage to the hippocampus showed major learning deficits (e.g. Kimble and Dannen, 1977).

Lesions are used not only to examine the roles of particular brain structures, but also to investigate recovery of function from brain damage. Lesions do not invariably produce enduring deficits; over time, functions lost immediately after injury can return. Experimenters can examine how various manipulations might encourage or retard recovery of function: for example, certain drugs may accelerate recovery, or certain training programmes or kinds of experience might also improve recovery. Astute behavioural analysis is necessary in order to determine whether functional recovery represents a full return of capacities present before injury, or whether recovered function is achieved by reorganizing spared abilities to compensate for an irrecoverable loss. Through addressing these kinds of question, physiological psychologists can use behaviour to shed light on important physiological processes, and can provide information of potentially great clinical significance.

Electrical stimulation of the brain

In contrast with the lesion method, which looks at how behaviour changes in the absence of particular biological structures, methods based on direct brain stimulation look at how behaviour is affected by artificially activating certain structures. These structures are usually stimulated by passing an electric current through thin electrodes surgically implanted in the brain. Traditionally, this approach has been less popular than the lesion method, perhaps because it is less easy to determine how the manipulation is producing its effect. For example, changing the parameters of the stimulating current may change behavioural responsiveness, but it may be difficult to explain this in terms of effects on the electrophysiological properties of neurons. Moreover, prolonged, artificial activation of a specific structure or pathway may bear little relation to its normal mode of activation.

Another reason for its restricted use is that, in animals, direct brain stimulation rarely produces discrete patterns of behaviour. Behaviours associated with stimulation of various brain regions are often disorganized and difficult to interpret. One area where this method has been applied with some success is in the study of sexual behaviour. Stimulation of a forebrain region called the medial preoptic area, located just in front of the hypothalamus, will provoke male rats to mount and copulate with female rats (e.g. Malsbury, 1971).

As with the analysis of lesion effects, careful behavioural testing may be necessary to reveal the functional consequences of brain stimulation. Thus stimulation of a midbrain region called the periaqueductal grey produces no easily observable effect in terms of elicited behaviour, but it causes profound analgesia, or insensitivity to pain (e.g. Mayer and Liebeskind, 1974). This discovery proved to be very significant to the study of how pain perception is modulated by the nervous system.

Drugs

There are drugs available with very specific actions on the nervous system: they are used by physiological psychologists to modify activity within particular neurotransmitter pathways in the brain. Drugs are often defined as agonists or antagonists. Agonists produce a physiological response at a particular receptor (in a similar fashion to neurotransmitters), and change the likelihood of neural firing. Antagonists, on the other hand, bind to specific receptors in the same way as agonists, but have no intrinsic biological activity. The result of this lack of pharmacological effect is that they act to block receptors, and so tend to work in opposition to agonists (or to the brain's own neurotransmitters). Another class of drugs, called indirect agonists, act to increase neurotransmitter levels by blocking the re-uptake of released neurotransmitters. Cocaine, for example, increases the amount of dopamine present in the synapse by preventing its re-uptake from the synapse back into the neuron which released it.

Drugs can modify neurotransmitter function in other ways too. For example, amphetamine directly stimulates the release of dopamine from neuron terminals. Drugs can also reduce neurotransmitter activity: thus, for example, alpha-methyl-paratyrosine reduces dopamine transmission by inhibiting the synthesis of dopamine, and in this way depresses dopaminergic neurotransmission. Effects such as these are usually short-lived, their durations primarily determined by the time it takes the body to render the drug inactive. However, some drugs can permanently damage specific neurons in the brain, or can permanently inactivate specific kinds of neurotransmitter receptor.

Drugs may be given orally, or they may be injected into a body cavity or into the blood supply. These methods are sometimes collectively referred to as systemic drug administration. With systemic administration, the drug is available to act on any tissue in the body which has receptors to which the drug will bind. This presents difficulties in determining the critical site of action of a drug, since the relevant receptors may be distributed widely throughout the brain, and may also be located on other organs – e.g. the heart, liver and kidneys. Some insight into the critical site of drug action can be obtained if comparison drugs are available which act in the periphery but fail to get into the brain. However, to describe fully the involvement of different neurotransmitter pathways in behaviour it is necessary to inject drugs directly into specific regions of the brain. Here, a thin, metal tube (cannula) is implanted through the animal's skull, such that the tip is located in the region of interest, and tiny volumes of drug solution are injected through the cannula.

Drugs have been used by physiological psychologists in so many different ways and in the study of so many different aspects of behaviour that it is difficult to give characteristic examples; instead, some of the experimental uses of drugs are illustrated in the account given in 'Using Various Methods'.

Recording neural activity

The simplest way of recording neural activity is by use of the electroencephalograph (EEG): electrical contacts are placed at various points across the scalp, and the overall electrical potential of the underlying cortex is detected and plotted over time. Increased sensitivity in detection devices now allows the recording of electrical activity from different regions of the brain, allowing some determination of differential involvement by various brain regions. Although the EEG record is typically the product of millions of neurons firing at many different frequencies, computer analyses can allow various contributing patterns to be differentiated from what at first glance may appear to be random noise. EEG analysis has been central to our modern understanding of the different stages of sleep, each defined according to characteristic features of wave amplitude and frequency. Analysis of EEG has been used as an adjunct to the study of drug actions on brain and behaviour in animals, providing additional physiological data to strengthen the study of drug effects on behaviour (e.g. Ongini and Longo, 1989).

New techniques for recording the activity of the whole brain or of its component parts have recently become available. Most significant is the development of positron emission tomography (PET), a method which provides real-time monitoring of neural activity throughout the brain, with a resolution in the order of millimetres. The device used to image the brain in this way is called a PET scanner. The method works as follows. For normal functioning, all neurons require a copious supply of the chemical glucose: the more active a given neuron, the more glucose it needs. For PET scanning, glucose molecules are 'tagged' with a radioactive isotope and injected into the animal's or person's bloodstream. These glucose molecules are taken up by the brain's neurons in proportion to their rates of activity. As the radioactive isotopes attached to the glucose molecules decay, characteristic radioactive by-products are emitted, and these are detected by a special sensor surrounding the head. A computer analyses these signals to determine the locations and rates of activity of the emission sites. A contour map of the brain in terms of neural activity can thus be generated. PET imaging has been used to determine which structures are active during various psychological processes, e.g. reading, performing mathematical calculations, interpreting speech, solving problems, memorizing information. The method has also been used with varying degrees of success to investigate possible brain dysfunction in certain psychiatric conditions, e.g. schizophrenia.

EEG and, especially, PET are powerful tools for the study of global brain function or the involvement of particular brain structures in behaviour. However, there are certain constraints on their usefulness: first they are limited by their coarse levels of resolution (particularly EEG), which prevents detailed analysis of some brain systems and of small groups of neurons; second, their physical size (particularly PET equipment) limits their use in naturalistic settings.

Monitoring the activities of small groups of neurons can be achieved more invasively by implanting electrodes into the brain and recording changes in electrical potential as the neurons are activated. The electrodes can be fixed into place such that the animal (rarely human) can continue to interact with its environment. Thus the environment can be manipulated to study the relationship between the activities of specific neurons and the animal's behaviour within very specific circumstances. The advent of especially fine microelectrodes now permits the monitoring of the activity of individual neurons (single-unit activity) in freely moving animals. The study of single-unit activity has been particularly productive for the investigation of the neural substrates of learning and memory. In 1971, O'Keefe and Dostrovsky identified individual cells in the rat hippocampus which became active only when the rat was at a specific location within a test enclosure. These location-specific neurons were dubbed 'place cells', and their unexpected properties contributed to a theory which held that one of the primary functions of the hippocampus is the acquisition and integration of spatial information in memory (O'Keefe and Nadel, 1978). However, since then, single-unit studies have also implicated the hippocampus in the learning of non-spatial information (e.g. Berger *et al.*, 1986), and the precise role of this structure in memory processes remains unclear. Nevertheless, these studies further demonstrate how psychological theory both informs – and is in turn informed by – physiological studies.

Microdialysis

The methods described above for recording neural activity address physiological function at different levels of analysis: whole brain, component structures, small groups of neurons (e.g. particular nuclei), and finally individual neurons.

The recently developed technique of *in vivo* microdialysis goes one step further, providing a method for measuring neurotransmitter release in real time. In simple terms, a probe is inserted into a region of the brain in which there is an abundance of terminals which release a particular kind of neurotransmitter. The tip of the probe is permeable, and permits the diffusion of neurotransmitters into the probe. A neutral solution called the dialysate, similar to the cerebrospinal fluid which bathes the brain, is passed down through one chamber of the probe into the permeable tip, and is then recovered by a second chamber of the probe. During the course of its circulation, the dialysate becomes enriched with neurotransmitters released by neurons near the tip of the probe. The quantities of neurotransmitter present in the dialysate are measured by devices capable of sensitive chemical analysis.

Microdialysis has a wide range of applications in physiological psychology. It has been used to confirm proposed mechanisms of drug action, for example by demonstrating that amphetamine produces enhanced release of dopamine (e.g. Carboni *et al.*, 1989), and to examine critical sites of drug action by determining how neurotransmitter release in response to drugs varies between different sites in the brain (e.g. Kuczenski *et al.*, 1991). The time course of drug effects on behaviour can also be related to the time course of their effects on neurotransmitter availability. In this way, the study of how psychoactive drugs affect behaviour is powerfully enhanced. However, microdialysis has also been employed to examine how neurotransmitter function changes during the commission of various behaviours or in association with presumed psychological states. For example, changes in levels of neurotransmitter can be plotted while an animal is feeding, or in situations presumed to evoke stress in an animal, or during sexual activity (e.g. Wenkstern *et al.*, 1993). Furthermore, it has been found that brain dopamine levels increase in response to the presentation of stimuli which have previously been associated with reward – such as food (e.g. Phillips *et al.*, 1993). This provides a physiological basis for the theory that stimuli associated with reward often acquire many of the motivational properties associated with the reward itself (e.g. Beninger, 1983).

Present limitations on the method include its insensitivity to a large number of neurotransmitters. This selectivity may blind the researcher to the critical neurotransmitter changes involved in behavioural regulation, or may result in the technique determining the direction of research, rather than vice versa.

Measuring behaviour

Many consider the analysis of directly observed behaviour to be the simplest approach to the study of behaviour. This is far from true. In studying animal behaviour, the natural ecology of the animal and its specific behavioural adaptations must not be overlooked. Although there are many aspects of behaviour that are common to whole classes of animal, each species also has its own species-specific repertoire of behaviours. Very different behaviours may be employed by different species to achieve the same functional end, just as a particular environmental event might result in very different behavioural responses by different species. These factors might be regarded as presenting problems for identifying or selecting behaviours for analysis; they also highlight the problems which inevitably arise in trying to relate animal behaviour to the human situation. However, the diversity of behaviour and the nature of its continuous, complex interactions with environmental factors (many of which may be unrecognized by the experimenter) also create difficulties when we try to quantify behaviour.

Thus, although it might seem that simple movements or species-specific acts – e.g. grooming – should present few difficulties in terms of measurement, it may be difficult to define clear start-points and end-points for quantifying the movements, and further problems arise in trying to quantify the magnitude of the movements. Even for such simple behaviours, frequency, duration and magnitude may vary independently of each other – if so, which (if any) should be the critical measure? Focusing on a specific behaviour may also conceal the contributions of other behaviours to the effects observed. Thus, for example, reduced food intake might be explained not by reduced hunger on the part of an animal, but by the fact that the animal is persistently engaged in some other kind of behaviour during its period of access to food.

Appetitive behaviours, such as feeding, are often considered to be quite easily related to psychological processes. From the study of behaviours such as feeding, drinking and sexual behaviour – motivated activities common to all mammals and necessary for biological viability – inferences are often made concerning the motivational processes underlying the behaviours, and the involvement of reward mechanisms in their regulation. Thus, physiological interventions which increase or decrease the expression of these behaviours might be used to infer the biological substrates which control their motivational properties, or the mechanisms which subserve their rewarding properties. Distinguishing between alternative interpretations for observed changes in behaviour, as we have seen, requires detailed behaviour analysis.

Further caution is required in experiments where a particular psychological state is the focus of investigation. For example, tasks may be devised to engender anxiety, fear or aggression as psychological states. The tasks may have differing degrees of face validity (in people as well as other animals), and may differ in the extent to which extraneous factors complicate their interpretation. As in other fields of psychology, it is unwise to focus exclusively on the results of a single experimental procedure.

The situation becomes still more complex when trained behaviour is measured. In studies of the physiology of learning, it is of course necessary to establish a learned response on the part of the animal. This response might be naturalistic, as in training a rat to find food in a particular location, or it might be less appropriate to the natural ecology of the animal, as with training a rat to press a lever for food reinforcement. It is important to determine whether changes in learned behaviour are the product of an altered ability to perform the learned response (e.g. motor deficits causing impaired responding), or of a change in learning ability. However, learned behaviours are often used to assess psychological functions other than learning itself. For example, lever-press responding in an operant chamber can provide a baseline against which to assess the effects of various behavioural or physiological manipulations. Clearly, in such complex behavioural procedures there are many points at which a given manipulation can produce a change in measured behaviour, and disentangling the factors critical to the experimental outcome requires skilful experimental design and analysis.

Using various methods to address a problem in psychobiology: an example

Finally, it is worth looking at how these techniques have been used in concert to study a particular problem in psychobiology.The example used here is drawn from research into the biological bases of reward. Much of the relevant research has been directed toward understanding the mechanisms of action of drugs of abuse. There is a clear social context for this research: increased recreational drug use in western societies has highlighted the need for a better understanding of the physiological and psychological factors which underlie drug abuse.

How has psychobiology contributed to this understanding? We shall address this question by looking at the effects of one particular abused drug, cocaine. It was mentioned earlier that cocaine inhibits dopamine reuptake by blocking the presynaptic transporter which transfers dopamine from the synapse back into the terminal. Hence cocaine enhances dopaminergic transmission throughout dopamine pathways in the brain. In terms of simple, observed behaviour, the most obvious consequence of cocaine's pharmacological action is an increase in overall activity. This may be measured, for example, by counting the frequency with which an animal moves across certain fixed points within a test arena. As the dose of cocaine is increased, so its locomotor activity increases (e.g. Scheel-Kruger *et al.*, 1977), until (at high doses) the animal begins to engage in repetitive, seemingly purposeless actions called stereotyped behaviours – for example, repeatedly circling in the same spot, or repeatedly traversing the same part of the test arena. At extremely high doses, toxic effects such as seizure or death may occur. This dose-related profile of effects is typical of other drugs – such as amphetamine – which also enhance dopaminergic activity. Hence cocaine's behavioural effects are consistent with its presumed effects on dopamine neurons.

The effects of cocaine on locomotor activity can be used to explore further its mechanism of action. Consistent with the dopaminergic hypothesis of cocaine's effects, drugs which act as antagonists at dopamine receptors attenuate cocaine-induced locomotor activity. Drugs which block one of the various kinds of postsynaptic dopamine receptor (the D-1 dopamine receptor) are especially effective at blocking the stimulatory effects of cocaine, suggesting that the effect might be mediated by the actions of dopamine at D-1 dopamine receptors specifically (Cabib *et al.*, 1991). To examine further the mechanisms involved, cocaine has been injected into various dopaminergic regions of the brain. In this way, it has been found that cocaine most reliably elicits locomotor stimulation when injected into a nucleus located at the base of the striatum in the limbic forebrain: the nucleus accumbens (Delfs *et al.*, 1990); cocaine's actions here seem to underlie its effects on motor activity. Lesions to the nucleus accumbens impair the effects of systemically administered cocaine (Kelley and Iversen, 1976), and microdialysis has revealed increases in dopamine levels in the nucleus accumbens following cocaine injection (e.g. Carboni *et al.*, 1989).

Locomotor activity is a simple behaviour, and may not be considered relevant to the study of cocaine's rewarding effects. However, studies of the rewarding effects of cocaine have yielded analogous results in terms of the drug's mechanism and sites of action. One procedure used to study the reinforcing effects of drugs is the self-administration model. Here, animals are surgically fitted with an indwelling intravenous catheter, through which drugs can be infused directly into the bloodstream. The other end of the catheter is attached to an infusion pump, which the animal can activate to deliver drug by pressing a lever in an operant chamber. Thus the animal is given control over the infusion of drug to itself. Drugs with addictive potential in people, such as cocaine and morphine, are very readily self-administered by a range of species; indeed, the method has been adopted to screen for the abuse potential of drugs. Again, as with the locomotor effects of cocaine, the reinforcing effects – determined by high rates of self-administration – are mimicked by drugs which increase dopaminergic activity (e.g. Bergman *et al.*, 1989). The rewarding effects of cocaine are disrupted by systemic injections of drugs which impede dopamine transmission (e.g. Woolverton, 1986). Microdialysis has revealed that self-administration of cocaine is accompanied by increased dopamine levels in the nucleus accumbens (Pettit and Justice, 1991), and lesions of the accumbens (or of other components of the dopamine system with which it is associated) attenuate cocaine self-administration (e.g. Roberts *et al.*, 1980). Together, these methods – drugs (administered systemically and directly into the brain), lesions, microdialysis, simple and complex behavioural procedures – are beginning to provide a coherent picture of the means by which cocaine produces its effects. Of course, the findings presented here are very partial; as we noted earlier, no single brain structure subserves any behaviour in isolation, and indeed several other brain regions are implicated in cocaine's effects. In addition, there are results which do not fit easily within this framework: for example, animals will not self-administer cocaine directly into the nucleus accumbens (Goeders and Smith, 1983), and the size of the locomotor response to stimulant drugs does not appear to depend upon dopamine levels in the nucleus accumbens (e.g. Kuczenski *et al.*, 1991). Nevertheless, these problems are currently being tackled by further studies, using many of the methods already described. By these means, psychobiologists are currently contributing to a massive expansion in our understanding of the biological bases of drug abuse and the nature of reward.

In many fields of science, the kinds of question asked are determined to some extent by the techniques available. This has sometimes been the case in psychobiology, and in part explains the methods-orientated nature of this chapter. Nevertheless, from this account it should be clear that many diverse problems are being addressed by physiological psychologists in a range of different ways. Moreover, it should be apparent that studies of the biological bases of behaviour often have implications for the development of therapeutic approaches to many conditions associated with brain dysfunction. Such conditions include those associated with easily identifiable physical pathologies – such as Parkinson's disease, Alzheimer's disease, stroke – as well as those which lack obvious pathological markers, such as mental illness and drug addiction.

Further reading

ASHTON, H. (1992) *Brain Function and Psychotropic Drugs*, Oxford, Oxford University Press.
CARLSON, N.R. (1994) *Physiology of Behavior*, 5th ed., London, Allyn & Bacon.
JULIEN, R.M. (1995) *A Primer of Drug Action*, 7th ed., New York, W.H. Freeman.
SAHGAL, A. (Ed.) (1993) *Behavioural Neuroscience: A Practical Approach*, Vols. 1 and 2, Oxford, Oxford University Press.
THOMPSON, R.F. (1993) *The Brain: A Neuroscience Primer*, 2nd ed., New York, W.H. Freeman.

References

BENINGER, R.J. (1983) 'The role of dopamine in locomotor activity and learning', *Brain Research Reviews*, 6, 173–96.
BERGER, T.W., BERRY, S.D. and THOMPSON, R.F. (1986) 'Role of the hippocampus in classical conditioning of aversive and appetitive behaviours', in: ISAACSON, R.L. and PRIBRAM, K.H. (Eds) *The Hippocampus*, Vol. 4, New York, Plenum Press.
BERGMAN, J., MADRAS, B.K., JOHNSON, S.E. and SPEALMAN, R.D. (1989) 'Effects of cocaine and related drugs in nonhuman primates, III: Self-administration by squirrel monkeys', *Journal of Pharmacology and Experimental Therapeutics*, 251, 150–5.
CABIB, S., CASTELLANO, C., CESTARI, V., FILIBECK, U. and PUGLISI-ALLEGRA, S. (1991) 'D1 and D2 receptor antagonists differently affect cocaine-induced locomotor hyperactivity in the mouse', *Psychopharmacology*, 105, 335–9.
CARBONI, E., IMPERATO, A., PEREZZANI, L. and DICHIARA, G. (1989) 'Amphetamine, cocaine, phencyclidine and nomifensine increase extracellular dopamine

concentrations preferentially in the nucleus accumbens of freely moving rats', *Neuroscience*, **28**, 653-61.

CARLSON, N.R. (1994) Physiology of Behaviour, 5th Ed., London, Allyn & Bacon.

DELFS, J.M., SCHREIBER, L. and KELLEY, A.E. (1990) 'Microinjection of cocaine into the nucleus accumbens elicits locomotor activation in the rat', *Journal of Neuroscience*, **10**, 303-10.

GOEDERS, N.E. and SMITH, J.E. (1983) 'Cortical dopaminergic involvement in cocaine reinforcement', *Science,* **221**, 773-5.

GREGORY, R.L. (1961) 'The brain as an engineering problem', in: THORPE, W.H. and ZANGWILL, O.H. (Eds) *Current Problems in Animal behaviour*, Cambridge, Cambridge University Press, 307-30.

HETHERINGTON, A.W. and RANSON, S.W. (1942) 'Hypothalamic lesions and adiposity in the rat', *Anatomical Record*, **78**, 149-72.

KELLEY, P.H. and IVERSEN, S.D. (1976) 'Selective 6OHDA-induced destruction of mesolimbic dopamine neurons: abolition of psychostimulant-induced locomotor activity in rats', *European Journal of Pharmacology*, **40**, 45-56.

KIMBLE, D.P. and DANNEN, E. (1977) 'Persistent spatial maze-learning deficits in hippocampal-lesioned rats across a 7-week postoperative period', *Physiological Psychology*, **15**, 409-13.

KIRCHGESSNER, A.L. and SCLAFANI, A. (1988) 'PVN-hindbrain pathway involved in the hypothalamic hyperphagia-obesity syndrome', *Physiology and Behavior*, **42**, 517-28.

KUCZENSKI, R., SEGAL, D.S. and AIZENSTEIN, M.L. (1991) 'Amphetamine, cocaine, and fencamfamine: relationship between locomotor and stereotypy response profiles and caudate and accumbens dopamine dynamics', *Journal of Neuroscience*, **11**, 2703-12.

MALSBURY, C.W. (1971) 'Facilitation of male copulatory behavior by electrical stimulation of the medial preoptic area', *Physiology and Behavior*, 7, 797-805.

MAYER, D.C. and LIEBESKIND, J.C. (1974) 'Pain reduction by focal electrical stimulation of the brain: an anatomical and behavioral analysis', *Brain Research*, **68**, 73-93.

O'KEEFE, J. and DOSTROVSKY, T. (1971) 'The hippocampus as a spatial map: preliminary evidence from unit activity in the freely moving rat', *Brain Research*, **34**, 171-5.

O'KEEFE, J. and NADEL, L. (1978) *The Hippocampus as a Cognitive Map*, Oxford, Clarendon Press.

ONGINI, E. and LONGO, V.G. (1989) 'Dopamine receptor subtypes and arousal', *International Review of Neurobiology*, **31**, 239-55.

PETTIT, H.O. and JUSTICE, J.B. Jr. (1991) 'Effect of dose on cocaine self-administration behavior and dopamine levels in the nucleus accumbens', *Brain Research*, **529**, 94-102.

PHILLIPS, A.G., ATKINSON, L.J., BLACKBURN, J.R. and BLAHA, C.D. (1993) 'Increased extracellular dopamine in the nucleus accumbens of the rat elicited by a conditional stimulus for food: an electrochemical study', *Canadian Journal of Physiology and Pharmacology*, **71**, 387–93.

ROBERTS, D.C.S., KOOB, G.F., KLONOFF, P. and FIBIGER, H.C. (1980) 'Extinction and recovery of cocaine self-administration following 6-hydroxydopamine lesions of the nucleus accumbens', *Pharmacology, Biochemistry and Behavior*, **12**, 781–7.

SCHEEL-KRUGER, J., BRAESTRUP, C., NIELSEN, M., GOLEMBIOWSKA, K. and MOGILNICKA, E. (1977) 'Cocaine: discussion on the role of dopamine in the biochemical mechanism of action', in: ELLINWOOD, E.H. and KILBEY, M.M. (Eds) *Cocaine and Other Stimulants*. New York, Plenum Press, 373–407.

SCHMALTZ, L.W. and THEIOS, J. (1972) 'Acquisition and extinction of a classically conditioned response in hippocampectomized rabbits', *Journal of Comparative and Physiological Psychology*, **79**, 328–33.

WENKSTERN, D., PFAUS, J.G. and FIBIGER, H.C. (1993) 'Dopamine transmission increases in the nucleus accumbens of male rats during their first exposure to sexually receptive female rats', *Brain Research*, **618**, 41–6.

WOOLVERTON, W.L. (1986) 'Effects of a D1 and D2 antagonist on the self-administration of cocaine and piribedil by rhesus monkeys', *Pharmacology, Biochemistry and Behavior*, **24**, 531–5.

Chapter 9

Cognitive Neuropsychology

M. Jane Riddoch and Glyn W. Humphreys

Behaviour may be studied in many different ways. Neuropsychology is concerned with the study of the behaviour of people with known brain damage, and this is done both in order to understand the function of the damaged region within the normal brain, and to understand the functional components that go together to create complex behaviours.

What exactly do we mean by the term 'behaviour'? We are capable of many complicated perceptual and cognitive abilities. We are able to recognize a friend within a crowd of other people with no apparent effort, we can communicate our feelings to others by either the spoken or written word, and we can traverse a town with a maze of apparently similar streets and arrive at a predetermined destination. However, this apparent ease of everyday functioning leaves us at a loss to explain cases where, following brain damage, patients fail to recognize their therapist or even members of their own family from one day to the next; why patients can understand complex sentences (such as 'what is the name of the instrument we use to tell of the passage of the hours?') but fail to understand a simple sentence such as 'put the pen on the pencil' (e.g. putting the pencil on the pen instead); or why some patients may fail to complete one half of a drawing (see Figure 9.1).

How can these complex perceptual and cognitive abilities be classified and interpreted? The traditional neuropsychological approach has been to ascribe different cognitive functions to the different lobes of the brain. In this way it has been found that the occipital lobes are concerned with vision, the parietal lobes are concerned with spatial abilities, the temporal lobes are concerned with memory and (in the left hemisphere) with some language functions, while the frontal lobes are concerned with executive functions (such as the selection of which task to perform) and (again within the left hemisphere) some language functions. In each case, we can observe deficits in the general functions described (vision, spatial abilities, memory and language and so forth) following damage to the relevant lobe.

More recently a 'cognitive neuropsychological approach' has developed, with its roots in the information-processing approach of cognitive psychology. Here attempts are made to identify the components that go to make up complex abilities, usually by performing experiments with non-brain damaged people. For instance, it has been shown that if people are read lists of words,

Figure 9.1 *Drawing of a man by a person suffering damage to the right parietal lobe of the brain (note the omission of detail on the left relative to the right side of the figure)*

and then are asked to recall the list in the order given (so-called 'serial recall'), performance is usually very good for the first and last items in the list, but relatively poor for the intervening items (Baddeley, 1986). Such findings have been used to suggest that memory consists of at least two sub-processes: short-term memory (or working memory) and long-term memory. The good perform-ance on the initial words in the list is thought to reflect the workings of long-term memory – the subject has a little time to rehearse these items even though further words are being presented, and this is sufficient to transfer the information to long-term memory from short-term memory. However, as more words are presented, it becomes more difficult to rehearse them. Short-term memory itself is thought to have a limited capacity; unless information is rehearsed and transferred to long-term memory, it will be displaced by subse-quent information as it enters the store. Thus performance is poor for the intervening items in the list. The final items in the list remain in the short-term store since there is no further input of information, and hence these items remain available for report. *Cognitive neuropsychologists* have used such ideas derived from experimental cognitive psychology in order to help understand the behaviour of patients after brain damage. Additionally, findings from such patients can help inform about the nature of the normal system. For instance, amnesic patients show a different pattern of performance from normal subjects on a serial recall task such as that described above; in particular, amnesics show abnormally poor performance for the initial items in the list, but (interestingly) normal performance on the final items. That is, they show a *selective* pattern of deficit (rather than being poor at all aspects of performance). This selective pattern of performance has been used to argue that amnesic subjects have a deficit in transferring new material into long-term memory while their short-term memory remains intact (hence their good performance on the final items in the list) (e.g. Baddeley and Warrington, 1970).

Until very recently, the work of cognitive neuropsychologists was not related to underlying brain structures for reasons that we will discuss more fully in the next two sections. However, more recently, sophisticated brain scanning techniques have become available (e.g. functional magnetic resonance imaging [MRI] and positron emission tomography [PET]) that allow observation of the activation of particular brain regions whilst cognitive operations are being performed. Coupled with the more traditional evidence from studies of lesioned patients, these new techniques are enabling us to build detailed accounts of how the components of cognitive tasks are performed in the brain. We no longer need to refer to very general functions such as vision, language and memory, located in the lobes of the brain, but to particular processes involved when (for instance) we recognize faces, formulate speech or recall a route home. We will discuss more fully these new advances in our understanding of how the brain controls behaviour towards the end of this chapter.

Localization of function

The beginnings of neuropsychology as we know it today can be traced back to the last century, although it was probably not identified as a separate discipline within psychology until much later. Localization of language function within a particular area of the brain may be attributed first to Franz Joseph Gall (1778–1828). Gall described two cases where some form of language dysfunction resulted from brain damage (Gall, 1825). The first was the case of a 26-year-old man who had received a sword injury. The sword penetrated near the base of the nose on the left-hand side entering the left anterior frontal lobe of the brain (at the front of the brain on the left) (see Figure 9.2). As a result of this injury, the man became paralysed on the right side of his body, he had double vision, impaired smell and taste and, most interesting as far as cognitive functioning is concerned, he lost the ability to recall proper names (e.g. the names of his friends), although he had no difficulty in naming objects. The second case involved a patient who had suffered a stroke. This man was unable to pronounce any of the words he wished to say although he understood all that was said to him (Gall, 1825). As a result of these observations, Gall argued that language was located in the brain in the region of the left frontal lobe.

Workers subsequent to Gall reported that while damage to the front portions of the left hemisphere produced language disturbances in many cases,

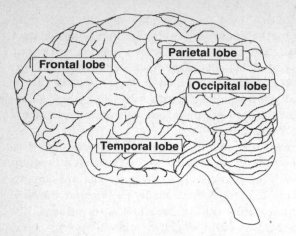

Figure 9.2 *Side view of the human brain indicating the location of the different lobes*

damage to the right hemisphere did not affect speech (Broca, 1861). On the other hand, the parietal lobes were found to be more involved in the analysis of the spatial dimensions of the world (Hécaen, 1962). Thus patients suffering parietal damage may find it difficult to rotate an image in their head, to bisect the centre of lines etc. Such work led to the accounts of general cognitive functions, such as language and spatial processing, being assigned to particular lobes of the brain.

During Gall's lifetime, the ability to determine the precise location of damage to the brain was relatively crude. Indeed, analysis of the areas of damage could only take place once the patient had died and a post-mortem examination could be performed. Nowadays, many sophisticated techniques are available and it is possible to obtain detailed information about the living brain in such patients. For instance, a CT scan (a computerized transaxial tomograph) provides a two-dimensional representation of slices of the brain as a result of pictures produced from a rapidly rotating X-ray source. MRI scans are superficially similar to CT scans, although the way they are generated is different (images are derived from measured changes in the magnetic resonance of the brain), and they provide yet more accurate images. PET scanning requires that subjects are injected with radioactive isotopes, which (for example) are taken up as a function of the amount of oxygen within particular regions of the brain. Since the uptake of oxygen in different brain regions changes as a function of the task performed, PET scans can indicate which brain areas are functioning whilst particular cognitive operations take place. PET studies have also shown that damaged areas of the brain have reduced blood flow, and, furthermore, brain areas can be *functionally* impaired on PET even if they are not *structurally* impaired, as shown on MRI scans. Such functional impairments can come about if a lesion in one brain area prevents another (structurally intact) area from operating normally. Such techniques have proved invaluable in the medical management of conditions such as head injury, tumours etc.

Also, they provide much more information about the functioning of the brain than was provided by the detailed observations of past researchers. Had either of Gall's patients been scanned, not only would damage to the front parts of the brain have been observed, it may also have been possible to demonstrate that slightly different brain regions were affected in the two cases. This would allow the different language impairments to be traced back to contrasting regions within the frontal lobe. As we shall discuss below, the different language processes impaired in the two patients may also now be related to normal language functions measured by means of PET techniques in normal subjects performing different language tasks.

Of course, to understand behaviour more fully, we need to do more than describe the relation between a given behavioural impairment and a given brain lesion: we need to understand the component processes that together enable a particular task to be performed. This is one of the prime aims of cognitive psychology, which stands as one of the pillars of modern-day cognitive neuropsychology.

The distributed view of brain function

A major critic of the early localisationist view of brain function (i.e. that brain regions were specialized for particular behavioural functions) was the English neurologist John Hughlings Jackson (1835-1911). Jackson argued that the symptoms observed in a patient following a lesion of a particular area did not necessarily mean that the impaired function was located in the damaged area but rather that the patient's behaviour was the result of the concerted action of the unimpaired areas of the brain. He proposed that general cognitive abilities, such as language and memory, are distributed throughout the brain, rather than being localized within any small brain region. So, whilst a frontal lobe lesion may interfere with the ability to speak, other language abilities may remain unimpaired (e.g. the ability to understand what is said) (Jackson, 1915).

We can use the account of a recently reported case to illustrate this argument. The patient was a 67-year-old labourer who suffered a stroke damaging the left occipital lobe (Coslett and Saffran, 1989). The occipital lobes are concerned with the processing and recognition of visual stimuli and are located at the back of the brain. The patient's speech and auditory comprehension were quite unimpaired (which we would expect following Gall's observations that language disturbances follow damage to the left frontal lobe). The patient was, however, totally unable to read single letters or words and was unable to name pictures. Surprisingly, if given a task where a written word has to be matched to one of four pictures, the patient performed at a very high level (an example of this sort of task is shown below in Figure 9.3). He was also able to sort 'food' words (e.g. grape) from words that looked very similar (e.g. graph). Similarly, given a series of pictures, he was able to sort them successfully according to whether they were edible or inedible. These tasks do not require

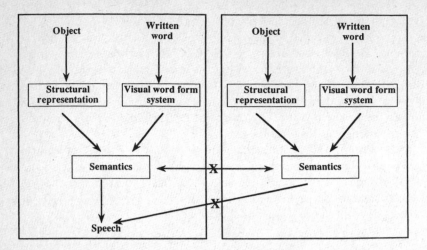

Figure 9.3 *Coslett and Saffran's (1989) allocation of language processes to the left and right hemispheres of the brain on the basis of observations of patients with optic aphasia (the Xs represent damage to the normal system)*

spoken output, but they do require the *intact recognition* of the stimulus material; that is, the ability to read words and to recognize pictures.

The stroke damaged the left occipital lobe of this patient. The effect of such damage may have been to disrupt the recognition of pictures and letters within the left hemisphere. However, the right occipital lobe was intact and it is possible that the patient was using right hemisphere recognition systems in order to perform the picture–word match tests. Coslett and Saffran suggest that the brain lesion disrupted the links between the two hemispheres (in addition to the left occipital lobe damage); as a result, the visual information arriving in the right hemisphere is prevented from accessing the left hemisphere speech areas (see Figure 9.4) (Coslett and Saffran, 1989). The suggestion is that the patient was able to use the intact right hemisphere in order to perform picture–word match tasks and to sort pictures and words according to a given criterion; however, when overt naming was required, the integrity of links between the right hemisphere recognition systems and left hemisphere speech systems was necessary in order to transmit information from the right hemisphere in the system for overt speech in the left hemisphere. Coslett and Saffran argue that language processes should not just be taken to reflect spoken output. Other processes are necessary; these include the ability to recognize letters or words, and the ability to know what words mean (so that you know that words such as 'grape' and 'graph' refer to different things). These other processes are located in areas of the brain other than the frontal lobes and, indeed, as the case we have described suggests, may also be located in the 'silent' right hemisphere.

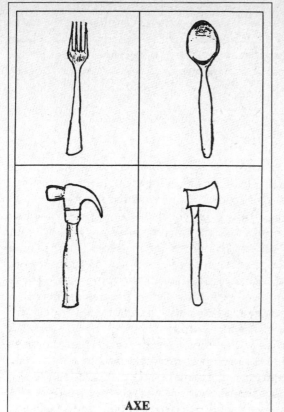

AXE

Figure 9.4 *One item from a picture–word match test: the distractor items are chosen to be visually similar to the target item*

Hughlings Jackson also thought that the nervous system was arranged in a functional hierarchy of layers. Each successively higher level would control more complex aspects of behaviour. Brain damage was more likely to affect the higher levels of the hierarchy; as a consequence, the resultant behaviour would reflect the operation of the lower levels. For example, as far as language is concerned, we might suppose that 'high-level' abilities, such as formulating the plan of what you want to say, may be more susceptible to damage than 'lower level' abilities, such as simply repeating back what is being said. However, this now seems incorrect. Patients can have intact 'high-level' abilities, whilst failing at apparently more simple, 'lower level' tasks. Simple repetition may be disrupted, for example, if there is damage to processes dealing with speech input, even if the processes involved in formulating complex speech output are intact. What seems more important here is whether the abilities share common component processes, rather than whether one is more complex than the other. The search to specify the processes mediating given tasks characterizes modern cognitive neuropsychology.

Although Jackson's criticisms of the localization of general cognitive abilities seem well founded, they should not be taken to refute a finer-grained approach to localization. Localization of function may still be possible when general cognitive abilities are broken down into their components; for example, language deficits may be understood and related to the sites of brain lesions if language is decomposed into separate processes concerned with (e.g.) the recognition of words, the retrieval of their meaning and the retrieval of the associated names.

Cognitive Neuropsychology

In the 1970s a new discipline emerged: cognitive neuropsychology. Rather than building on the neuropsychology of earlier years, where the main interest was the functioning of the various parts of the brain, cognitive neuropsychology was more closely linked with cognitive psychology. Cognitive psychology typically involves an information-processing approach to the study of the brain, in which cognitive functions are broken down into a series of sequential processing stages. For example, reading a word aloud may be decomposed into stages concerned with (a) visual recognition of the word, (b) retrieval of its associated name, and (c) retrieval of the articulatory programme necessary to pronounce the word. Experimental cognitive psychologists are largely concerned with empirical work with normal subjects while cognitive neuropsychologists are concerned with the patterns of impairment shown by brain-damaged subjects and the relationship of these patterns to normal functioning. For instance, within sequential information-processing accounts, it may be possible to lose some functions whilst others are spared (e.g. words may be visually recognized even if access to name information is impaired). Studies of patients with selective deficits in cognitive tasks can also help define the functional stages making up the tasks.

The initial accounts of cognitive functions derived by cognitive neuropsychologists made no reference to brain structures. It was felt that while it was useful to have some knowledge of the major functions of the different brain regions, it was important to appreciate that many complex functions require the integrated working of a number of different brain areas (cf. Jackson, 1915) and that the best way to identify component processes was by the manipulation of different variables in experimental paradigms. To illustrate this let us consider reading: what processes operate to allow us to comprehend a single word? We first must be able to distinguish between particular letter combinations that form words from letter combinations that do not (e.g. BREAK from KREAB). In order to pronounce the word correctly, at least two procedures may be followed. In one, we can obtain the pronunciation by applying letter-to-sound rules (these can also be used for non-words – you could say what KREAB would sound like even though you had never seen it before). In the other, we can associate the spelling of the word with the pronunciation (see above). We also need to be able to attach meaning to the word (so that we know that even though GRAPE and GRAPH look very similar they have very different meanings). A patient's reading may be assessed in an experimental way in order to determine whether these component processes are intact or not. For instance, in order to assess the ability to distinguish between words and non-words, the patient may be asked to carry out a 'lexical decision' task, for instance by ticking the words in a given list of items (e.g. VATER, STEAK, LATER, STEEK etc.). A test of the ability to apply letter-to-sound rules correctly would be to ask the patient to read aloud a non-word (such as KREAB). The ability to associate pronunciations with the spelling of the whole can be assessed by asking the patient to read irregular words aloud (words that violate the spelling-to-sound rules in English such as PINT, which if pronounced regularly, using spelling-to-sound rules, would be pronounced to rhyme with MINT and HINT). A test of comprehension would consist of the patient select-ing the word closest in meaning to a target word from a number of alternatives (e.g. given the target word STAKE to be paired with one of POST, MEAT, STREET). Note that, even if a patient has difficulty articulating language, tests may be conducted to assess whether the intonal aspects of the reading system are intact. For instance, processes involved in accessing pronunciations can be assessed using picture–word matching where a patient is asked to point to a picture associated with the name of a non-word (e.g. PHOCKS, with pictures of a FOX, a PHONE and a LOCK), or an irregular word (e.g. STEAK, with pictures of MEAT, a POST and a STREET). The former tests whether the spelling-to-sound system for 'assembling' pronunciations is intact; the latter tests whether the system for 'addressing' pronunciations from the spelling of whole words is intact. Note that by decomposing tasks in this way we get to a much finer grained analysis of behaviour. General functions such as language, vision, memory and so forth become particularized so that we can assess the specific operation of cognitive subsystems.

The application of detailed tests of this sort reveals the point at which performance may be breaking down and will allow therapy to be directed effectively.

Assumptions underlying cognitive neuropsychology

There are at least three major assumptions underlying cognitive neuro-psychology. These are

(1) The concept of modularity: i.e., for any complex cognitive function, the component processing parts of that function may be seen as autonomous.
(2) Brain damage can impair modules differentially.
(3) Observing the behavioural consequence of damage to a module reveals how that module functions in the normal brain.

Thus, complex behaviour (such as our ability to recognize words or to use objects addressed by those words appropriately) is thought to occur as a result of the collective working of a number of different processing components or modules. Observations of patients with selective brain damage, together with detailed experimental work with non-brain damaged individuals have led cognitive neuropsychologists to develop models of reading (Ellis and Young, 1988), speech (Ellis and Young, 1988), action (Riddoch *et al.*, 1989), face recognition (Bruce and Young, 1988), and visual object recognition (Humphreys and Riddoch, 1987). Humphreys and Riddoch's model of visual object recognition is illustrated in Figure 9.5.

A cognitive neuropsychological approach to visual object recognition

According to this model, visual object recognition is thought to result from processing at a number of distinct stages, some of which may occur simultaneously (e.g. the early processing of colour, depth, movement and shape); and some of which occur sequentially (e.g. the processing of shape and access to stored knowledge). The model was derived from the observations and descriptions of patients with selective visual problems.

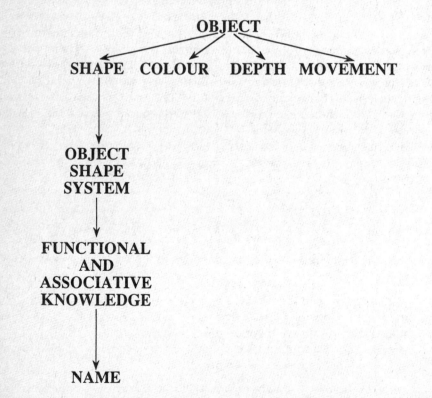

Figure 9.5 *A simplified version of Humphreys and Riddoch's (1987) model of visual object recognition*

(1) Deficits in the early visual processing of colour, depth and movement.   Work with animals has shown that cells in the occipital lobe may respond selectively to certain forms of visual input; for instance, cells in an area termed V4 have been shown to respond to colour but not, for example, to movement (Livingstone and Hubel, 1987; Zeki, 1980). Interestingly, a number of patients have been reported who have lost the ability to perceive colour consciously (Meadows, 1974). They report the world in white and black and shades of grey. The quality of their lives is diminished: food without colour is not so appetizing (imagine grey strawberries and cream!), but their ability to interact with their world remains unchanged. In at least some cases, object recognition itself is not affected, nor is the appreciation of other forms of visual information such as movement (Heywood *et al.*, 1987).

Other cells, in an area termed MT (in the monkey this is situated along the border between the occipital and parietal lobes), have been shown to respond selectively to movement, but not, for example, to colour (Livingstone and Hubel, 1987; Zeki, 1974). Again, in the neuropsychology literature it is possible to find cases of patients with selective deficits in this sphere (Vaina, 1989; Zihl *et al.*, 1983; Zihl *et al.*, 1991). The patient reported by Zihl and his colleagues had a greatly impaired ability to perceive motion (1983; Zihl *et al.*, 1991). Her interactions with the world were much affected by this disorder. For instance, she reported difficulties when filling a glass with water since she had no appreciation of the level of liquid rising in the glass; at one moment it appeared at one point; at the next, the glass overflowed. People in a room would be first at one place and then another; she was unable to see them moving from the door to a chair. We should also note that the patient's colour-processing and object-recognition abilities were unaffected by her lesion.

Cells in other areas of the brain have been shown to be sensitive to depth perception (Fischer and Poggio, 1979; Livingstone and Hubel, 1987). Here, let us consider the case of a young soldier wounded by a machine-gun bullet during the First World War (Holmes and Horrax, 1919). The sophisticated techniques we have available today to locate precisely areas of brain damage were not available at that time; however, Holmes and Horrax indicate that the bullet entered the brain through the posterior portion of the right angular gyrus and left via the upper part of the left angular gyrus (a region on the border between the occipital, parietal and temporal lobes). The soldier regained consciousness after several days and was observed to be alert and intelligent. He showed no trace of weakness, incoordination or disturbance of muscle tone, and he could move his limbs easily and naturally. Yet, although he showed no obvious abnormality of gait, he would typically walk with short, slow steps with his hands held out in front of him. Furthermore, despite being able to see (he was able to identify objects and people), he would collide with obstacles in his path, always to his great surprise and discomfort. On questioning, he explained that he had not realized that the objects were so near to him. The young soldier's difficulties were the result of an impaired perception of depth and the distances between objects. This case provides a very clear example of how important normal depth perception is to everyday functioning, with the patient's difficulties resulting from a very circumscribed lesion.

Findings such as these suggest that different areas of the brain are specialized for processing different aspects of visual input. The important thing to note about the patients described above is that their deficits are *selective* and therefore may be taken as supportive of the notion that different forms of processing may take place in different modules in the brain.

(2) Deficits in shape processing So far we have considered modularity in terms of the evidence in favour of separate processing systems for particular types of visual information (systems specializing in the processing of colour, motion or depth perception). There is also specialized processing of the shape of objects; furthermore, as is indicated in Figure 9.4, our ability to recognize objects appears to require us to process visual information at a number of different levels. The levels are hierarchically organized, so that a problem early on in the series of processes required will affect the processing of information at later levels. Lissauer in 1890 was the first to propose such a hierarchical organization and to apply it to neuropsychological impairments of object recognition. He initially distinguished between difficulties in 'on-line' visual processing (he termed these apperceptive agnosia) and difficulties in accessing our memories from vision (so-called associative agnosia) (Lissauer, 1890). Since the 1960s a number of detailed investigations of visually agnosic patients have been performed and it has become clear that a two-level hierarchy is too simple a concept. Let us first consider 'on-line' visual processing. What processes may be necessary for us to 'see' a simple two-dimensional square? Look at Figure 9.6. We are able to see a square in all three of the examples even though different processes are involved in each case. For instance, we need to be able to compute contours from changes of intensity in the image in order to see the square in Figure 6a; In Figure 6b we need to be able to *derive* contours (based on projecting their continuation across the missing segments); while in Figure 6c we need to be able to separate the shape of the square from the other shapes present. There therefore appear to be at least three mechanisms of shape processing. If these are separate processes they may be independently susceptible to brain damage.

Let us consider three people who all have severe difficulty in recognizing objects from sight: D.F., F.G.P. and H.J.A. D.F. was a 34-year-old businesswoman when she suffered carbon monoxide poisoning from a faulty gas heater, causing damage to the back of the brain in the region of the occipital lobes (Milner *et al.*, 1991). F.G.P. had also been a businesswoman but had retired and was aged 68 years when she complained of difficulty in recognizing faces and objects (Kartsounis and Warrington, 1991). Scans showed no particular abnormality of her brain. The third patient, H.J.A., a businessman aged 61, suffered a stroke causing bilateral damage in the region leading from the occipital to the temporal lobes (Humphreys, Riddoch, Quinlan, Donnelly and Price, 1992; Humphreys, Troscianko, Riddoch, Boucart, Donnelly and Harding, 1992; Riddoch and

Figure 9.6 *The outline of a square is readily seen in Figure 6a as a result of changes in intensity between the square and its surround; in Figure 6b the contours of the square are derived by projecting their continuation across the missing segments and in 6c the square can be separated from other pictured objects by grouping the object contours appropriately*

)

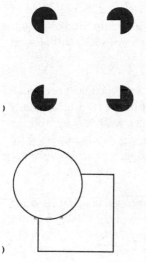

)

)

Humphreys, 1987a). The CT scan showed damage in the region of the occipital lobes. All three of these patients were very impaired at recognizing practically all kinds of seen objects (if they felt the objects with their hands they were often able to identify them), but none the less they were able to perform simple everyday activities such as dressing, eating and avoiding obstacles in their path (such as furniture). Detailed study of the reports of these patients show that they differed in the *degree* of visual impairment; in particular, they differed in their abilities to perceive simple shapes.

(a) *Contour perception*: D.F. failed on a simple test of shape perception known as the Efron test (Efron, 1969). In one form of this test, two figures are presented at a time and the task is to decide whether they are the same shape or not. Importantly, the figures are matched for brightness, preventing this being used as a cue. While D.F. performed very little better than chance on this task, F.G.A. and H.J.A. performed well.

(b) *Ability to derive implicit contours*: Study Figure 9.6b. The figure consists of four circles each with a segment missing. These circles appear to be located at the points of an 'illusory' square, the square is illusory since its

177

boundaries do not in fact exist but are suggested by the positions of the missing segments in the four circles. Whilst F.G.A. had no difficulty in comparing two shapes when their outlines were explicit (the Efron test), she was unable to detect shapes when boundary information had to be computed by continuation. Thus, she described Figure 9.6b as 'four little curves'. H.J.A., on the other hand, could detect subjective contours with such simple shapes.

(c) *ability to separate figure from ground*: When given a number of different shapes that overlap each other (see Figure 9.6c), and asked to trace around the contours of the individual shapes, H.J.A. was very impaired relative to normal observers. He found it difficult to determine which part belonged to which shape. H.J.A.'s shape processing is therefore also impaired although he can both perceive contours and derive implicit contours with simple shapes.

Our ability to perceive shape, which we find such an effortless process, is clearly no simple matter. We are able to see shapes explicitly (the Efron test), implicitly (e.g. shapes derived from subjective contours), and we are able to separate one shape from another. These abilities may be separately impaired by brain damage, consistent with shape processing in the intact brain comprising a number of separable processing stages.

(3) Deficits in accessing stored knowledge We noted earlier that Lissauer divided deficits in visual object recognition according to whether they resulted from deficits in on-line visual processing or whether they represented deficits in accessing stored knowledge. In the same way that case studies of neuropsychological patients show that on-line visual processing does not represent a single process, so too case studies show that stored memories, accessed by vision, can take a number of forms. For instance, take a cat. You know that it is a relatively small animal covered with soft fur which may be long or short depending on the species. You know that people keep cats as pets, and that they are deemed to be useful in that they catch mice. You know cats vary greatly in colour. Some of this stored knowledge may be used directly for visual recognition. For instance, size and shape information may be important; however, the knowledge that they catch mice is not likely to play a direct role when we need to distinguish between pictures of a cat, a dog and a rabbit shown in isolation. Such information may become important, however, if the animal is seen only briefly but seems to be chasing another animal into a mouse hole. Given the principle of modularity, it is possible that these different kinds of knowledge are represented in different modules; that is, stored knowledge of the visual appearance of objects (such as that a cat has pointed rather than round ears) may be distinct from stored functional knowledge (a cat can be kept for catching mice) or associative knowledge (a cat is frequently associated with warm soft places in which to sleep). We will discuss this notion of modular knowledge stores in the light of three further cases who all also had marked

difficulties in visual recognition: J.B. (Riddoch and Humphreys, 1987b), D.W. (Riddoch and Humphreys, 1992) and E.E. (Riddoch *et al.*, in preparation). Unlike the cases we have described above, these three patients had no impairments in on-line visual processing; however, as we shall show, they differed in their ability to access stored knowledge from vision.

(a) *Separate knowledge systems?*: J.B. was involved in a road traffic accident, which caused a large lesion to the parietal/occipital region of his left hemisphere. Following this, his recognition of many common objects was substantially impaired. If shown a line drawing of an object and then asked a series of probe questions about it, his performance was very poor. Typically, he was able to give general information about the item (e.g. information about an object's superordinate category) but was very poor at responding to specific questions concerning stored functional and associative knowledge. For example, when shown a drawing of a 'horse', he was asked questions such as: 'Can it be kept as a pet?'; 'Does it eat meat?'; 'Are you more likely to find in on a race course or by a swimming pool?'. Although able to decide that the object was an animal, J.B. often failed to answer any more specific questions correctly. Interestingly, J.B. was rather better at answering item-specific questions when he was given the *name* of the item rather than when he was given a *picture* of it, suggesting that specific knowledge about the object was not lost, but was rendered inaccessible from vision. This brings us back to the point we were making earlier about the different *kinds* of stored information; it was clear that J.B. had difficulty in accessing stored functional and associative knowledge from vision but what about knowledge about the visual properties of objects? To test this, J.B. was asked to decide whether line drawings such as those illustrated in Figure 9.7 could exist in real life or not. This is termed an object decision task. Such decisions require a patient to decide whether the shape of an object is familiar or not, but they do not require the retrieval of functional or associative knowledge. Interestingly, J.B. could perform at a high level. From this it seems that the ability to access stored knowledge of object shape can be separated from the ability to access stored functional and associative knowledge.

J.B.'s deficit can be interpreted as a difficulty in accessing functional and associative knowledge along with normal access to stored visual knowledge (Riddoch and Humphreys, 1987b). Given the separation of visual knowledge from functional and associative knowledge, it may also be possible to find patients with deficits in each of the different knowledge systems, rather than having problems in accessing the knowledge.

(b) *The object shape system*: D.W. had suffered from epilepsy since the age of 20 and, at the age of 45, suffered a fit while standing on a ladder. He sustained a head injury in the resultant fall, causing damage both to the

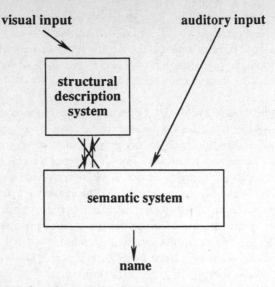

Figure 9.7 *J.B. shows that the stored knowledge systems we can access from vision can be separated into stored knowledge of object shape (intact in his case) and stored functional and associative knowledge (which he cannot access from vision but can access from the spoken word) (see also Figure 9.5) (The Xs represent damage to the normal system)*

front (the frontal lobes) and the back (the occipital lobes) of the brain. Unlike J.B., D.W. made numerous errors on the object decision task that J.B. did well on; D.W. found it difficult to distinguish between real and unreal objects. When we probed D.W.'s knowledge of objects by asking him to tell us about them, he again did not do well. For instance, when asked to give a definition for a giraffe, D.W.'s reply was: 'A giraffe spends most of its time jumping. It has strong back legs and small front legs. It chews the cud. It's of medium size but I can't think what it looks like. It's light brown in colour.' When asked about a carrot he said: 'I don't know if it's a fruit or a vegetable. It's curved, red in colour and quite sweet. I would say it is more ball shaped than cylinder shaped.' Interestingly, only some kinds of knowledge were impaired in the case of D.W. This was apparent when we asked him to provide a name in response to a definition rather than the other way round. So, in one set of definitions we stressed the visual appearance of objects (e.g. a bee was: 'a small black and yellow striped flying insect') and in the other we stressed functional characteristics of the objects (now a bee was: 'an insect that lives in a hive and makes honey'). D.W. did poorly on the 'visual definitions', failing to produce the correct name on over half the trials; in contrast his naming from the 'functional definitions' was at a normal level. This pattern of performance supports the suggestion that visual and functional knowledge are separated in the brain. D.W. had impaired visual knowledge, along with relatively good functional knowledge.

(c) *Stored functional and associative knowledge*: What sort of performance might we expect from someone whose deficit affects stored functional knowledge? Such a person should be able to perform object decision tasks but should have difficulty when required to discriminate between items that are functionally and associatively related to each other. Problems might also be encountered when item names, rather than pictures are used. One such person is E.E. who had a stroke at the age of 74, largely affecting the occipital and temporal lobes of her left hemisphere. Her speech was markedly affected; she could speak, but her speech made little sense in that words were used inappropriately, or new words were created; for instance, when asked to name a picture of a helicopter she said it was a 'neggerty apple'. She knew this was not correct, and went on to say 'it goes round when it's going on its journey'. She experienced similar difficulties when asked the function of items; thus when asked what she would do with a kettle, she said 'Boil some stuff in - bananas, potatoes or water'. More often, however, her responses were entirely inappropriate. She named the picture of a gorilla as an 'umbrella' and a mouse as a 'group with a ticket'. E.E. was given picture–word matching tasks in which she had to point to the correct picture of an item from among four; having been given the target item's name she performed well if the distractors were unrelated to the target (e.g. the picture of fox when the four pictures were a fox, a shoe, a fork and a potato) (see Figure 9.2); she also performed quite well if the distractor items were visually similar to the target item (e.g. the picture of a knife when the distractor items were a chisel, nail file and a paint-brush). However, in contrast with this, she performed very poorly when she had to distinguish between items on the basis of categorical relations (e.g. when asked to select the picture of a fox from four pictures which included a fox, a deer, a horse and a cow). It might be argued that this last test is difficult on two counts: the distractors are both categorically and visually similar to the target item. However, E.E. also performed poorly in tests where the distractors were only semantically and not visually related to the target item. For instance, when asked to determine whether a picture of a lamp or a picture of a torch was more closely associated to the target picture of a battery, she chose the lamp. She made errors on this test whether spoken words or pictures were used as test items, suggesting that the problem was not simply one of access to functional or associative knowledge from vision. The ability to distinguish between associatively and functionally related items appeared very difficult for E.E. She had similar difficulty when she was asked to select the correct name for a face. For instance, when shown a picture of John Major (the current British Prime Minister), she said 'I know who he is ever so well'. She was asked whether he was an actor or a politician and correctly answered that he was a politician. She was also correct in indicating that he was a Conservative rather than a Labour politician. She was then given two names from which to choose – John Major and Edward Heath (a former British Prime Minister). She said it was neither of them, but reiterated that he was a member of the Conservative Party. She then said that she thought it was Douglas Hurd (Douglas Hurd is a high-ranking politician in the Conservative Party). E.E. seems to be able to retrieve information from the correct semantic area for a word or an object, but then appears unable to distinguish between close semantic alternatives.

From such results, we can conclude that E.E. had a general deficit in functional and associative knowledge which was apparent whatever the nature of the material she was given. Paralleling her difficulties with recognizing pictures were difficulties with recognizing printed words. She was unable to read words or even to identify individual letters; however, she was able to discriminate between words and non-words very well (equivalent to her good object decisions).

(d) Specific memories for door handles?: Other patients have been reported who have even more intriguing problems with the semantic system. Some appear very counter-intuitive; for instance, patients have been reported with a recognition problem restricted to body parts (Dennis, 1976), countries (McKenna and Warrington, 1978) and indoor objects (Yamadori and Albert, 1973). More significantly, a number of patients have been reported who show a selective impairment in their ability to recognize living relative to non-living things (Hart *et al.*, 1985; Mehta *et al.*, 1992; Riddoch and Humphreys, 1987b; Sartori and Job, 1988; Sheridan and Humphreys, in press; Warrington and Shallice, 1984). The converse impairment has also been shown (Hillis and Caramazza, 1990; Sacchett and Humphreys, 1992; Warrington and McCarthy, 1983, 1987). This particular area is one of the most controversial areas of cognitive neuropsychology at the present time. Questions that remain as yet unresolved include: (1) Are there separate forms of associative knowledge for different types of input (e.g. one for words, one for visual objects), or one knowledge store for all inputs?; and (2) What is the nature of the information represented in the object shape system? Are perceptual attributes of an object (such as colour, texture, taste, sound) properties of this system or properties of the functional/ associative system? We will return to these questions in a little more detail below in the section on 'Alternative methods of conceptualizing cognitive architectures'.

To sum up cognitive neuropsychology

In the preceding section, we have attempted to demonstrate that cognitive systems are best understood as information-processing devices and, as such, are describable as a series of independent processing components each with a specific function. We have used visual object recognition as an example, and have tried to show that object recognition depends on a number of independent processing components, each with a specific function. These components may be separately impaired as a result of brain damage. This form of functional architecture has been derived on the basis of evidence from neuropsychological dissociations of performance (i.e. evidence of relative impairments in one capacity, while, at the same time, another capacity remains relatively unimpaired – consider EE's good performance on object decision tests relative to her poor performance on tests of functional and associative knowledge outlined above).

Alternative methods of conceptualizing cognitive architectures: connectionist networks

Cognitive neuropsychology has been used to derive the *functional* architecture of complex cognitive systems (such as the system for visual object recognition). Current theorists have now become interested in the question of how such a functional architecture may be implemented in the physical system of the brain. One possibility is that each of the functional components we have described above may be isolated to specific brain areas (cf. the localization account of Gall, 1825). Brain damage may affect one (or more) component(s) of a cognitive system, but the remainder of the system should continue to function. Impaired performance should only be seen in tasks that require the intact operation of the damaged component. Allport (1985) has pointed out that if cognitive architectures were implemented in this way, we should expect patients to show *complete* failure on one set of tasks, while performance on another set should be normal. In fact, this pattern of performance only rarely occurs; more patients show a relative reduction in performance on one set of tasks relative to another set. It may therefore be more useful to consider an alternative possibility, namely that particular functional sub-components of a complex cognitive ability reflect patterns of activation within an interacting network (cf. the distributed view of brain function: Jackson, 1915). The same elements may be involved in different functions; the uniqueness of the function is specified by the *pattern* of activation across the network. Recently, attempts have been made to model cognitive abilities in computers, using networks based on artificial neurones or processing units. These models are often termed connectionist networks because their ability to perform complex tasks is based on the patterns of connectivity between many processing units, each one of which may only carry out a simple function (such as summing incoming values and giving an output if the input values exceed some threshold). Some of the characteristics of connectionist networks are as follows:

(1) The network consists of units which are connected together (typically each unit is connected to many units).

(2) Activated units may either activate or inhibit other units with the magnitude of activation or inhibition dependent on the weight of the connection between two units. Weights on connections correspond to something like the strength of a synapse between two neurons in the brain.

(3) A unit may only affect other units if it has reached a certain threshold of activation.

(4) A network is characterized by the properties of its constituent units, and by the different strengths of connections between the units.

(5) Networks can have different structures or layers.

(6) A representation of a concept may be stored in a distributed manner by a pattern of activation throughout the network.

(7) The same network can store many different patterns without them interfering with each other if they are sufficiently distinct.

(See Hinton and Anderson, 1981; McClelland *et al.*, 1986; Rumelhart *et al.*, 1986.) Currently, attempts are being made to use connectionist networks to model cognitive behaviour by training the networks to associate various inputs to particular outputs. The models typically make use of several layers to perform with any complex behaviour. One layer may consist of input units which are set up to encode different patterns of activation (e.g. corresponding to stimuli such as objects, words etc). Another layer may be used to represent outputs from the network. The connections between input and output layers (and perhaps between other intermediary layers) can be altered, so that a given input can (over a number of training cycles) generate the appropriate output. Once lesioning has occurred, such networks can show many properties that seem to correspond to human abilities; for instance, they may generalize to give an appropriate output to a new stimulus that is similar to previously encountered stimuli; they may give the complete output when given only partial input and so forth. Such characteristics may correspond to our ability to (e.g.) pronounce non-words such as VIB (note that this is similar to words we have previously learned to pronounce), and (e.g.) our ability to recognize objects when they are partially occluded. Attempts have been made to model the effects of brain damage on human performance by 'simulating' a lesion in the network. In general, the effect of damage to such a network is to *reduce* performance, not to lose it altogether (cf. Allport, 1985).

In a recent paper, Farah (1994) has argued that the localization account is probably incorrect and that it is more plausible to consider the implementation of cognitive functions in terms of a distributed network. She uses examples from three sources of neuropsychological impairment in order to substantiate her argument. We shall focus on one of these examples as it relates to the account of the processes involved in visual object recognition we have outlined above, and also because it presents an account of how cognitive processes may be simulated using a parallel distributed network on a computer.

Modular representations

In our account of visual object recognition deficits given above, we remarked on the fact that a number of patients have been reported with a particular problem in recognizing selective categories of items; in particular, living things relative to non-living things. Using a modular account to accommodate such evidence, we might argue that our stored knowledge of objects is subdivided into separate components dealing respectively with further subdivisions distinguishing between living and non-living things (Warrington and Shallice, 1984).

Distributed representations

Warrington and Shallice (1984) described two patients with a selective deficit in the recognition of living relative to non-living things. However, whilst the patients were markedly worse at recognizing, defining or answering questions about items from the impaired category relative to the spared categories, some degree of impairment was also apparent with the spared categories. Thus, the definitions produced by Warrington and Shallice's (1984) patients for living things were impoverished in both visual and functional detail. Farah and McClelland (1991) attempted to simulate the underlying knowledge system which when lesioned would produce category-specific errors similar to those deficits observed in patients with brain damage. The system is illustrated in Figure 9.8. It consists of three separate pools of processing units, representing respectively the names of items, the visual characteristics of items and a 'semantic' memory which is further subdivided into visual and functional semantic memory pools. With the semantic system, all units are interconnected. Hence there are not separate compartments for 'visual' and 'functional' knowledge, rather a distributed pattern of activity across the visual and functional units in the semantic system.

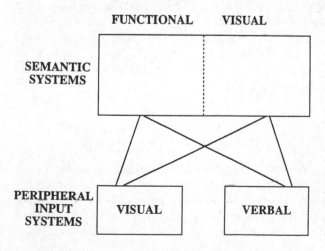

FUNCTIONAL **VISUAL**

SEMANTIC SYSTEMS

PERIPHERAL INPUT SYSTEMS

VISUAL **VERBAL**

Figure 9.8 *Farah and McClelland's connectionist model derived to explain category-specific deficits*

Given this architecture, if the functional units are lesioned, there must be some effect also on the visual units. The model was trained to associate (i) the correct semantic and name portions of its pattern when given the visual portion of its pattern at input, and (ii) the correct visual and semantic portions of its pattern given the name portion as input. After learning, the model was selectively damaged by disconnecting different proportions of the visual or functional semantic units, and performance was then reassessed. Selective impairments of living *or* functional things were produced. If 'visual' units in the semantic system were lesioned, the model performed better with patterns corresponding to functional objects than with patterns corresponding to living things; however there was also a minor impairment for patterns for functional objects. The reverse was found if the 'functional' units in the sematic system were lesioned.

This example illustrates how relatively simple connectionist models can capture some of the puzzling aspects of the behaviour of brain-damaged patients in terms of the residual operation of a distributed processing system. In Farah and McClelland's model, living things were particularly impaired after damage to the 'visual' units within the semantic system because living things were more richly represented in terms of their visual properties within this system. Correspondingly, non-living things were particularly impaired after damage to the 'functional' units because they were more richly represented in terms of their functional properties. To consider how this might come about, imagine the properties of living and non-living things. Living things tend to be described in terms of their visual or perceptual properties, non-living things in terms of their functional properties (what you do with them).

Nevertheless, some constraints undoubtedly exist on the degree to which information is distributed within the brain. It is most unlikely that the brain is a single network of the type simulated by Farah and McClelland's distributed semantic memory. Indeed, our earlier discussion of patients such as D.W. demonstrated limits on the amount of distribution in our stored knowledge systems. Recall that D.W. had largely preserved functional knowledge about objects (e.g. when given verbal definitions stressing functional properties). From this, it seems reasonable to distinguish a memory system concerning the shape of objects (impaired for D.W.) from the kind of semantic system modelled by Farah and McClelland. This might be so even if knowledge is distributed within both knowledge systems.

Back to the brain?

Cognitive neuropsychologists have tended to stress component parts of complex cognitive functions without reference to the underlying brain structures. However, recent advances in neurological scanning techniques are dramatically changing this situation, and returning neuropsychological interest to the brain.

As indicated at the start of this chapter, PET studies involve the injection of radioactive isotopes into the bloodstream allowing blood flow to particular regions of the brain to be measured during cognitive activities. For instance, areas of the brain involved in a task may have a greater uptake of oxygen than non-active areas. The PET scanning technique detects such differences in up-take across different tasks, enabling investigators to learn which neural areas are differentially involved in the tasks. The experimental procedures typically in-volved in PET use a subtractive technique. Subjects are asked to carry out two cognitive tasks which are thought to differ in just one component. Oxygen uptake in the brain is measured for both tasks, and the subsequent picture of neural activity for one task is then subtracted from that in the other, ideally to reveal the area of neural activity that differs in the two tasks; this is taken as the site of the component process that distinguishes the tasks. To illustrate this, we will consider some work on visual word recognition. Earlier we listed some of the processes that may mediate the reading of simple printed words, and included one process in which words were recognized as familiar visual stimuli. This process of visual recognition of words has been studied by Petersen and his colleagues (Petersen *et al.*, 1989; 1990). One experiment used words and word-like visual stimuli. There were three sorts of word-like stimuli: in one, stimuli consisted of strings of letter-like forms that were matched for many of the visual features of actual letters. In another, stimuli were strings of random consonants. The third set of word-like stimuli were letter strings that followed the spelling rules of English (so they could be pronounced) but they were not real words (e.g., TWEAL); such stimuli are known as *pseudowords*. All four sorts of stimuli led to activation in the posterior part of the brain in an area known as the lateral extrastriate cortex. However, by subtracting activation in the letter-like and consonant string conditions from those in the pseudoword and word condi-tions, activation further forward in the left hemisphere in the medial extrastriate cortex was found. This reveals that there is an area specific to the visual processing of words and pronounceable non-words in the left hemi-sphere (Petersen *et al.*, 1990). When subjects are asked to make rhyme judg-ments about visually presented word pairs there is activation further forward in the brain still in the region of the lateral temporoparietal cortex. Petersen *et al.*, suggest that this region is involved in phonological processing (Petersen *et al.*, 1989). Activation in the front of the brain in the left inferior frontal area occurs when subjects are asked to make associations to words rather than simply naming them aloud. Petersen *et al.*, propose that this area is the site of func-tional/semantic information about words (Petersen *et al.*, 1988).

PET studies, such as those conducted by Petersen and his colleagues, are beginning to provide an important link in studies of cognitive processing in the brain. Such studies are closely linked to functional, information-processing models of cognition, since such models (like the model of word recognition outlined in this chapter) provide frameworks for interpreting PET data – they enable suitable tasks to be paired together, so that the subtractive experimental technique can be applied. Furthermore, the studies provide an important source of converging evidence for helping to understand disorders of cognition in brain-damaged patients. In all, we may look forward to an even greater cooperation in the future between the methods of study outlined in this chapter – neuropsychological studies of cognition, cognitive analyses of normal people, computational modelling – and on-line analyses of functional brain states during cognitive tasks. This cooperation across different methodologies should provide a richer functional and anatomical description of cognition than could ever have been imagined when workers such as Gall first began research in the field.

Acknowledgements

The work in this chapter has been supported by grants from the MRC to both authors.

Further reading

COLTHEART, M., PATTERSON, K. and MARSHALL, J.C. (Eds) (1980) *Deep Dyslexia*, London, Routledge & Kegan Paul.

ELLIS, A.W. and YOUNG, A.W. (1988) *Human Cognitive Neuropsychology*, London, Lawrence Erlbaum.

EYSENCK, M.W. and KEANE, M.T. (1990) *Cognitive Psychology: A Student's Handbook*, Hove and London, Lawrence Erlbaum.

FARAH, M.J. (1990) *Visual Agnosia*, Cambridge, MA, MIT Press.

HUMPHREYS, G.W. and RIDDOCH, M.J. (1987) *To See but Not to See: A Case of Visual Agnosia*, London, Lawrence Erlbaum.

HUMPHREYS, G.W. and RIDDOCH, M.J. (1993) *Object Agnosias*, in KENNARD, C. (Ed.) *Baillieres Clinical Neurology*, London, Bailliere Tindall, 339–59.

McCARTHY, R.A. and WARRINGTON, E.K. (1990) *Cognitive Neuropsychology: A Clinical Introduction*, London, Academic Press.

RIDDOCH, M.J. and HUMPHREYS, G.W. (Eds) (1994) *Cognitive Neuropsychology and Cognitive Rehabilitation*, Hove, Lawrence Erlbaum.

ROBERTSON, I. and MARSHALL, J.C. (Eds) (1993) *Unilateral Neglect: Clinical and Experimental Studies*, Hove, Lawrence Erlbaum.

SHALLICE, T. (1988) *From Neuropsychology to Mental Structure*, Cambridge, Cambridge University Press.

References

ALLPORT, D.A. (1985) 'Distributed memory, modular subsystems and dysphasia', in NEWMAN, S. and EPSTEIN, R. (Eds) *Current Perspectives in Dysphasia*, London, Churchill Livingstone.

BADDELEY, A.D. (1986) *Working Memory*, Oxford, Oxford University Press.

BADDELEY, A.D. and WARRINGTON, E.K. (1970) 'Amnesia and the distinction between long- and short-term memory' *Journal of Verbal Learning and Verbal Behaviour*, **9**, 176–89.

BROCA, P. (1861) 'Remarques sur le siège de la faculté du langage articulé suivie d'une observation d'aphémie', *Bulletin de la société anatomique de Paris*, **36**, 398–407.

BRUCE, V. and YOUNG, A. (1988) 'Understanding face recognition', *British Journal of Psychology*, **77**, 305–27.

COSLETT, H.B. and SAFFRAN, E.M. (1989) 'Evidence for preserved reading in "pure alexia" ', *Brain*, **112**, 327–59.

DENNIS, M. (1976) 'Dissociated naming and locating of body parts after a left anterior temporal lobe resection', *Brain and Language*, **3**, 147–63.

EFRON, R. (1969) 'What is perception?', *Boston Studies in Philosophy of Science*, **4**, 137–73.

ELLIS, A.W. and YOUNG, A.W. (1988) *Human Cognitive Neuropsychology*, London, Lawrence Erlbaum.

FARAH, M.J. (1994) 'Neuropsychological inference with an interactive brain: a critique of the locality assumption', *Behavioural and Brain Sciences*, **17**, 43–61.

FARAH, M.J. and MCCLELLAND, J.L. (1991) 'A computational model of semantic memory impairment: modality specificity and emergent category specificity', *Journal of Experimental Psychology: General*, **120**, 339–57.

FISCHER, B. and POGGIO, G.F. (1979) 'Depth sensitivity of binocular cortical neurones of behaving monkeys', *Proceedings of the Royal Society, London, B*, **204**, 409–14.

GALL, F. (1825) *Sur les fonctions du cerveau et sur celles de chacune de ses parties*, Paris, Boucher.

HART, J., BERNDT, R.S. and CARAMAZZA, A. (1985) 'Category-specific naming deficit following cerebral infarction', *Nature*, **316**, 439–40.

HÉCAEN, H. (1962) Clinical symptomatology in right and left hemisphere lesions', in MOUNTCASTLE, V. B. (Ed.) *Interhemispheric Relations and Cerebral Dominance*, Baltimore, MD,: Johns Hopkins University Press.

HEYWOOD, C.A., WILSON, B. and COWEY, A. (1987) 'A case study of cortical colour "blindness" with relatively intact achromatopic discrimination', *Journal of Neurology, Neurosurgery and Psychiatry*, **50**, 22–9.

HILLIS, A. and CARAMAZZA, A. (1990) 'Category-specific naming and comprehension impairment: a double dissociation', *Brain*, **114**, 2081–94.

HINTON, G.E. and ANDERSON, J.A. (1981) *Parallel Models of Associative Memory*, Hillsdale, NJ, Lawrence Erlbaum.

HOLMES, G. and HORRAX, G. (1919) 'Disturbances of spatial orientation and visual attention with a loss of stereoscopic vision', *Archives of Neurology and Psychiatry*, **1**, 385–407.

HUMPHREYS, G.W. and RIDDOCH, M.J. (1987) 'The fractionation of visual agnosia', in HUMPHREYS, G.W. and RIDDOCH, M.J. (Eds) *Visual Object Processing: A Cognitive Neuropsycholological Approach*, London, Lawrence Erlbaum.

HUMPHREYS, G.W., RIDDOCH, M.J., QUINLAN, P.T., DONNELLY, N. and PRICE, C.A. (1992)

'Parallel pattern processing and visual agnosia', *Canadian Journal of Psychology*, **46**(3), 377–416.

HUMPHREYS, G.W., TROSCIANKO, T., RIDDOCH, M.J., BOUCART, M., DONNELLY, N. and HARDING, G.F.A. (1992) 'Covert processing in different visual recognition systems', in MILNER, A.D. and RUGG, M.D. (Eds) *The Neuropsychology of Consciousness*, London, Academic Press.

JACKSON, J.H. (1915) 'On the nature of duality of the brain', *Brain*, **38**, 80–103.

KARTSOUNIS, L.D. and WARRINGTON, E.K. (1991) 'Failure of object recognition due to a breakdown of figure–ground discrimination in a patient with normal acuity', *Neuropsychologia*, **29**, 969–80.

LISSAUER, H. (1890) 'Ein fall von seelenblindheit nebst einem beitrage zur theorie derselben', *Archiv für Psychiatrie und Nervenkrankheiten*, **21**, 222–70.

LIVINGSTONE, M.S. and HUBEL, D.H. (1987) 'Psychophysical evidence for separate channels for the perception of form, colour, movement and depth', *Journal of Neuroscience*, **7**, 3416–68.

McCLELLAND, J.L., RUMELHART, D.E. and GROUP, P.R. (Eds) (1986) *Parallel Distributed Processing*, Vol 2: *Psychological and Biological Models*, Cambridge, MA, MIT Press.

McKENNA, P. and WARRINGTON, E.K. (1978) 'Category-specific naming preservation: a single case study', *Journal of Neurology, Neurosurgery and Psychiatry*, **41**, 571–4.

MEADOWS, J.C. (1974) 'Disturbed perception of colours associated with localised cerebral lesions', *Brain*, **97**, 615–32.

MEHTA, Z., NEWCOMBE, F. and DE HAAN, E. (1992) 'Selective loss of imagery in a case of visual agnosia', *Neuropsychologia*, **30**, 645–55.

MILNER, A.D., PERRETT, D.I., JOHNSTON, R.S., BENSON, P.J., JORDAN, T.R., HEELEY, D.W. *et al.* (1991) 'Perception and action in "visual form agnosia" ', *Brain*, **114**, 405–28.

PETERSEN, S.E., FOX, P.T., POSNER, M.I., MINTUN, M. and RAICHLE, M.E. (1988) 'Positron emission tomographic studies of the cortical anatomy of single word processing,' *Nature*, **331**, 585–9.

PETERSEN, S.E., FOX, P.T., POSNER, M.I., MINTUN, M. and RAICHLE, M.E. (1989) 'Positron emission tomographic studies of the processing of single words', *Journal of Cognitive Neuroscience*, **1**, 153–70.

PETERSEN, S.E., FOX, P.T., SNYDER, A. and RAICHLE, M.E. (1990) 'Activation of extrastriate and frontal cortical areas by visual words and word-like stimuli', *Science*, **249**, 1041–4.

RIDDOCH, M.J. and HUMPHREYS, G.W. (1987a) 'A case of integrative agnosia', *Brain*, **110**, 1431–62.

RIDDOCH, M.J. and HUMPHREYS, G.W. (1987b) 'Visual object processing in optic aphasia: a case of semantic access agnosia', *Cognitive Neuropsychology*, **4**, 131–85.

RIDDOCH, M.J. and HUMPHREYS, G.W. (1992) 'The smiling giraffe: an illustration of a visual memory disorder', in CAMPBELL, R.R. (Ed.) *Mental Lives*, Oxford, Basil Blackwell.

RIDDOCH, M.J., HUMPHREYS, G.W. and PRICE, C.J. (1989) 'Routes to action: evidence from apraxia', *Cognitive Neuropsychology*, 6, 437–54.

RIDDOCH, M.J., HUMPHREYS, G.W., BATEMAN, A. and FORDE, E. (in preparation) 'The neggerty apple: a case of semantic access agnosia'.

RUMELHART, D.E., MCCLELLAND, J.L. and GROUP, P.R. (1986) *Parallel Distributed Processing*, Vol 2: *Foundations*, Cambridge, MA, Bradford MIT Press.

SACCHETT, C. and HUMPHREYS, G.W. (1992) 'Calling a squirrel a squirrel but a canoe a wigwam: a category-specific deficit for artefactual objects and body parts', *Cognitive Neuropsychology*, 9(1), 73–86.

SARTORI, B. and JOB, R. (1988) 'The oyster with four legs: a neuropsychological study on the interaction of visual and semantic information', *Cognitive Neuropsychology*, 5, 677–709.

SHERIDAN, J. and HUMPHREYS, G.W. (1993) 'A verbal-semantic category-specific recognition impairment', *Cognitive Neuropsychology*, 10, 143–84.

VAINA, L.M. (1989) 'Selective impairment of visual motor interpretation following lesions of the right occipital-parietal area in humans', *Biological Cybernetics*, 61, 347–59.

WARRINGTON, E.K. and MCCARTHY, R.A. (1983) 'Category-specific access dysphasia', *Brain*, 106, 859–78.

WARRINGTON, E.K. and MCCARTHY, R.A. (1987) 'Categories of knowledge: further fractionations and an attempted integration', *Brain*, 110, 1273–96.

WARRINGTON, E.K. and SHALLICE, T. (1984) 'Category-specific semantic impairments', *Brain*, 107, 829–54.

YAMADORI, A. and ALBERT, M.L. (1973) 'Word category aphasia', *Cortex*, 9, 112–25.

ZEKI, S.M. (1974) 'Cells responding to changing image and size disparity in the cortex of the rhesus monkey', *Journal of Physiology*, 243, 827–41.

ZEKI, S.M. (1980) 'The representation of colours in the cerebral cortex', *Nature*, 284, 412–18.

ZIHL, J., VON CRAMON, D. and MAI, N. (1983) 'Selective disturbance of movement vision after bilateral brain damage', *Brain*, 106, 313–40.

ZIHL, J., VON CRAMON, D., MAI, N. and SCHMID, C. (1991) 'Disturbance of movement vision after bilateral posterior brain damage', *Brain*, 114, 2235–52.

Part V

Social Psychology

Chapter 10

Interpersonal Processes

Raymond Cochrane

In 1897 N. Triplett wrote a report for the *American Journal of Psychology* in which he reported that children improved the speed of reeling in a fishing line when they were performing in the presence of other children doing the same task. He did not ask them to engage in competition, but it appeared that the presence of other children meant that a child reeled the line much faster than the same child could when performing the same task alone. Other people influence our behaviour, and we influence the behaviour of other people all the time. The other person does not even have to be present to exert an influence over what we do and think. Someone may dress in a certain way because they anticipate meeting someone who might like that style of dressing. They may dress that way because, in the past, someone has told them they look nice in that particular shirt or whatever. Triplett's finding that the presence of other people improved performance has been elaborated and refined over the last century. We now know that having other people present usually improves performance where speed or strength are required (for example an athletics competition such as a track race or weight lifting), but the presence of other people can inhibit performance where it is dependent upon accuracy and precision. It is said, for example, that basketball players are much better at free-throw shooting in practice than in front of a large crowd (Kimble, 1990).

In this chapter we will be looking at the ways in which people relate to each other. This will start with how we perceive and explain the behaviour of other people whom we might or might not know; we will then move on to the process of getting to know other people, such as in the development of friendship and other intimate relationships.

Perceiving and knowing others: early impressions

We were probably all told as children (and in turn we will probably tell our own) not to 'Judge a book by its cover'; in other words, don't be taken in by first appearances. Despite this folk wisdom, we find that we cannot help ourselves in doing just that. Indeed, it is very difficult to imagine how we could possibly avoid making some judgements on the basis of external appearances. Imagine the two situations depicted in Figure 10.1. Most of us would have an immediate

---

SHORT STORY A.
A blue Volvo Estate, registration M779TPP, is being driven slowly down a quiet street. It stops outside a large new house and out steps a woman. She is in her mid-thirties, is very well dressed and has curly blonde hair. She opens the boot of the car, takes out a bag, looks up and down the street and walks into the front garden of the house.

SHORT STORY B.
A white Ford Consul, registration HHK 343P, is being driven slowly down a quiet street – one wing of the car is of a different colour and the exhaust is held on with wire. It stops outside a large new house and out steps a man. He is in his early 20's, wearing greasy jeans and a cut-away tee shirt, revealing several tattoos on his upper arms. He has a shaven head, a thin moustache and one earring. He opens the boot of the car, takes out a bag, looks up and down the street, and walks into the front garden of the house.

Figure 10.1 *Two short stories*

reaction to story A and judge that the person so described might be a well-to-do, middle-class woman who has just been shopping in town and is returning to her home, and looking forward to examining the exciting purchase she has made, which is probably an item of clothing. Story B gives us a different impression: the man is most probably a burglar or some other kind of criminal up to no good or, at best, he may be a workman taking out a bag of tools. Further, we would probably be quite pleased to offer assistance to the woman in the first story, but might be less willing to do so for the man in the second. Now, there might be a grain of truth in the images that emerge; women are much less likely to be burglars than are men; people with expensive cars are much less likely to engage in some types of crime than are people with cheap cars. The two people described in the stories are giving us very different impressions, and this is probably deliberate; they will be aware of the image they are projecting and will have their own reasons for projecting this image. The woman may well want to create an impression that she is respectable, trustworthy and personable, while the young man may want to present a threatening, intimidating and somewhat ugly image.

What is it that we notice about people when we first encounter them? The most obvious things we will notice about a stranger on first contact are their gender, their build, their clothes, facial features and hair colour, and an overall impression of their attractiveness. We are more likely to notice this last characteristic if the stranger is of the opposite sex. We will also register the person's skin colour but, again, only if it is different from our own. We will not only notice these factors, but our impression or stereotype of the kind of person that we have met will be built up from these impressions. So, for example, we all 'know' that women and men have different characteristics. A commonly shared stereotype is, for example, that men are more aggressive than women, while women are more caring than men. Most people judge a thin stranger as more likely to be quiet, tense and suspicious than an overweight stranger, who will be assumed to be talkative, weak, dependent and lazy. Research has shown that, particularly in judging women, hair colour is also important. Blonde women are thought to be much more sociable, fun loving and sexually active than are brunettes, who are commonly considered to be more intelligent, conscientious and dependable. The stereotype of the redhead is, of course, that she is excitable, short-tempered and very emotional (Hinton, 1993).

Most people also believe that the face reveals a great deal about a person's character. So thin lips indicate that the person is intense and conscientious, while large lips indicate the person is friendly and generous. If someone has a predominance of what are called 'baby features' (large eyes, large forehead, smooth skin and a rounded chin) then we know them to be warm, naïve, weak and submissive – a bit like a baby. Adult features, on the other hand (relatively small eyes, small forehead, wrinkles and an angular chin), indicate that the person is strong, dominant and perceptive (Hinton, 1993).

So, when we first encounter a stranger, our mind automatically computes a stereotype made up of the various elements related to each of these impressions. Although these stereotypes may often be wrong, they do serve a useful function in that they give us a starting point for each new interaction. Without them we would be totally at a loss as to how to initiate an interaction with a stranger. They become problematic, however, if they resist change when evidence which points to the limitations of the accuracy of stereotypes becomes available.

If we do get past the initial encounter and strike up a conversation with a stranger, we will start noticing other things which will help modify our initial impression. The person's voice provides us with many clues as to their status, character and intention. A deep voice is considered authoritative, while a squeaky voice is usually taken to indicate that the person is not to be taken seriously. Accent, at least in Britain, is thought to provide a basic clue to the person's social class. If, when they open their mouth, a perfect BBC type of accent emerges we are prone to assume that they are well educated, probably wealthy and come from a respectable family. If, however, they have a distinct regional accent then this will elicit other images; for example, the cockney accent of London is associated with cheerfulness, the person is assumed to be streetwise, happy and none too honest. Research shows that the first impression created by a Birmingham accent is that the person is rather stupid, quarrelsome and usually miserable!

But there will be non-verbal cues as well, so that if a person looks us in the eye we will more likely expect them to be honest and record that they probably like us. If they do not look us in the eye, they may be regarded as shifty or having taken an instant dislike to us. There is virtual universal recognition of the meaning of facial expressions too, so that nearly everyone can distinguish between whether a stranger looks happy or sad, for example (Argyle, 1988). We may notice too that our hypothetical stranger might be wearing make-up to hide some of their original facial features. What is the meaning of eye make-up, for example? Well, if it is applied by a woman in a moderate amount, it makes her look as though she is pleasant and sexually attractive. Too much eye make-up, however, is taken to indicate that a woman is likely to be promiscuous and unreliable. Think what the wearing of eye make-up by a man indicates to someone he encounters.

Even within a few seconds of meeting another person, then, we will have assimilated a wealth of information about that person and formed a judgment of them which may later be difficult to shift. If the interaction continues, we will undoubtedly find out more about them: for example, their interests and opinions, what they think of us, and whether or not they like us.

The journalist, Walter Lippman, first used the term 'stereotype' in the 1920s. It was taken over from a technical term used in printing where it refers to some type which is fixed in a frame and which can be used for multiple impressions. To a psychologist, the term 'stereotype' refers to a cognitive simplification which is used to guide how we perceive people around us, and how we process the information they present. So, sterotypes have their uses, but they also produce their problems. For example, almost universally, 'out groups' are perceived as more negative than are members of the 'in group'. The 'out group' may refer to people of the opposite gender, or of a different racial or ethnic background from the perceiver. Stereotypes also tend to exaggerate any group differences which may exist in reality, and they lead to an under-estimation of the variability that occurs within groups. So, for example, a man may believe that a particular behaviour is 'typical of women', but does not stereotype his own sex as having typical behaviour patterns.

Stereotypes, which have existed for a long time and seem very resistant to erosion, are also often based on factually incorrect assumptions. For example, the belief that may be held by some men that women are poor drivers is not borne out by statistics on road accidents. Where this is the case, the person holding the stereotype can be said to have a distorted perception of reality. This perhaps would not matter so much if, when reality produced evidence which undermines the stereotype, it changed. But another characteristic of stereo-types is that they are very resistant to change, and we all have ways of incorporating inconsistent evidence within the stereotype. So the 'Scotsmen are mean' stereotype may not be weakened by an example of a Scotsman being generous. He will either be defined as an exception to the rule, or his generosity will be perceived as having an ulterior motive. Where stereotypes are resistant to change in the face of contradictory evidence, they can lead to inappropriate responses or inappropriate decisions being made such as not offering a job to the best qualified, and potentially most productive employee, because of their gender.

Understanding other people's motives: social judgments

However, we do not just record impressions of other people and fit them into neat categories within our pre-existing conceptual framework; we also make judgments about their motives. Imagine this scene: a car is being driven down a main road at 70 mph when suddenly it swerves, skids out of control, crosses an embankment and ends up in a field. Because this is a made-up story we can have a happy ending, so the occupants escape unhurt. How might a person explain this episode? Well, it depends very much on who was driving. If the person doing the explaining was the driver, then he or she will be most likely to use explanations such as the fact that the road was in a poor state of repair, there was a tight bend, it was raining heavily, or they were avoiding a dog on the carriageway. However, if the person whose mind we are exploring was explaining how this incident had occurred to someone else, they would perhaps attribute the road accident to the fact that the person was a bad driver, driving too fast for the conditions, had become distracted, perhaps they were drunk, or very tired. One of the best known theories in social psychology which attempts to account for how we explain our own and other people's behaviour is known as 'attribution theory' (which was first put forward in a systematic way by Jones and Davis in 1965). As the example given illustrates, there is a strong tendency to use explanations based on *internal* causes when explaining other people's behaviour, especially when that behaviour is in some way problematic. However, we are much more likely to use *external* causes when explaining our own apparently bad or inappropriate behaviour. So common is this tendency that it has come to be known as the 'fundamental attribution error'. It seems almost universal that we over-emphasize internal causes and under-emphasize external causes of other people's behaviour, even when there may be clear evidence of external pressures forcing them to behave in the way they do. So, a Police Officer carrying out his/her duty in strict accordance with the law may nevertheless be imputed with unpleasant and mean-spirited motives if his/her behaviour obstructs what we want to do. A striking example of this was shown experimentally by Jones and Harris (1967). American college students were told that they had to write an essay which was either in favour of Castro's Cuba or against Castro's Cuba: they had no choice. Other students, who knew that the essay writers had no choice over which stance they took, were then asked to judge the authors' true attitudes. The common assumption was made that those students who had been told to write a pro-Castro essay did in fact have more positive attitudes towards Castro than did those students who wrote the anti-Castro essay, even though it was apparent all along that they were just following the instructions of the experimenter.

Once we have come to a judgment about another person on the basis of their appearance, their speech patterns, their behaviour, and we have made a judgment of their disposition by observing their behaviour, we go out of our way to seek evidence to support these judgments. This is known as 'confirmatory hypothesis testing', and helps to account for the fact that stereotypes are difficult to change. We may do this by completely ignoring contradictory evidence, or by remembering confirmatory evidence much more clearly than evidence that tends to conflict with our pre-existing views. Our tendency to seek this supportive evidence becomes even stronger if we have become publicly committed to a particular point of view, for example by communicating our opinions of someone to a third party. We can see examples of this all around us. Sometimes it is only to be expected, as when a politician defends the discredited policies of his/her party by being very selective in the evidence to which attention is paid. Sometimes it is a little bit more subtle than this, as when a smoker chooses to remember that granddad, who smoked 40 cigarettes a day, lived to be 90, and ignores the mass of statistical evidence showing that cigarette smoking dramatically increases the risk of lung cancer and heart disease.

Social psychologists have also demonstrated this phenomenon experimentally. Darley and Gross (1983) asked people to watch a video of a 9-year-old girl taking an intelligence test. One half of the observers were told that the girl came from a professional, well-educated family, and the other half that she came from a poorly educated, manual working-class background. Prior to seeing her take the test it is not surprising, given what we have learned, that the subjects in the first group made higher predictions of the girl's IQ than those who were in the second group. After making these predictions, the subjects then watched the video of the intelligence test, in which the girl got about half the questions right and half of them wrong. Those in the first group, who had predicted higher intelligence for the girl, used the evidence of a 50 per cent success rate in the test to support their view that she was highly intelligent. The members of the second group, who watched exactly the same video, used the fact that she got half the questions wrong to support their assumption that she was not very bright. In this case evidence, which was identical in an objective sense, was used to strengthen two completely opposite stereotypes.

Not only do the judgments we make of other people affect how we subsequently process information about them, they can also affect the behaviour of the person themselves. The classic demonstration of this was performed in 1968 by Rosenthal and Jacobson. Their study, which is one of the most ingenious and important in the whole of social psychology, involved giving schoolchildren in America an intelligence test and then giving teachers feedback on how the children had done. However, the feedback was not derived from the intelligence test, but the teachers were told that some children, chosen *completely at random*, were very bright and showed great academic promise, while other children, also chosen at random, did not show this promise. When the researchers returned a year later and administered another intelligence test, it was found that those children whom the teachers had been led to believe had great academic potential had shown substantially greater gains in IQ than those whom the teachers believed to be ordinary. This effect was most marked with younger children. Thus, our judgments of other people, which are perhaps based on stereotypes, can become self-fulfilling prophecies.

The way in which we judge other people on the basis of first or early impressions is thus crucial to whether, and how, any longer term relationship with them will develop, and it is to this that the next section of the chapter addresses itself.

Interpersonal attraction and the development of friendships

So far, we have considered the factors that influence the initial judgment we make of other people. Now we will turn to the question of how a mere contact may lead to an acquaintanceship being formed, and then possibly a friendship, and even beyond that to a lifelong partnership. The importance of physical appearance has already been mentioned, but it is of vital importance apparently in the process of developing a friendship and liking for another person. Even very young children choose as their preferred best friends other children who are perceived as physically attractive by independent adult raters (Dion and Berscheid, 1974). Adults also are influenced in their perception of children by their physical appearance: more physically attractive children are attributed fewer negative characteristics, and are less likely to be blamed for misdemeanours than are less attractive children (Dion, 1972). It is clear that the life experiences and social relationships that people develop are strongly influenced by their physical appearance, with more attractive people having more positive experiences and the opportunity to make more social relationships. A survey of undergraduate students' social interactions by Reis *et al.* (1982) showed that students who were independently rated as physically attractive had far more social interaction during the four-week period that was studied than did unattractive students – this effect being particularly strong for men, but less so for women. What happened was that attractive males spent far more time interacting with females than did unattractive males. The same was true the other way round, i.e. unattractive women spent less time with men, but they made up their total amount of social interaction by more interaction with other women.

Well, it seems certain that physical attractiveness does influence the quality and quantity of people's social interaction, and hence their potential for making friends and establishing long-term relationships. The question remains, though: what constitutes physical attractiveness? Is it true that 'Beauty lies in the eye of the beholder', or is it the case that there are some people whom everyone recognizes as attractive, and others who are universally considered ugly? It would be very comforting to indicate that the former proposition was true but, unfortunately, for those of us who are towards the less attractive end of the dimension, it is the latter statement that is the case. Study after study has shown that there is very good consensus between people over what constitutes physical attractiveness in their own sex, and even more consistency over what constitutes physical attractiveness in the opposite sex (Hinton, 1993). The constituents of physical beauty have been analysed, initially with considerable attention given to body shape and proportion. Recently, too, attention has been turned to the components of facial beauty in both men and women. A series of studies by Cunningham and his colleagues (Cunningham, 1986; Cunningham *et al.*, 1990) have done very detailed 'facialmetric' measurements on photographs of faces, and found that such factors as the size of the eyes, the area of the face occupied by the nose and the chin, the width of the lips etc., all correlate very well with rated physical attractiveness.

These findings of universals in physical attractiveness have led to the intriguing question of how is it that less attractive, or even downright ugly people, do make friends and, indeed, very frequently get married or enter into long-term heterosexual relationships. If it is the case that we would all prefer to make friends with physically attractive people, and have physically attractive people as sexual partners, why are there not even more lonely people about in this world than there actually are? There are at least two answers to this question. The first attempt to resolve the paradox was made by Walster *et al.* (1966). They suggested a 'matching hypothesis' which predicted that people make a rough judgment of their own physical attractiveness and then seek friends, and more especially sex partners, of roughly equal attractiveness. Early research was not kind to this hypothesis, however, and even Walster's own experiments showed that, when choosing preferred partners, the person's own physical attractiveness did not enter into the equation: everyone chose more attractive people of the opposite sex. Latterly some studies have yielded results consistent with the hypothesis, however. What appears to happen is that while people will choose very attractive partners in the abstract, when they add in their own subjective estimate of the probability of liking being reciprocated, preferences are modified (Duck, 1988). In other words, it is well recognized by everyone that more attractive people will have more offers of social interaction and, therefore, be less likely to accept any particular offer. Thus, while a relatively unattractive person may ideally prefer to have as a friend or partner a highly attractive member, let us say, of the opposite sex, they are realistic in gauging their chances of success in interesting the other person, and so modify their actual behaviour in the light of this estimate of probability. This is borne out by evidence that married couples have roughly similar levels of attractiveness on average. That is, when wives and husbands in successful marriages are independently judged for their physical attractiveness, partners seem to be in the same general area on the scale (Cate and Lloyd, 1992).

The second and probably more important answer to the question of the significance of physical attractiveness in the development of long-term relationships lies in the sequencing of information that becomes available to potential friends. Obviously, physical appearance is an instantly available piece of information when we meet another person. If, however, even minimal interaction takes place, we soon learn some other things about that person which may subsequently become more important than physical appearance. This assumes that the relationship gets beyond merely the handshake stage and some conversation takes place. Very early in this kind of conversation other important factors about the new person will emerge. A great deal of research has been done on the way in which 'mere acquaintances' get translated into friends. An overwhelmingly important variable that has emerged from study after study is that the degree of *similarity* between the two people's views, attitudes, opinions, beliefs, personality and value systems is a virtual prerequisite for the development of friendship (Cate and Lloyd, 1992). If you look around at any sets of friends with whom you are acquainted you will probably notice that they are similar in many observable characteristics such as age, race, gender, perhaps the clothes they wear, and possibly even their size and shape. However, it is on psychological characteristics that similarity really becomes a potent determinant of friendship. In one of the classic studies in social psychology Newcomb (1961) looked at the pattern of friendship development of new students going to the University of Michigan. He found that, on the basis of measuring the attitudes of students on arrival at their college hall of residence, he was able to predict with surprising accuracy which of them would become friends and which would not. This link between similarity and attraction has been demonstrated experimentally a number of times by Byrne (1971) and many others. A simple experimental paradigm is used in which the naïve subject of the experiment (usually a student) is induced into interacting with at least two other people who are also supposed to be naïve subjects but who, in reality, are actors. One of the actors is usually instructed to agree with more or less everything the real subject says and does, while the other is instructed to contradict them. These studies almost all show that, when the real subject is given the opportunity to prolong the interaction with one or other of the actors, the actor who has feigned agreement is universally chosen. There appears to be no truth in the old saying that 'opposites attract'.

Because we find, for example, that long-term married couples have views and opinions and outlooks very similar to each other, we should not overlook the possibility that they have come to be similar rather than that they were similar to start with. Indeed, this possibility has been explored, but it does appear to be the case that only those who were initially quite similar developed sufficiently close relationships to enable marriage even to be contemplated. Indeed, there is no evidence that married couples become more similar over the years; they remain just as similar as they were when they first entered their relationship.

Why should this be the case? Why should we prefer to have as friends those who tend to agree with us and be like us? Well, there are several explanations of this phenomenon, none of which is entirely satisfactory on its own. What has come to be known as 'balance theory' suggests that we are more comfortable when our beliefs and views are consistent than when we are inconsistent, or when we have views challenged. Thus, if we meet someone else who has similar views to our own, we are less likely to receive a challenge to our own views and, therefore, less likely to upset our cognitive equilibrium. This theory is based on the premise that inconsistency in cognitions is uncomfortable, and we will strive to avoid it wherever possible. Thus, whatever we say, we really do not like arguing the point with our friends; we prefer to seek out or maintain relationships with people who generally agree with us.

Byrne, who was instrumental in describing the process of similarity leading to attraction, had a slightly different view. He suggested (Byrne and Clore, 1967) that having someone agree with you is a way of confirming your own view of the world. Because we all have a degree of uncertainty about whether our perception of the social environment is accurate, we seek out this so-called 'consensual validation' because it reinforces our own view of the world. Having constant disagreements with someone leads to a shaking of our confidence that our views are appropriate.

A simpler model than either of these just suggests that having interaction with people who agree with one is reinforcing because those interactions tend to be emotionally pleasant. Although it could be considered challenging or arousing to have constant arguments with one's friends or partners, in fact that is more likely to lead to negative affect and, therefore, be unpleasant in the long run. Probably all three of these explanations are true for some interactions and for some of the time, and may all be required to give a complete explanation of the similarity-attraction link.

The third pillar underpinning the foundation of friendship, along with physical appearance and psychological similarity, is reciprocity of liking. We nearly all of us acquire a very strong need to be liked by other people, to receive positive feedback from other people, and to be held in high esteem by other people. Indeed, so powerful is this need in most of us that we will do a great deal of psychological, and even physical, work to achieve it. We will go out of our way to present an image of ourselves that we believe to be attractive to other people; we will modify our behaviour to be closer to that which we subjectively estimate other people would like us to exhibit; we will work hard to make sure other people only see the most attractive side of us; and we will give presents of material goods, compliments and even sexual favours in order to make other people like us a bit more, or retain their friendship. The other side of this coin is, of course, that we will prefer to avoid people who we believe do not like us, and who have a negative view of us. Unless there is some possibility of converting them to holding a positive view of us, we would prefer not to be in their company, as interacting with them provides us with strong negative feedback about ourselves which is aversive to most people. It is not surprising, then, that during a sequence of social interactions that may or may not lead to friendship, each party is constantly looking for clues as to the other's feelings towards them.

While reciprocity of liking is undoubtedly a foundation stone for the development of friendships, and even marriages, it does appear that being liked by someone constantly over a long period loses some of its potency. An important experiment was performed in 1965 by Aronson and Linder. Basically, this demonstrated that the acquisition of positive regard from another person was more potent than constant positive evaluation throughout an interaction. This was applied by Aronson to the situation of marriage, and has become known as the 'Law of marital infidelity' (Kimble, 1990). This suggests that if a husband (or wife) constantly shows affection for their partner, pays them compliments and pays attention to them during a long relationship, this will gradually come to have less significance for the recipient. The *same* level of attention or affection received from a stranger is perceived by the recipient as much more exciting and much more reinforcing. Thus, apparently happy marriages may be interrupted not because of any fundamental problems within the marriage, but because of the lowered potency of constant regard. The third party in these situations may be very ordinary and not actually offer a great deal more in terms of enhancement of self-esteem or passionate love than the abandoned spouse.

Romantic love

It will have become clear that many of the studies of relationship development have concerned the development of heterosexual, marital-type relationships. This is not only because such relationships are of enormous intrinsic interest, but also because they are very common and are very commonly developing during the time when subjects (usually undergraduate students) are available for being researched! Some intrepid social psychologists have tried to go beyond the analysis of friendship patterns to the analysis of romantic love (Hendrick and Hendrick, 1992). This is a difficult task because most people believe that falling in love is a very subjective and powerful emotional experience, and are reluctant to believe that it can be carefully analysed by scientific research. It must be admitted that some of the explanations offered are not in themselves intrinsically romantic but, nevertheless, they do account for this phenomenon which is extremely widespread and widely experienced in our society. Figure 10.2 contains the common elements of the experience

---

COMMON ELEMENTS OF THE EXPERIENCE OF ROMANTIC LOVE

1. Experienced by almost everyone at some time.
2. Subjectively defined as positive.
3. Marked by intense levels of arousal.
4. But *no* unique physiological patterns.
5. Desire for intimacy, both physical and psychological.
6. Almost always associated with sexual attraction and sexual exchange.
7. Strong elements of emotional bonding.
8. Tends to be most important relationship – others may be sacrificed.
9. Desire to give selflessly and care for the other person.
10. Desire for exclusivity in relationship.

Figure 10.2 *Common elements of the experience of romantic love*

of falling in love and being in love, but what we need to ask is: how does a possibly chance encounter between person A and person B develop such overwhelming emotional connotations, while a chance encounter between person A and person C, who to the external observer may appear very similar to person B, ends in no time at all without a relationship having developed?

There have been several explanations for this phenomenon put forward, but the one that is most well validated in terms of its consistency with other psychological theories, and its consistency with the evidence that is available, is that based on another variant of attribution theory. This suggests that people will believe they have fallen in love when (a) they have become repeatedly highly aroused in the presence of another person and (b) when there are strong environmental pressures to label that arousal as being due to having fallen in love. This explanation only works because of the observation that all kinds of intense arousal have the same physiological concomitants. Whether we are aroused because we are angry, because we are fearful, because we are ecstatic, or because of sexual excitement, the 'symptoms' of this arousal are identical. You will know the feelings: butterflies in the tummy, sweaty palms, heart rate increasing, possibly flushing of the face and neck, and, in prolonged arousal, inability to sleep and to concentrate on anything except the situation. Indeed, this kind of arousal can be induced by drugs such as adrenalin, or by simple exercising such as running on the spot.

As it is the case that all kinds of intense arousal are effectively the same in physiological terms, we only understand them in emotional terms because of cognitive attributions of the reasons for them. Often this attribution is very simple: if we are crossing the road and a fast-moving bus is bearing down on us, we will rapidly interpret our heightened state of arousal as fear, and react accordingly. Similarly, if we find ourselves in a social situation where we are repeatedly insulted by another person, we will interpret the physiological state we experience as due to embarrassment or anger.

At certain stages in peoples' lives we may consider that they are in a psychological set of being ready to fall in love and hence be more likely to attribute physiological arousal, which was generated by a variety of causes, as being the result of love. In our society the most obvious life stage at which this occurs is in young adulthood, and it is no coincidence that it is at this time of life too that, for many people, there is a strong propensity to seek out arousing situations. What do young people do for recreation? Well, they may go to entertainments which involve loud music, flashing lights, dance, close contact with lots of other people, with the underlying themes of physical threat and sexual promise. They may go to cinemas where the films that are shown almost always have a strong emotionally arousing content, be it based on violence, humour, pathos, sex, or excitement based on adventure or horror. This is also a time of life when sexual desires are at their peak, and the opportunities for sexual gratification are most available. Attribution theory suggests that if two people repeatedly experience these intense emotional arousals in each other's presence they *may* 'misattribute' some portion of this intense arousal to 'being in love'.

Of course, the attribution explanation only accounts for the experience of falling in love and not for the persistence of the same strong feelings over a longer time period. Walster and Walster (1978) contrasted short-term passionate love with what they called 'companionate' love. Passionate love is associated with the enormous swings in emotional arousal just described but, for most couples, is unlikely to last for more than a few months or a few years at the most. Companionate love, on the other hand, is much more similar to friendship in that it involves mutual reinforcement on a continuing basis, the exchange of mutual regard and reciprocal liking, and must be based on a considerable degree of psychological similarity. Only if companionate love overlaps and replaces passionate love will a long-term relationship develop, and remain stable.

An overview of the development of long-term friendships

It is easiest to summarize all of the mountain of research that has been done on the development of interpersonal relationships as a series of stages or filters through which relationships must pass if they are to endure.

Obviously, the first stage is coming into contact with a potential friend in the first place. The major determinants of this are physical proximity (we are more likely to meet people who live next door to us than people who live five miles away), but this in itself is associated with other important social and psychological characteristics. We are more likely to meet people who are similar to us in terms of age (e.g. at school, college or work), have roughly the same educational level as ourselves, come from the same kind of social class background, from the same religious and racial groupings and, later, people from the same occupational groups as ourselves. Who we come into contact with, and thus those people who are available for potential friendships, is far from random. However, within the vast number of contacts we all make, only a few develop into friendships. Unless we are so lonely and isolated that we are desperate for anyone's friendship, we must consciously or unconsciously make a selection of people with whom we wish to interact further.

At the second stage we will have regard for obvious physical and social characteristics which make the person potentially attractive as a friend or lover. Thus physical appearance and social characteristics such as being of relatively high status or wealthy, or obviously socially skilled, will make a person a more desirable potential friend, while the absence of those characteristics will make the person less desirable as a friend. Our perception may be modified to a certain extent by our subjective estimate of our own qualities along similar dimensions but, for one reason or another, we will target certain individuals as those we believe likely to provide us with sufficient reinforcements to maintain continuing interaction.

Having, by accident or design, engaged in a longer interaction with some selected individuals, we will be rapidly working out the degree of psychological similarity between us and them. As we have seen, those people who are more similar to us are more likely to pass through this third filter and remain candidates for long-lasting relationships. Other people who are perceived to be less similar may be put in the category of acquaintance, to be interacted with occasionally, and at a non-intimate level, but only those who provide us with evidence of sufficient psychological similarity to ourselves will remain candidates for friendships.

Even when friendships develop, some last longer than others, and some become more central to the person's existence than do other relationships. Kelley (1983) analysed the elements that are necessary to lead to the persistance of relationships for many years, and even a whole life-time (Kimble, 1990). According to Kelly, several psychological features characterize long-lasting friendships (including marital-type relationships). These include companionate love (which need not be with a sexual partner but refers to the high level of reinforcement to be gained from a relationship); common investments of the two people such as in a house or a child, or some other shared activity such as a business; an estimate of the subjective cost of ending a relationship (i.e. what would be lost if the partner were lost?); the relative unavailability of attractive alternative relationships that could supply similar levels of reinforcement; and private promises of commitment to maintaining the relationship through difficult periods. When all of these conditions are fulfilled a long-lasting and mutually gratifying relationship may develop between two people which, over time, becomes robust enough to withstand temporary setbacks and even prolonged separation.

Further reading

CATE, R.M. and LLOYD, S.A. (1992) *Courtship*, Newbury Park, CA, Sage.
DUCK, S. (1992) *Human Relationships*, 2nd ed. London, Sage.
HENDRICK, S.S. and HENDRICK, C. (1992) *Romantic Love*, Newbury Park, CA, Sage.
HEWSTONE, M. (1989) *Causal Attribution*, Oxford, Blackwell.
HAYES, N. (1993) *Principles of Social Psychology*, Hove, Lawrence Erlbaum.

References

ARGYLE, M. (1988) *Bodily Communication*, London, Methuen.
ARONSON, E. and LINDER, D. (1965) 'Gain and loss of esteem as determinants of interpersonal attraction', *Journal of Experimental Social Psychology*, **1**, 156–72.
BYRNE, D. (1971) *The Attraction Paradigm*, New York, Academic Press.
BYRNE, D. and CLORE, G.L. (1967) 'Effectance arousal and attraction', *Journal of Personality and Social Psychology*, **6**, Monograph 1–638.

CATE, R.M. and LLOYD, S.A. (1992) *Courtship*, Newbury Park, CA, Sage.

CUNNINGHAM, M.R. (1986) 'Measuring the physical in physical attractiveness: quasi-experiments on the sociology of female facial beauty', *Journal of Personality and Social Psychology*, **50**, 925-35.

CUNNINGHAM, M.R., BARBEE, A.P. and PIKE, C.L. (1990) 'What do women want? Facialmetric assessment of multiple motives in the perception of male facial physical attractiveness', *Journal of Personality and Social Psychology*, **59**, 61-72.

DARLEY, J.M. and GROSS, P.H. (1983) 'A hypothesis-confirming bias in labelling effects', *Journal of Personality and Social Psychology*, **44**, 20-23.

DION, K.K. (1972) 'Physical attractiveness and evaluations of children's transgressions', *Journal of Personality and Social Psychology*, **24**, 207-13.

DION, K.K. and BERSCHEID, E. (1974) 'Physical attractiveness and peer perception among children', *Sociometry*, **37**, 1-12.

DUCK, S. (1988) *Relating to Others*, Milton Keynes, Open University Press.

HENDRICK, S.S. and HENDRICK, C. (1992) *Romantic Love*, Newbury Park, CA, Sage.

HINTON, P.R. (1993) *The Psychology of Interpersonal Perception*, London, Routledge.

JONES, E.E. and DAVIS, K.E. (1965) 'From acts to dispositions: the attribution process in person perception', in BERKOWITZ, L. (Ed.) *Advances in Experimental Social Psychology*, Vol. 2, New York, Academic Press.

JONES, E.E. and HARRIS, V.A. (1967) 'The attribution of attitudes', *Journal of Experimental Social Psychology*, **3**, 2-24.

KELLEY, H.H. (1983) 'Love and commitment', in KELLEY, H.H., BERSCHEID, E., CHRISTENSEN, A., HARVEY, J.H., HUSTON, T.L., LEVINGTON, G., McCLINTOCK, E., PEPLAU, L.A. and PETERSON, D.R. (Eds) *Close Relationships*, New York, W.H. Freeman.

KIMBLE, C.E. (1990) *Social Psychology: Studying Human Interaction*, Dubuque, IA, W.C. Brown.

NEWCOMB, T.M. (1961) *The Acquaintance Process*, New York, Holt, Rinehart & Winston.

REIS, H.T., WHEELER, L., SPIEGEL, N., KERNISS, M.H., NEZLEK, J. and PERRI, M. (1982) 'Physical attractiveness in social interaction', *Journal of Personality and Social Psychology*, **43**, 979-96.

ROSENTHAL, R. and JACOBSON, L. (1968) *Pygmalion in the Classroom: Teacher Expectation and Pupils' Intellectual Development*, New York, Holt, Rinehart & Winston.

TRIPLETT, N. (1898) 'The dynamogenic factors in pacemaking and competition', *American Journal of Psychology*, **9**, 507-33.

WALSTER, E. and WALSTER, G.W. (1978) *A New Look at Love*, Reading, MA, Addisan-Wesley.

WALSTER, E., ARONSON, V., ABRAMS, D. and ROTTMAN, L. (1966) 'Importance of physical attractiveness in dating behavior', *Journal of Personality and Social Psychology*, **4**, 508-16.

Chapter 11

Social Processes in Transitions from Youth to Adulthood

Christine Griffin

> KKB: What's your ideal job?
> PN60: I'd like the job of the Queen.
> KKB: Why? What does she do?
> PN60: Well – she gets paid a lot of money for doing nothing. . . . Put it like this, she gets paid for breaking bottles against ships and we get arrested for breaking bottles on the street. (Bhavnani, 1991, p. 183).

The above exchange is taken from a study of political issues relevant to young Black and White working-class people in 1980s Britain. This extract records an interview with one of the research participants ('PN60') by the researcher, Kum-Kum Bhavnani ('KKB'), and it ends the book which gives a full account of the study, *Talking Politics: A Psychological Framing for Views from Youth in Britain* (Bhavnani, 1991). This exchange refers to one of the key elements in the transition to adulthood for young people, that of looking for a job. It illustrates a particular area of inequality between the secure and cushioned circumstances of the British monarchy and the far harsher conditions faced by many of her young working-class 'subjects'.

This chapter will examine the nature of *social processes* in relation to the various transitions involved in the shift from youth to adulthood. The period between childhood and adulthood is characterized by a series of transitions which operate in the spheres of education, leisure, sexuality, family life and the job market. 'Youth' or 'adolescence' is above all a time of change for most young people as they move between some of the major social institutions, leaving full-time education, entering the job market (though not necessarily finding a job), leaving their family of origin, and so on.

The boundaries of 'youth' or 'adolescence' are notoriously difficult to define. Some researchers associate the beginning of adolescence with the onset of puberty, but this can vary considerably between individuals. If puberty starts with the onset of menstruation (or menarche) in girls, what would be the equivalent for boys? It is frequently assumed that the onset of puberty is a relatively clear-cut event but, for most of us, female and male, a range of hormonal and physiological changes take place over a period of a few weeks to months or even years. In addition to this, there are considerable variations in the age at which such changes occur in different individuals (Coleman and Hendry, 1990).

It would be a mistake to see these changes as solely biological or physiological, since several studies have shown that the age of menarche and most other developmental changes in females and males vary according to the general health and dietary level of the population. Poverty, poor housing and an inadequate diet will tend to depress the age at which many developmental changes occur.

This chapter will concentrate on the social processes involved in transitions to adulthood for young people, despite the difficulties in defining the upper and lower limits of 'youth'. In contemporary western societies, 'youth' is usually taken to refer to the 'teenage' years between 13 and 19, but the precise age limits are perhaps less important for our purposes than the many social and cultural changes which occur during this time.

It is important to remember that 'adolescence' is a fairly recent invention: until the late nineteenth century no such concept existed. The notion of a particular age stage which is defined largely in terms of physiological changes around puberty emerged in the 1880s. Before that time 'youth' was a period between childhood economic dependence and adulthood which had no clear association with the teenage years nor with the onset of puberty. The move to adult status was more likely to be understood in terms of the movement of Christian religious conversion. The medical and sexual construction of 'adolescence' which is so prevalent in contemporary western societies was consolidated by the work of the early US psychologist G. Stanley Hall, whose two-volume text *On Adolescence* was published in 1904.

Whilst biological definitions of 'adolescence' have been extremely influential in psychological studies, few researchers would deny the vital role played by social, economic and environmental dimensions in shaping transitions to adulthood. For young people in contemporary western societies, the shift from childhood to adult status is marked by a *series* of transitions. There is not simply one neat moment of transition. Childhood is defined mainly as a time of dependence and innocence, even though many children are far from innocent beings, and millions are compelled to be financially independent, especially in Third World countries. Adulthood is seen as a period of independence (especially for men), heterosexual maturation, full-time employment (especially for men) and a move from the parental home to marriage and parenthood. The two key transitions in the move from youth to adulthood concern the shift from full-time education to the job market, and various pressures to attain a 'mature' sexuality and family life. The latter revolves around the strong association between adult gender identity (femininity and masculinity), and getting a boy- or girlfriend of the opposite sex, followed eventually by monogamous marriage, heterosexual intercourse and parenthood preferably in that order. 'Mature' sexuality means *hetero*sexuality, particularly in a 'stable' relationship.

Wendy Hollway's interview study with adult heterosexual couples involved an analysis of the discourses through which they constructed gender and sexuality (Hollway, 1989). This included a section on these respondents' reminiscences about 'growing up properly' as a girl or a boy. Whilst such material cannot be taken as equivalent to young people's experiences in 1980s or 1990s Britain, it does bear considerable similarity to the results of other interview studies with young people (e.g. Griffin, 1985; Lees, 1986).

For the men in Wendy Hollway's study, 'growing up properly' as a boy meant getting a girlfriend by 'being pushy' and *actively* 'pulling a bird'. For the women, the mark of entry to 'mature' femininity involved getting a boyfriend, but in a *passive* mode by 'attracting boys' (Hollway, 1989). So the transition into 'mature' sexuality is a *gendered* one in which young women and men are expected to, and often do travel very different routes.

A key process in this transition is that of getting a boy or girlfriend of the *opposite* sex. Heterosexuality is defined as normal, natural and ideal: it signifies adult femininity and masculinity. Although the situation is changing slightly, young people who do not have a girl or boyfriend of the opposite sex are frequently seen as 'frigid' or 'immature'. Those who identify as lesbian, gay or bisexual are still likely to be treated as 'sick', 'deviant', psychologically troubled or sexually immature by teachers, peers, therapists and parents.

The assumption that 'normal' young people should have a full-time job and a relationship with a member of the opposite sex which eventually leads to marriage and parenthood in a nuclear family unit is *normative*. That is, these are powerful and *dominant* ideas which try to dictate how 'normal' young women and men should behave. Anyone who does not conform to this ideal pattern can then be defined as 'deviant'. Rising youth unemployment levels during the mid-1980s and into the 1990s meant that many thousands of school leavers in Britain were unable to find a job, especially if they were working class and/or Black. Some adults, especially conservative politicians and journalists, were quick to condemn such young people as 'irresponsible', 'unemployable' or 'feckless', ignoring the lack of reasonably paid jobs (or places on training schemes) with prospects which were available for young people. So those who do not fit into what is defined as the 'normal' pattern could be labelled as deficient or even as a 'danger to society'. Beyond a certain point, however, it became increasingly difficult to blame individual young people for their own unemployment as the number of jobs available decreased at a rapid rate. So arguments about 'feckless youth' are always changing with the economic, political and social circumstances of the time.

One additional element in transitions to adulthood concerns the move towards the full adult status and citizenship that comes with enfranchisement, or being eligible to vote (at 18 in the UK), and the various other age-specific legally defined points which mark out the boundaries of adult status. Gillian Jones and Claire Wallace have taken this approach to understanding young people's experiences in their book on *Youth, Families and Citizenship* (1992). They argue that citizenship provides a more useful means of appreciating the changing position of young people than entry to adulthood, because the latter is so closely associated with a biological model of 'adolescence', and they prefer a social and political framework for understanding the rights and responsibilities (or lack of them) of 'youth'.

Kum-Kum Bhavnani's interview study which was quoted at the start of this chapter provides more detailed insights into young people's understandings of enfranchisement and political power. The young White and Black working-class people interviewed by Kum-Kum Bhavnani introduced three points into discussions of democracy, voting and party politics. These can be summarized as follows:

(a) that politics is boring,
(b) that politics is difficult to understand,
(c) that there was no point in voting. (Bhavnani, 1991, p. 139)

Other psychological researchers have identified similar views as reflections of respondents' 'apathy', 'cynicism' or 'disaffection' (e.g. Coffield *et al.*, 1986; Ullah, 1985). For Bhavnani, however, such points could be more usefully discussed in terms of the concept of 'disenfranchisement'. That is, 'the young people did have views and arguments to present about issues considered to be in the realm of the political, but . . . certain aspects prevented them from participating in the democratic process' (Bhavnani, 1991, p. 149). In this sense, 'disenfranchisement' refers to the removal of political privileges, particularly of voting rights. Some of these young people argued that the lack of political accountability of elected representatives and the lack of any discernible social change as a consequence of voting for any of Britain's major political parties explained their view of voting as a waste of time. In this sense, the latter could be seen as a relatively rational or pragmatic response to the situation as perceived by these young people, rather than simply a reflection of cynicism or apathy.

This example illustrates that transitions to adulthood must always be understood in social, historical and political *context*. Access to the enfranchised status of the adult voting citizen in a democratic society is not a straightforward process. Most young people may become eligible to vote at 18, but this movement does not have equivalent connotations for all young people. It is shaped by *power relations* structured in dominance which are based around class, 'race', gender, disability and sexuality, such that those in subordinated groups tend to feel excluded from or marginal to the political process.

This example also illustrates the important role of the researcher in framing the way in which young people (or other research participants) are represented. All researchers will be 'biased' to some extent in their choice of research topic and analysis, but some adopt a more sympathetic approach to their respondents. It is important for all researchers to undertake systematic studies and to treat respondents seriously whilst not taking their words or actions at face value (Griffin, 1985).

The main elements involved in transitions from youth to adulthood concern the move from full-time education to the job market; pressures to get a 'steady' boy- or girlfriend of the opposite sex as a precursor to marriage and parenthood; and the shift towards 'responsible' adult status and full citizenship. Each of these elements involves a series of *social processes* through which young people negotiate the path to adulthood. For example, getting a job entails decisions about whether to continue in full-time or part-time education, searching for work, approaching prospective employers, considering government training schemes and whether one is eligible for social security or unemployment benefit. It might involve weighing up the demands and expectations of relatives, friends, teachers and careers advisers, assessing the state of the local job market, and so on. All of these various psychological, social and economic elements play a part in the search for employment, which involves a complex series of social processes.

Dealing with pressures to enter a 'steady' heterosexual relationship, to get a job and to be a 'responsible' and 'mature' citizen is not specific to young people. Most adults also experience similar pressures, but for young people these circumstances have a particular resonance because such social processes all imply a transition to *adult* status. Various theoretical approaches have been used in an attempt to understand the nature of transition from youth to adulthood.

Key theories of transitions to adulthood

Social psychological research on transitions from youth to adulthood overlaps with studies in education, sociology, cultural studies and criminology: the boundaries between the different academic disciplines are not rigid. The main theoretical approaches to the study of *social processes* in this area are *psychoanalytic theory, social learning theories and life-span developmental theories*, and the *structuralist and post-structuralist theories* of feminist, Marxist and other radical analyses. None of these theoretical frameworks is specific to studies of youth and adolescence: they all reflect different approaches to the analysis of developmental processes. A more detailed discussion of these various theories can be found in Coleman and Hendry (1990), Furnham and Stacey (1991) and Griffin (1993), but for the purposes of this chapter I will present only a brief outline of each approach.

Mainstream approaches

Psychoanalytic theories.   Emerging from the work of Sigmund Freud in the early years of the twentieth century, psychoanalytic theories rest on the notion of adolescence as an upsurge of *instincts* which are assumed to occur as a consequence of puberty (Coleman and Hendry, 1990). This instinctional upheaval is assumed to cause increased emotional turbulence and a certain vulnerability of the adolescent's personality. Two factors are associated with these changes. First, the adolescent's sexuality is presumed to turn outside the family circle in search of appropriate 'love objects', thereby severing longstanding ties with their parents. Second, a range of psychological defences is employed to deal with the upsurge of instincts and anxieties which are seen as maladaptive, and this leads to a vulnerability of the personality.

This conception of emotional turmoil and adolescent vulnerability under-lies the *storm and stress model*, which pervades the mainstream psychology of adolescence. The latter is represented as a time of inevitable psychic and hormonal turbulence through which we move towards the supposed stability and maturity of adulthood. Nor is this assumption confined to the psychological textbooks: it forms an integral part of 'popular' or 'common sense' conceptions of adolescence.

According to the psychoanalytic perspective, adolescence can be charac-terized by *disengagement* from the dependent status of childhood in the family of origin, and *regression*, or the manifestation of behaviours more usually associated with earlier stages of development. Examples of such regressive behaviour, according to the psychoanalytic perspective, include the idolization of celebrities such as pop stars and sports people, and fluctuating emotions or mood, depression and non-conformity. The work of Erik Erikson is associated with a version of the psychoanalytic perspective, in that Erikson emphasizes the importance of identity formation and the possibility of identity crisis as integral features of the transition to adulthood (Erikson, 1968).

Psychoanalytic theories are primarily concerned with the emotional and sexual lives of individuals, and this 'internal' psychological focus can make it difficult to appreciate the role of wider social factors. The emphasis on the storm and stress model means that adolescence can be seen as a period of *inevitable* emotional turmoil, in contrast with adulthood which is assumed to be a time of relative stability. Some research has indicated that youth is not necessarily characterized by turbulence (Coleman and Hendry, 1990) and adult-hood is seldom a period of stability. Finally, psychoanalytic theories reinforce the assumption that genital heterosexuality is the key sign of mature adult sexual expression, and the end-point of a developmental period of maturation, which reproduces the heterosexual norm.

Social learning theories. Such frameworks are more prevalent in socio-logical research, although social learning theories have had an important influ-ence on social psychological approaches to *socialization*. Whilst the psychoanalytic perspective emphasizes the importance of internal psychologi-cal processes, social learning theories place greater stress on forces and factors *external to the individual* in shaping the course of the transition to adulthood. The latter is seen as a key moment in the lifelong process of socialization, which can be defined as 'the process whereby individuals in a society absorb the values, standards and beliefs current in that society' (Coleman and Hendry, 1990, p. 7). We do not simply soak up *all* contemporary values and standards, however. Certain values, cultural practices and norms are *dominant*, and some of the key institutions of society, such as the education system and the family, are involved in the transmission of such dominant values.

The second point to make here is that we are not passive recipients of dominant messages. From infancy onwards, socialization is an *active process* involving continual negotiation and transformation. For example, one pervasive assumption about young people is that they are particularly gullible and easily manipulated by media pressures and advertising campaigns. There has been considerable unease that major tobacco companies might be sponsoring prestigious sporting events in order to 'target' young consumers as a group of particularly vulnerable potential cigarette smokers. Whilst some advertising campaigns may well target particular groups of young people, the latter are not necessarily such a 'soft touch'. Studies of young people's use of video and music technology indicate that the recent popularity of 'sampling' rests on an ethos of do-it-yourself entertainment, in which young people are taping audio and video material for their own use (Willis *et al.*, 1990). This material is copyrighted, and such taping is illegal, but major companies are certainly not profiting from such practices. On the contrary, young people are demonstrating their ability to subvert pressures to purchase the packaged products of the leisure industries by using existing technology to create their own videos and musical forms.

The second element of social learning theories, apart from the emphasis on the process of socialization, is the concept of *roles*. Many (though by no means all) of the standards, cultural practices and values involved in the socialization process are associated with particular *social positions* or roles in a given society. That is, certain sets of expectations will be linked to the positions of daughter, son, school student, parent, teacher, and so on. Some of these positions or roles may be more amorphous, such as 'trouble-maker' or 'hooligan'. Many of these sets of expectations are differentiated by gender, class, 'race' and sexuality as well as age. For example, 'deviance' for young men is strongly associated with aggression and macho bravado: being seen as a 'bad boy' has connotations of being *hyper*-masculine, and probably non-academic. For young women, 'deviance' frequently has connotations of sexuality, such that being seen (or seeing yourself) as a 'bad girl' is associated with being seen as sexually 'promiscuous' in heterosexual terms, and probably also with being non-academic. For young women, such 'deviance' involves being seen as *un*-feminine. As Sue Lees's work indicates, these labels are less concerned with what young women actually *do*, but with the ways in which labels such as 'slag' and 'slut' are used by young men and women, and by teachers (Lees, 1986).

We all occupy a diverse and complex set of social positions, from formal roles such as daughter/son, through to more informal and flexible positions in particular friendship groups. The expectations associated with each of these social roles will often contradict one another. For example, children of all ages are expected to respect their parents and do what they are told, but many youth sub-cultural groups value anti-authoritarian attitudes and defiance of 'boring' or restrictive adult society.

The primary *agents of socialization* are school, family life, the state, the mass media and friendship groups, and each may transmit conflicting messages. Academic success is valued in school, but unemployment may mean that, in some households, a young person's family can demand that they leave school at 16 and get a job rather than stay on to study for further qualifications. Sometimes these conflicts are particular to certain sectors of the population. Young women, for example, are still not expected to excel academically, at least not in competition with their male peers, or in subjects which are seen as particularly 'masculine', such as physics or maths (Walden and Walkerdine, 1985). To perform well in these areas is to be unfeminine and to deviate from dominant expectations about gender and femininity. However, many young women, like their male peers, are expected to do well in school, regardless of gender, and these two sets of messages can conflict and cause considerable distress for some young women.

Since adolescence or youth is characterized by a series of major transitions, it has been the focus for considerable research attention to the socialization process. The assumption here is that we can see the latter at work most clearly at moments of change. Social learning theories would view adolescence/youth as a period of potential turmoil because of these transitions within and between major *social* institutions such as school, the job market, family life and peer groups, whilst psychoanalytic and more psychologically orientated theories would view adolescence/youth as a period of potential (or even inevitable) turmoil as a consequence of physiological, psychic and other *internal psychological* changes. Social psychological research straddles the divide between the two approaches by considering the relative impact of internal and external factors on young people's lives.

Role conflict and role change provide the focus for social learning theories, as do deviance and conformity with prevailing social norms. All of the approaches discussed so far view adolescence/youth as a period of 'storm and stress', whether this is assumed to be caused by physiological, psychological or social/cultural forces. Before we move on to consider the more radical approaches of feminist, Marxist and anti-racist researchers, and of structuralist and post-structuralist perspectives, we will take a brief look at a relatively recent development in mainstream social-psychological research.

Lifespan or developmental psychology. This approach is *multidisciplinary*, not confined to either psychology or sociology, and it emphasizes the *active role* that individuals can take in their own development. Both individual young people and their families are seen as *dynamic* entities, each influencing the other in a constant process of change. This approach considers the various influences of physiological, biological and psycho-social factors on young people (Coleman and Hendry, 1990).

The above theories all fall within the *mainstream* or traditional perspectives of psychological or sociological research on youth and adolescence. Other influential mainstream approaches, which there is insufficient space to consider here, include Erik Erikson's theory of adolescent identity development, and theories of social cognition (see Coleman and Hendry, 1990, for more detail). I want to turn now to look at various *radical* perspectives in research about young people's lives.

Radical approaches

Many different theories fall within the radical perspective, and there is insufficient space to do them full justice here (see Brake, 1984 and Griffin, 1993, for more detail). Whilst mainstream approaches are more concerned with searching for the causes of constructed social problems such as 'delinquency' or 'teenage pregnancy', a radical perspective would be more interested in how 'delinquency' and 'teenage pregnancy' came to be constructed as social problems in the first place, looking at the implications of this for the treatment of particular groups of young people. Radical perspectives would tend to *deconstruct* such taken-for-granted social categories, arguing in relation to 'delinquency', for example, that this concept is applied selectively to young working-class people, particularly young men. Their upper class peers behave in unpleasant and offensive ways without being treated as the products of 'deprived' cultural or family background or seen as evidence of a general decline in the fabric of society (Muncie, 1984). Geoffrey Pearson's historical analysis of the origins and subsequent uses of the term 'hooligan' is a good example of this approach (Pearson, 1983).

Radical perspectives examine the ways in which young people are treated and positioned *differently* as a consequence of gender, class, 'role', disability and sexuality, so that when an upper class 'Hooray Henry' gets into a drunken fight at the end of term at his public school, this is treated as unfortunate behaviour for a young man of wealth and privilege. When his working-class counterpart acts in a similar way after a football match this is frequently taken as evidence of a widespread 'hooliganism' which threatens the very basis of British (or rather English) society (Pearson, 1983). Radical analyses would understand this differential treatment in terms of *power* relations, or, according to Kum-Kum Bhavnani:

> . . . the cognitive structurings of social reality [are] . . . embedded in the social relationships of structured domination and subordination. (1991, p. 181)

Radical analyses argue that the social processes involved in the transition to adulthood are gender-, class- and 'race'-specific. Pressures to get a job are seen to steer young people from an unequal and inadequate education system into an exploitative job market in which the more privileged groups of young people will do disproportionately well, while the majority of their peers are relegated to an economic 'scrap-heap' of unemployment, training schemes and low-paid, low-status jobs (Hollands, 1990; Willis, 1977). Pressures to enter a stable heterosexual relationship are argued to prepare young people, and particularly young women, for a future which is centred around the domestic world, servicing a husband and family (Griffin, 1985). Entry to the status of 'responsible' adult citizenship is viewed as part of a 'democratic' system which stresses the importance of equality and freedom while simultaneously operating a society of marked and growing social and economic inequalities (Jones and Wallace, 1992).

This radical perspective, which treats social processes as operating in the context of power relationships which are structured in dominance, is very different from the mainstream approach to youth and adolescence. Research which adopts a radical perspective is marked by an opposition to the status quo, often arguing that young people provide a convenient focus for *moral panics* over constructed social problems, as John Clarke and his colleagues argued in *Resistance through Rituals*, a key text in radical analyses of youth cultures:

> 'Youth' appeared as an emergent category in post-war Britain, one of the most striking and visible manifestations of social change in the period . . . It was signified as a social problem by the moral guardians of the society – something we "ought to do something about" '.
> (Clarke *et al.*, 1975, p. 9)

For radical researchers the way in which young people are located as the source of particular 'social problems' is at least as relevant and worthy of study as their experiences of school, family life, leisure or the job market. The way that 'youth' is treated by the main social institutions can be just as important as what young people are actually doing, and the two cannot always be disentangled so readily.

Radical analyses tend to adopt explicit political positions, as feminist, Marxist and/or anti-racist. It would be easy to discuss them as 'biased' for this reason, unless we take account of the argument that *all* research is biased, but only radical studies 'come clean' about this. The mainstream approach either advocates a reinforcement of the status quo (a conservative position), or some minor reform of traditional practices (a liberal position). It would not call for radical changes.

There are two other ways in which radical approaches differ from mainstream analyses in their treatment of young people and transitions to adulthood. First, many radical studies are critical of the developmental model, which constructs youth as a period characterized by the physiological, psychological and social turmoil which is assumed to be associated with 'maturation' (e.g. Walkerdine, 1990). Radical researchers argue that development is seldom a straightforward or linear process, and that those characteristics associated with adult 'maturity' are frequently specific to certain sectors of the population, operating in a *normative* way to define particular groups as deviant, abnormal or deficient. One example here is the association of full-time employment and a steady heterosexual relationship (preferably within marriage) with responsible adulthood, which was mentioned earlier in this chapter. This association positions young people who are unemployed and those who are not seeking a heterosexual relationship on the margins of mature adult status.

Second, some radical theories would not make such a clear-cut distinction between individual subjects and external social forces (e.g. Hollway, 1989). Such researchers argue that it is never possible to separate internal psychological attributes from external social factors, since the two areas are always inextricably connected in complex ways. The distinction between individual subjects and 'society', it is argued, reinforces the victim-blaming thesis, in which individual young people are blamed for their unemployment, poverty or poor educational attainment.

Not all radical approaches take this line, however. *Structuralist* theories would view external social forces and institutional structures as primary elements shaping the conditions of young people's lives. Marxists and feminists would argue that these social structures are fundamental to capitalist and patriarchal systems which exploit and oppress particular groups of young people, including young women, working class and Black youth (e.g. Griffin, 1985; Willis, 1977). The approaches which would dissolve the distinction between individuals and society are usually termed *post-structuralist*. These analyses can be difficult to read since the language is often complex, but they ask different questions from mainstream and structuralist studies, and their insights can be valuable (e.g. Walkerdine, 1990).

Research methods

The research methods which have been used to investigate the various social processes involved in transitions to adulthood include all the main techniques employed in the social sciences. These comprise experimental studies, social surveys and questionnaire-based research, field studies and naturalistic projects which are conducted in young people's everyday contexts rather than within university departments or by creating artificial environments. They can involve structured and formal interview formats and more open, informal and unstructured interviews and observational studies. I have mentioned examples of studies involving all of these research methods in the course of this chapter, and each method has its own particular advantages and limitations. Each set of research techniques will be able to provide a different set of information about young people and their lives.

There is no one research method which is ideal for investigating young people's lives, since each method will be more suited to the specific research question under investigation. If, for example, a researcher wished to examine the extent and pattern of unemployment found amongst different groups of young people, then a social survey might be the most appropriate method. If she or he wished to examine young people's experiences of domestic violence, then informal interviews or systematic observation might be the most suitable method.

Since the focus of this chapter is *social processes*, it is worth considering some of the key features involved in a study of such phenomena. For research that will be concerned with *change* (or the lack of it), a *longitudinal* study would be ideal. Although these studies are relatively expensive and time-consuming, they provide a dynamic picture of young people's lives. Second, it is important to place *individuals* in the relevant *social context*, considering psychological, social, economic and cultural dimensions of their lives, so it might be advantageous to use *a range of research methods*, or to contact *a variety of sources*, including parents, friends and teachers as well as young people themselves. This approach is sometimes referred to as *triangulation*.

Recent research findings

Adults have devoted a great deal of attention to the activities and attitudes of young people, from nineteenth-century worries about the assumed evils of masturbation (especially for young men) to more recent anxieties about the supposed problem of 'teenage pregnancy'. Such concerns are reflected in the extensive research literature on numerous aspects of youth and adolescence, which cuts across the fields of psychology, sociology, education and criminology. Studies commissioned by research councils and government departments have examined young people's education and training, entry to the job market and family lives, especially amongst working-class groups (e.g. Carter, 1966; Veness, 1962). There was a marked expansion of youth research in the period following the Second World War, with the emergence from the 1950s of distinctive youth cultures such as Teddy boys, mods and rockers (Clarke *et al.*, 1975).

By the 1990s, we see a vast range of research studies concerned with young people's lives, and a comprehensive review of this literature would be a considerable task (see Griffin, 1993, for a fuller analysis). I want to focus on two examples of British youth research which include both mainstream and radical approaches. The first is a study from a major research initiative on young people funded by the Economic and Social Research Council in the late 1980s (see Bynner, 1992, for details). This study is an example of a mainstream approach to social psychological research on youth, in which Nick Emler and Dominic Abrams examined the distribution of domestic work amongst young women and men in Scottish households (Emler and Abrams, 1991). The second example adopts a radical approach to the study of young women with children and the way in which 'teenage pregnancy' is constructed as a social problem. Ann Phoenix's interview study with young women who are mothers adopts a feminist and anti-racist perspective, looking at the transition to motherhood for this group (Phoenix, 1990). These studies employ a range of research methods and adopt different theoretical approaches, but they are all concerned to examine social processes related to the transition to adulthood for young people.

Turning first to the Emler and Abrams study, they sent postal self-report questionnaires to 1600 Scottish 16- and 18-year-olds which asked about contributions to housework and use of resources in the home. Some 1296 young people returned completed questionnaires, and it is important to remember that this study looks at *self-reports* about domestic life, which may present a different picture when compared with other sources of information, such as an interview study with the young people's mothers for example. Emler and Abrams's study found marked differences between the sexes. That is, young women tended to report doing more domestic work than young men in all areas apart from household repairs, where young men predominated. Conversely, young women only benefited more often in their use of household resources in terms of the use of space to invite friends to stay.

The study also investigated sex-role attitudes using six questions concerning the domestic sphere and waged work. Young women tended to report more egalitarian beliefs than their male peers, and these beliefs appeared to be related to young people's contributions to domestic work, regardless of sex. That is, more egalitarian beliefs were associated with doing more household work and in more areas for young women and young men. This type of study provides some indication of gender differences in the pattern of self-reported domestic work in Scottish households, but only an interview and observational study would give a more dynamic picture of the social processes involved in the distribution of domestic work. That is, what are the processes through which young women end up doing more and young men relatively less domestic work? Arranging an observational study with an appropriate number of households would be an estremely difficult task, so we must rely on the information provided by Emler and Abrams's study in conjunction with interview-based projects. The type of information provided by research employing informal interviews is exemplified by Ann Phoenix's study with young women who became mothers in their teens.

Ann Phoenix's research was based on interviews with young women who became mothers between the ages of 16 and 19 (Phoenix, 1990). About 80 young women were interviewed three times, once in late pregnancy, about six months after the birth of the baby, and again just before their children were 2 years old. In addition to these interviews with young women who were approached at antenatal clinics in London, the research team also carried out a series of developmental tests with the young women's children in the final interview.

Much of the mainstream research with this group of women, especially in the USA, treats 'teenage pregnancy' as a major social problem, arguing that these young women's children suffer a range of psychological, social and economic deprivations *as a consequence of their mothers' youth*. 'Teenage pregnancy' has been blamed for events as diverse as the Los Angeles riots following the acquittal of the white policemen who were filmed beating up Rodney King, to the murder of Liverpool boy James Bulger by two pre-teenage boys. In this climate of moral panic, it is scarcely surprising that other researchers expected Ann Phoenix to identify these young women as a 'problem group'. In fact, she discovered that by the end of the study:

> . . . the women and their children were mostly doing fine, that lack of money was their major problem and that given their educational and family background it did not appear that their financial circumstances would necessarily have improved if they had deferred motherhood beyond their teenage years. (Phoenix, 1990, p. 1)

The importance of this study lies partly in the finding that poverty is the main problem for these young women, rather than their status as 'teen mothers', and this poses a major challenge to mainstream analyses. An additional element of the moral panic over 'teenage pregnancy' is the assumption that this is a particular 'problem' of young Black women, especially African-Americans. Ann Phoenix argued that the rate of births to young White women in the USA is above that in other industrialized countries. In conjunction with the project steering group, she decided not to make comparisons between young Black and White women in her British study, owing partly to the difficulty of separating groups of young Black women from their White peers given the incidence of mixed parentage amongst the young women (and their children). In addition, there was considerable cultural diversity between the young women who were of African-Caribbean origin or descent, and it would have been unwise to treat them as one group in terms of 'race' or ethnicity.

Above all, Ann Phoenix's book *Young Mothers?* demonstrates that it is not young women with children, or young Black women with children, or even young 'unmarried mothers' who are the source of 'social problems', but poverty, inadequate education and training provision, poor health care and housing facilities and high levels of unemployment amongst certain sectors of the population.

Apart from questioning dominant assumptions about 'teenage pregnancy', Ann Phoenix's study investigated the social processes involved in the transition to motherhood for these young women. The use of informal interviews alongside standardized developmental tests in a longitudinal study enabled the research team to present a dynamic and in-depth analysis of the psychological, social, cultural and financial dimensions of this transition. Most of these young women did not become pregnant because of ignorance about contraception or to gain council housing or social security benefits. Nor did their pregnancies lead to increasing poverty. Poverty, poor housing and unemployment were problems experienced by these young women before they became pregnant. Despite this, the quality of the degree of care for their children was comparable with that of older mothers, and many of these younger mothers were relatively satisfied with motherhood.

In conclusion, research on young people and transitions to adulthood provides one means of examining the various approaches to the study of social processes, from mainstream to radical theories, social surveys and questionnaires to informal interviews and observational studies. As with any research in the social domain, there are instances in which academic studies can provide valuable information on important political issues, sometimes acting as a counter to the prevailing 'common sense' views found in the 'popular' arena.

Taking the example of the constructed social problem of 'teenage pregnancy', we can contrast the *Guardian* book review quoted below with the words of one of the young women in Ann Phoenix's study. The two present two very different perspectives on the same phenomenon, the main distinction being that the text of a respectable newspaper such as the *Guardian* (or indeed any newspaper) is likely to carry more ideological weight than the words of those young people who are constructed as the focus of this particular 'moral panic'. If we want to understand the various social processes involved in transitions to adulthood, we have to be able to appreciate both sets of voices (and others as well).

Still, in his horrible way, Hitler was pointing to a problem that is constant and, in today's 'underclass', very serious. How do you stop single teenage mothers from breeding up tomorrow's football hooligans? (Stone, 1989)

It's [motherhood] made me more responsible. It's changed the sort of person I am. I used to be a trouble maker and get into fights all the time. People have been amazed at the change in my personality.
Q – How do you feel about that?
A – I'm happy with that.
Q – Has being a mother made any other difference in your life?
A – I feel less lonely. I feel more love being a mother.
(16-year-old single woman, six months after birth). (Phoenix, 1990, p. 244)

Further reading

BHAVNANI, K.-K. (1990) *Talking Politics: a Psychological Framing for Views from Youth in* Britain, Cambridge, Cambridge University Press.

COLEMAN, J. and HENDRY, L. (1990) *The Nature of Adolescence*, 2nd ed. London, Methuen.

GRIFFIN, C. (1985) *Typical Girls? Young Women from School to the Job Market*, London, Routledge & Kegan Paul.

PHOENIX, A. (1990) *Young Mothers?*, Cambridge, Polity Press.

WALKERDINE, V. (1990) *Schoolgirl Fictions*, London, Verso.

References

BHAVNANI, K.-K. (1991) *Talking Politics: a Psychological Framing for Views from Youth in Britain*, Cambridge, Cambridge University Press.

BRAKE, M. (1984) *Comparative Youth Cultures: the Sociology of Youth Culture and Youth Subcultures in America, Britain and Canada*, London, Routledge & Kegan Paul.

BYNNER, J. (1992) *ESRC 16–19 Initiative: the Route to Careers and Identities*, ESRC 16–19 Initiative Occasional Papers, Swindon, ESRC.

CARTER, M. (1966) *Into Work*, Harmondsworth, Penguin.

CLARKE, J., HALL, S., JEFFERSON, T. and ROBERTS, B. (1975) 'Subculture, cultures and class', in HALL, S. and JEFFERSON, T. (Eds) *Resistance through Rituals: Youth Subcultures in Post-war Britain*, London, Hutchinson.

COFFIELD, F., BORRILL, C. and MARSHALL, S. (1986) *Growing up at the Margins*, Milton Keynes, Open University Press.

COLEMAN, J. and HENDRY, L. (1990) *The Nature of Adolescence*, 2nd ed. London, Methuen.

EMLER, N. and ABRAMS, D. (1991) *The Sexual Distribution of Benefits and Burdens in the Household: Adolescent Experiences and Expectations*, ESRC 16–19 Initiative Occasional Papers, Swindon, ESRC.

ERIKSON, E. (1968) *Identity: Youth and Crisis*, New York, Norton.

FURNHAM, A. and STACEY, B. (1991) *Young People's Understanding of Society*, London, Routledge.

GRIFFIN, C. (1985) *Typical Girls? Young Women from School to the Job Market*, London, Routledge & Kegan Paul.

GRIFFIN, C. (1993) *Representations of Youth: The Study of Youth and Adolescence in Britain and America*, Cambridge, Polity Press.

HALL, G.S. (1904) *Adolescence: its Psychology and its Relation to Physiology, Anthropology, Sociology, Sex, Crime, Religion and Education*, New York, D. Appleton.

HOLLANDS, R. (1990) *The Long Transition: Class, Culture and Youth Training*, London, Macmillan.

HOLLWAY, W. (1989) *Subjectivity and Method in Psychology: Gender, Meaning and Science*, London, Sage.

JONES, G. and WALLACE, C. (1992) *Youth, Families and Citizenship*, Buckingham, Open University Press.

LEES, S. (1986) *Losing Out: Sexuality and Adolescent Girls*, London, Hutchinson.

MUNCIE, J. (1984) *The Trouble with Kids Today: Youth and Crime in Post-war Britain*, London, Hutchinson.

PEARSON, G. (1983) *Hooligan: a History of Respectable Fears*, London, Macmillan.

PHOENIX, A. (1990) *Young Mothers?*, Cambridge, Polity Press.

STONE, N. (1989) 'The gas chamber mentality', *The Guardian*, 14 December.

ULLAH, P. (1985) 'Disaffected black and white youth: the role of unemployment duration and perceived job discrimination', *Ethnic and Racial Studies*, **8**, 181–93.

VENESS, T. (1962) *School Leavers*, London, Methuen.

WALDEN, R. and WALKERDINE, V. (1985) *Girls and Mathematics: from Primary to Secondary Schooling*, Bedford Way papers, 24, London, Heinemann.

WALKERDINE, V. (1990) *Schoolgirl Fictions*, London, Verso.

WILLIS, P. (1977) *Learning to Labour: how Working Class Kids get Working Class Jobs*, Farnborough, Saxon House.

WILLIS, P., JONES, S., CANAAN, J. and HURD, G. (1990) *Common Culture: Symbolic Work at Play in the Everyday Cultures of the Young*, Milton Keynes, Open University Press.

Part VI

Applied Psychology

Chapter 12

Clinical Psychology

David Wales and Kevin Howells

Introduction: what is clinical psychology?

It has often been pointed out that 'clinical psychology' literally means 'bedside psychology', but although the term 'clinic' includes outpatient contact the recipients of psychological intervention are rarely bedridden or 'ill' in the usual sense (Woodworth, 1992). Despite the proposal of alternative titles such as 'consultant psychologist' or 'health care psychologist' the title 'clinical psychologist' has stuck. Clinical psychologists are health care professionals who mainly work in the fields of mental health or social services.

Confusion often arises regarding the similarities and differences between clinical psychology and other professions. This is not surprising given the overlap in basic psychotherapeutic skills of many health professionals, and the fact that often health professionals work very closely together and each contribute to the care of a client. Particular confusion arises between psychology and psychiatry. Whereas psychiatry has evolved as an applied branch of medicine concerned with 'mental illness', psychology derives from a mixture of philosophy and the natural sciences such as biology.

So what distinguishes clinical psychology from other mental health disciplines and when is a referral likely to be made to a psychologist? A distinction is often made on the basis of clinical psychologists' use of a 'scientist-practitioner' approach (which will be discussed below) and their emphasis on research. Referrals are often made to psychologists when the client is manifesting behavioural, emotional or cognitive problems for which the primary causes are psychological rather than medical or social. Very often referrals to clinical psychologists are made when a non-medical psychological framework is required to understand an individual's problem or when other strategies have proved unsuccessful.

Generally, people who are referred to a clinical psychologist are experiencing some form of distress or have a personal problem that they are having difficulty solving. Clinical psychologists have specialized training in the field of 'abnormal psychology' (Rosenham and Seligman, 1989; Davidson and Neale, 1994) which is concerned with the study of so called 'abnormal' behaviour. This helps them to understand what might be happening when things go wrong for an individual. It also means that there may be less stigma associated with seeing a psychologist than other mental health professionals – someone does not have to be 'mentally ill' to see a clinical psychologist.

'Abnormality' can be defined in a number of ways. It can simply mean a deviation from the 'norm' in a statistical sense. A very low or a very high IQ score might be abnormal in this way. It can also mean a deviation from social norms, referring to behaviour that is considered unacceptable by society. Criminal or 'anti-social' behaviour such as theft or arson may be considered abnormal in this sense. Abnormality may also refer to particular behaviour, thoughts and feelings which contribute to personal distress or suffering for an individual. While it is normal for everyone to feel, say, low in mood or unsure of themselves from time to time, if these experiences occur frequently or carry on for a long time or continually interfere with some aspect of a person's life they may be considered 'abnormal'. People who suffer from depression or anxiety may be abnormal in this respect.

The presenting problems that lead people to consult a clinical psychologist vary widely and include: emotional problems such as anxiety (e.g. phobias), depression, anger, guilt and bereavement; addictions and habit problems such as gambling, eating problems (e.g. anorexia), alcohol and drug abuse; sexual problems including dysfunction (e.g. impotence) and deviation (e.g. paedophilia); social and interpersonal problems such as social isolation, aggressive behaviour or relationship problems. Clinical psychologists also contribute to the treatment of physical problems where there is thought to be a psychological component present, such as in asthma or some types of headache, and in the treatment of pain (Marzillier and Hall, 1987).

It is worth mentioning briefly how abnormal behaviours are classified. A broad distinction was once made between *neuroses, psychoses* and *personality disorders*. Neuroses included phobias and obsessive-compulsive disorders. More recently the assumption that neurosis underlies these and other associated disorders such as post-traumatic stress disorder has been questioned (see Davidson and Neale, 1994) and the disorders are now identified independently. Collectively they are described as anxiety disorders (see Davidson and Neale, 1994). Psychosis refer to an impairment of mental functioning in which an individual experiences a distortion of reality. They may experience delusions. These are false beliefs maintained despite contradictory evidence (for example the belief that a family member is a secret agent spying on the individual). They may also experience perceptual disturbances such as hallucinations (for example seeing or hearing things that are not there). Psychosis may be present in mental illnesses such as schizophrenia or be caused by drug use or other processes which affect the functioning of the brain (American Psychiatric Association, 1994; Davidson and Neale, 1994; Rosenham and Seligman, 1989).

Personality disorders refer to enduring patterns of inner experience and behaviour that deviate markedly from the expectations of the individual's culture and are pervasive and inflexible (American Psychiatric Association, 1994). Many of the problems encountered by clinical psychologists have as much or more to do with longstanding maladaptive personality traits than with psychosis or other serious disturbance of mental state. Several surveys have shown that over a third of psychiatric patients are likely to meet current criteria for personality disorder (Kass *et al.*, 1985; Koenigsberg *et al.*, 1985).

Today, probably the most widely accepted classification of abnormal behaviours is that proposed by the *Diagnostic and Statistical Manual*, now in its fourth edition (DSM IV: American Psychiatric Association, 1994). The DSM IV distinguishes Clinical Syndromes (which include the major forms of 'mental illness' such as schizophrenia, mood disorders such as depression and disorders caused by organic damage to the brain, including various forms of dementia) and Personality Disorders. It stresses that personality disorders and mental illness can and very often do coexist. Table 12.1 lists a selection of the disorders described in DSM IV.

Table 12.1 *A selection of DSM IV disorders**

Anxiety disorders	Panic attack
	Agoraphobia
	Social phobia
	Obsessive-compulsive disorder
	Post-traumatic stress disorder
Mood disorders	Major depressive disorder
	Bipolar disorder
	Substance-induced mood disorder
Psychotic disorders	Schizophrenia
	Schizoaffective disorder
	Delusional disorder
	Substance-induced psychotic disorder
Disorders of infancy, childhood or adolescence	Mental retardation
	Learning disorders
	Motor skills disorder
	Pervasive developmental disorders (e.g. Autistic disorder)
Substance-related disorders	Alcohol-related disorders
	Cocaine-related disorders
	Nicotine-related disorders
Eating disorders	Anorexia nervosa
	Bulimia nervosa
Personality disorders	Avoidant personality disorder
	Schizoid personality disorder
	Dependent personality disorder
	Histrionic personality disorder
	Antisocial personality disorder
	Narcissistic personality disorder
	Compulsive personality disorder

* This table contains only a small selection of disorders listed in DSM IV for the purposes of illustration.

Historical background

The term 'psychology' literally means 'a study of the mind'. Many contemporary psychologists would feel unhappy with this definition. Some for instance would not be certain what is meant by 'the mind' and whether the dichotomy between mind and body is indeed a valid or necessary one. The term, however, reflects the origins of psychology as a branch of philosophy.

Initially psychology, still seen as part of philosophy and referred to as 'mental philosophy', was restricted to introspection or 'armchair psychology'. This involved the psychologist examining his or her own thoughts and generalizing from these to other people. From what we now know about the reliability of people's 'self-report' (what they say about themselves) and the great variance amongst people's experiences this method had considerable problems. Psychology departed from philosophy when it discarded introspection and adopted the general methods of the natural sciences to study mental processes.

During the nineteenth century in Great Britain psychological disorders were addressed by doctors, who established 'medical' or 'disease' models to account for such problems and attempted to treat them with medicines or other physical treatments. Pilgrim and Treacher (1992) have argued that the First and Second World Wars contributed significantly to the development of clinical psychology as it is today.

During the First World War, with large numbers of people suffering from 'shell-shock', some of the fundamental premises on which Victorian medical practices were based were challenged and the limitations of a purely biological psychiatry exposed. This allowed some practitioners to propose alternative psychological models to explain the effects of shell-shock and other neurotic complaints. These psychological models were clearly influenced by the psychodynamic theories of Sigmund Freud, who was not a clinical psychologist or a psychiatrist as such but a physician who was interested in how unconscious mental processes influenced people's behaviour and contributed to their psychological problems.

With the advent of the Second World War clinical psychology took another developmental step. With large numbers of people being recruited, selected and trained for duty, the army provided a demand for the techniques of psychometric assessment of individual differences. These had been developing over the previous decades. An example of such a technique is intelligence testing where intellectual functioning is measured and an individual classified by comparing their score with a relevant population. Some have claimed that an overriding interest in measurement deleteriously affected the development of clinical psychology, by consigning the profession to the role of assistants to psychiatrists (see Pilgrim and Treacher, 1992). This testing role was in fact the primary function of clinical psychologists immediately following the Second World War. Most clinical psychologists worked in large psychiatric or mental handicap hospitals assisting psychiatrists to make diagnoses and monitor treatment (Pilgrim and Treacher, 1992). The reaction against this role, however, contributed to clinical psychologists beginning to study ways of treating clients' problems rather than simply measuring them.

During the 1950s in the United Kingdom, the profession of clinical psychology became established in its own right and clinicians began to treat anxiety disorders with behaviour therapy. The influence of behaviourism was evident in the treatment methods of clinicians at this time, many of whom questioned the value of considering mental events (Eysenck, 1952, 1960; Ullman and Krasner, 1965). For these practitioners the notions of 'consciousness' and 'mind' were simply irrelevant to what they saw as the only public, observable and recordable aspect of people's functioning: behaviour. By the end of the 1960s clinical psychologists had firmly established their role as clinicians rather than technicians and had broadened the scope of therapeutic approaches they utilized beyond behaviour therapy.

The behavioural influence on the profession is still evident in the approaches used by clinical psychologists today. Clinical psychologists typically still stress the importance of assessing and changing behaviour itself and emphasize its importance as being observable and measurable and often the only important outcome variable when seeking change in people. Whilst clinical psychologists are still often concerned with assisting people to modify behaviour which is problematic, a considerable broadening of what constitutes 'behaviour' has occurred with an increasing emphasis on internal aspects of the person including language, thought and emotion. The 'cognitive revolution' in general psychology has had a major impact on clinical psychology, for example in the treatment of depression (Beck *et al.*, 1979).

The 1990s have seen the acceleration of a number of trends in the recent development of clinical psychology. In the United Kingdom, as in many other countries, the deinstitutionalization of people suffering from severe mental illness and learning disabilities has proceeded rapidly. Clinical psychologists increasingly find themselves working in a community setting, trying to maintain and improve upon clients' integration within community life. The shortage of clinical psychologists in the United Kingdom, coupled with the development of health services run on managerialist lines, has led to changing roles. Clinical psychologists increasingly contribute to the planning, organization and management of health services. The training of other professionals in psychological methods has also become a major role, though whether clinical psychology should be 'given away' so freely remains a contentious issue (see Pilgrim and Treacher, 1992).

Clinical psychology as a science

When clinical psychology adopted the methods of the natural sciences practitioners began to view clinical psychology as a science in its own right. A science can be defined by the methods it utilizes more so than the facts it assembles ('science is what scientists do'). Clinical psychologists have been described as 'scientist-practitioners' (Barlow *et al.*, 1984). This refers to the process of using scientific methods to direct clinical practice, which in turn contributes to the body of knowledge about presenting problems.

As Barlow *et al.* (1984) depict it, the scientific element of practice involves three primary and interrelated activities or roles for practitioners. In the first of these roles the practitioner is a consumer of new research findings (for example relating to as new assessment or treatment techniques) that he or she will put into practice. In the second role the practitioner is an evaluator of his or her own interventions through the use of empirical methods. In the third role the prac-titioner is a researcher producing new data to be reported to the scientific community.

The scientific process begins with the development of theories which seek to explain the occurrence of a particular problem or phenomenon. Very often theories are themselves influenced by earlier ideas or the results of previous study. In clinical psychology theories guide and influence the methods that practitioners use to understand and modify an individual's behaviour and are continually being proposed, modified, accepted or abandoned in response to clinical findings. The theories most valued by clinical psychologists (a) have some relevance to clinical problems, (b) have implications for the treatment of those problems and (c) are presented in terms that can generate hypotheses that can be tested. A good theory is one that can be 'falsified' or proved wrong by this process.

The methods and procedures that clinical psychologists use to test out theories must also conform to the standards required of a science aimed at 'falsification'. The end result of this scientific procedure for clinical psychologists is that they use treatment methods with their clients that have been shown to be effective or at least are being closely studied in terms of their effectiveness.

There are many definitions of the aim of psychological science. A common definition of this has been the 'understanding, prediction and control above the levels achieved by unaided common sense' (Allport, 1947). This notion may have authoritarian overtones when applied to human thought and behaviour, and as such serves to indicate the extent to which clinical psychology can be misused or at least misunderstood. It does however summarize the process that many psychologists use in their daily work of developing an understanding of people's problems through assessment, seeking to predict the course of those problems, instigating interventions aimed at changing (or controlling) those problems, and evaluating how successful these interventions have been.

Common activities of clinical psychologists

The major activities of clinical psychologists are not static. As has been indicated above, the core tasks of the profession have changed dramatically over time, and will undoubtedly change to some degree in the future. The following, nevertheless, are, and are likely to remain, important.

Assessment and formulation

Assessment, for clinical psychologists, involves the systematic gathering of information about the presenting clinical problem. The aim of assessment is to establish a better definition of the problem itself and the factors which have had a role in the development and maintenance of the problem. The process of assessment leads to a clinical *formulation* or hypothesis. We believe that the provision of an explicit formulation is, perhaps, the most important skill of the clinical psychologist. The formulation or hypothesis is based on the information that has been gathered and is informed by psychological theory and research findings. If clinical psychologists have a unique skill which distinguishes them from other professions, it is, perhaps, the ability to synthesize information about the presenting problem and to translate this information into a formal, theory-based formulation. Such a formulation needs to be tentative and subject to subsequent revision in the light of new information. It is the clinical formulation which dictates the nature of the interventions that may be required.

Assessment is usually carried out using some of the following modes of information gathering.

(a) Clinical interviewing: this involves a careful and detailed questioning of the client about the presenting problem, the way this problem has developed and factors which may influence its occurrence. Other people who are significant in the client's life (family members or friends for example) may also be interviewed to gain their impressions of the person's problems and confirm the client's version (see Kirk, 1989; Shea, 1988).

(b) Observation: this involves monitoring and recording aspects of the client's behaviour. Clinical psychologists have developed methods of 'sampling' behaviour and recording the results to make sure that observations reflect as accurately as possible what actually occurred (Barlow *et al.*, 1984; Bellack and Hersen, 1988).

(c) Self-monitoring: this procedure requires the client to monitor and record aspects of their own behaviour. Someone who has an alcohol problem may for instance monitor their drinking behaviour over a week and keep a dairy of their drinking pattern (Barlow *et al.*, 1984; Bellack and Hersen, 1988).

(d) Standardized tests: clinical psychologists have developed a range of standardized psychometric tests to measure particular aspects of people's behaviour. The best known of these tests are 'intelligence tests' such as the

Wechsler Adult Intelligence Scale Revised (WAIS-R: Wechsler, 1981). Tests like the WAIS-R allow clinical psychologists to measure a person's abilities on a set of specific tasks covering a range of intellectual functions. These results can then be compared with the norms from a large population. Tests such as the WAIS-R often form part of a larger battery which may be used, for example, to assess whether a person has suffered a brain injury and/or whether intellectual functioning has deteriorated for some reason.

Other tests take the form of questionnaires or rating scales which clients usually complete independently. They are thus referred to as 'self-report questionnaires'. The Beck Depression Inventory (BDI: Beck and Steer, 1987), for instance, is a self rating-scale containing 21 multiple-choice questions about the symptoms of depression, each containing four or five items ranked in order of severity. Wide-ranging questionnaires like the Millon Clinical Multiaxial Inventory (Millon, 1983) measure aspects of personality, personality disorder and also psychiatric symptomatology. The results of these questionnaires can then be compared with the results of large standardization groups. In the case of the BDI, this questionnaire provides an indication of severity of depression from the client's self-report, while in the case of the MCMI results can be compared with the scores of more than 40 000 individuals tested in the construction of the test.

There are standardized tests available to cover many aspects of human functioning (Bellack and Hersen, 1988). An important part of the clinical psychologist's job is to decide what test is best suited to the kind of assessment being carried out and to ensure the test measures what it is supposed to measure and does so reliably.

(e) Physiological assessment: this involves the measurement of physiological manifestations of psychological experiences. An example might be to measure heart rate or sweatiness of skin as an indication of anxiety (Barlow *et al.*, 1984).

A thorough assessment should obtain information from more than one source. Sometimes the information from these sources does not match up and this may provide important clues about how the client is experiencing and presenting their problem.

A good assessment should be objective, reliable and valid. *Objectivity* refers to the importance of assessing what a person actually does or says rather than our interpretation of these events. The advantage of some standardized tests is that they allow subjectivity to be minimized. *Reliability* refers to the importance of assessment procedures providing consistent results. Reliability can be measured by (a) getting two clinicians to complete the same assessment then comparing their results, or (b) by repeating the same assessment on different occasions, or (c) by developing a 'parallel form' of the assessment and comparing results on this with the original. *Validity* refers to the extent to which an assessment procedure measures what it is supposed to measure. There are many forms of validity. Validity is determined by how well a procedure appears to measure what it is supposed to (face validity), the extent to which it covers a representative sample of the behaviour being measured (content validity), how well the assessment compares with other assessments used for the same purpose (concurrent validity), and how well it measures a theoretical construct or trait (construct validity).

Many of the standardized tests available to clinical psychologists will provide information gained from research on objectivity, reliability and validity. When a clinical psychologist does not use a standardized test he or she must still consider these qualities.

Treatment

Treatment involves the use of psychological procedures to bring about *change* in thought, emotion or behaviour. Treatments may be conducted with individuals, with groups or families, or be applied to broad populations or services. There are many, indeed too many, forms of psychological therapy, many of them with an inadequate theoretical basis and/or little empirical evidence as to effectiveness. Some illustrative examples of effective treatments are given below.

Monitoring and evaluation

As scientists, clinical psychologists need to assess to what extent treatment interventions have been effective. This ensures that treatments which have not been effective are discontinued, that a more effective treatment is substituted, and that effective treatment does not continue for longer than is necessary. Evaluation might involve re-administering the standardized tests used during assessment to see if any changes have occurred. Increasingly, clinical psychologists are asked to evaluate the effectiveness of broad treatment services, in addition to looking at treatments for individuals. Thus a psychologist might be asked to determine whether, for example, a community-based psychiatric service is more effective than a hospital-based service.

Psychological therapies

When we consider the application of psychology to clinical situations we find that psychologists use a broad range of treatment approaches. These include approaches directly influenced by the psychoanalytic tradition of Freud and his followers and other approaches which emphasize helping clients through talking and listening such as counselling and psychotherapy. Psychologists have developed specialized approaches to help clients with specific problems such as psychosexual therapy for those with sexual problems and family therapy for those whose problems arise through difficulties within their family.

There are too many psychological therapies to mention them all in this chapter. Two broad approaches have, however, been particularly influential. The first of these has been influenced by learning theories which have given rise to behavioural therapies. The second approach has been influenced by cognitive theories. It is worth briefly reviewing the main points of these theories and how they are applied in contemporary clinical practice.

Behaviour therapy   *Parlovian theory*

This approach emphasizes *learning* in the explanation of behaviour and argues that behaviour which causes people problems is learned in the same way as non-problematic behaviour. Behaviour therapy recognizes two ways in which learning occurs. The first is through *classical conditioning* where an 'unconditioned stimulus' (e.g. food) leads to an 'unconditioned response' (e.g. salivation). These are said to be 'unconditioned' because the process occurs naturally or innately rather than being learned. When an initially neutral stimulus is paired with an unconditioned stimulus, however, it too becomes capable of eliciting the response. The initially neutral stimulus is said to be a 'conditioned stimulus' and the response a 'conditioned response' (see Chapter 7). This process has been used to explain how certain neutral events or situations come to elicit fearful or phobic responses in people when they are paired with some event that would normally elicit fear.

Behaviour can also be learned by the consequences it produces through what is referred to as *operant conditioning*. Behaviour that produces desirable consequences for the individual concerned may increase in frequency, in which case it is said to be *reinforced*; behaviour that produces aversive consequences may decrease in frequency and is said to have been *punished*. Reinforcers and punishments may be further distinguished as positive or negative depending on whether elements are added to or removed from the environment. The importance of this position is that, as the consequences of an individual's behaviour are delivered by the environment in which the behaviour occurs, then the principle determinants or causes of the behaviour are to be found *outside* the person.

The American psychologist Albert Bandura, however, argued that individuals may not only be rewarded by the environment but through self-reinforcement received through experiencing a sense of pride or achievement. He also recognized that people can experience 'vicarious reinforcement' by observing other people's behaviour being reinforced or punished. This in turn influences their own behaviour. Bandura described the processes of observational learning whereby people observe other people's behaviour and imitate it themselves. Once they have carried out the behaviour it can be reinforced or punished by its consequences as with any other operant behaviour (Bandura, 1977).

The probability of future occurrences of a particular behaviour depends on the pattern or '*schedule*' of reinforcement and punishment related to it. It is not necessary to reinforce *every* instance of a behaviour for the likelihood of it recurring to be maintained or increased. Much human behaviour is reinforced on what is called an *intermittent* schedule of reinforcement. An example of intermittent reinforcement can be found in the use of slot machines. A player only requires an occasional reward of a payout to reinforce the repeated behaviour of feeding money into the machines and pulling the lever.

Overall it is the balance of reinforcing and punishing experiences in an individual's learning history that dictates the presence or absence of a behaviour at a certain time and in a certain situation. Schedules of reinforcement and punishment are unlikely to be constant or steady over time, leading to often complex learning histories.

When applying psychology to abnormal behaviour it is useful to consider the *function* of the behaviour for the individual concerned (Owens and Ashcroft, 1982). Some problematic behaviour persists because it has come to perform a function for the individual: drinking, for example, may be a learned way of coping with stress. This may be particularly so when the stress has been present for a long time. One task for the clinical psychologist therefore is to assist the client to replace a maladaptive method of solving a problem with a more adaptive means. Very often this entails teaching the client new skills and behaviours as well as how to control problematic behaviour.

Techniques derived from behaviour theories utilize what is known about how people learn to behave to help them alter behaviour that is causing them problems. One behavioural technique that is used with such disorders as phobias is *systematic desensitization*. This assumes that phobic behaviours are learned or 'conditioned' and can therefore be 'unlearned' or 'de-conditioned'. It involves teaching clients techniques of relaxation which is known to counteract the physical symptoms of anxiety, and then systematically exposing them to the feared situation or object using an 'anxiety hierarchy'. People are encouraged to use relaxation to reduce the anxiety they feel. There have been hundreds of studies of systematic desensitization which demonstrate its effectiveness for many phobias (see Barlow, 1988 for a review of the psychological treatment of anxiety disorders). These studies also show that it is the *exposure* component, rather than the relaxation component, which is most important.

Many behavioural approaches aim to teach clients new skills to replace inappropriate or absent ones. Very often these teaching procedures utilize Bandura's concept of vicarious learning by having the therapist or someone else model appropriate ways of dealing with a situation. Suitable ways of behaving in problem situations can then be role-played by the client before they try out the behaviour in real life. One example of this is *assertiveness training* (see Wolpe, 1990) which instructs people how to speak up for their rights rather than behaving 'aggressively' or indeed 'passively'. Another example is *social skills training* which involves teaching people how to behave in social situations where they may have difficulty starting and maintaining a conversation, establishing a socially acceptable distance for the intimacy of the contact, or in using signals from body language to assist them in communication (Hollin and Trower, 1986a, 1986b).

Case Example: Ron, a 24-year-old single man, was referred to a clinical psychologist by his general practitioner whom he consulted after experiencing discomfort at social functions over the previous 12 months. He told the psychologist at their first meeting that he had had to leave his sister's wedding function early because he suddenly had difficulty breathing, broke out in a sweat and had an overwhelming sensation that he was going to pass out. These symptoms stopped once he left the function. He visited his GP soon after because he was worried he might have some form of coronary illness but examinations revealed no physical illness or disability. He said that the same experience occurred a month later at another social gathering and that he had become increasingly reluctant to attend social events as he was never certain if he was going to experience these sensations. Over the year he had turned down invitations to social functions because he thought the symptoms would occur. He said that he now felt worried that the symptoms might start at work and because of this had recently taken time off work. His employer had expressed concern and as a result Ron had consulted his GP again.

In discussion with the psychologist Ron described himself as a shy man who had always felt a little uncomfortable in social situations. The psychologist noticed that Ron appeared quite anxious as he spoke. Ron admitted that he felt anxious and had in fact experienced some of the symptoms he had been concerned about while waiting to see the psychologist.

At the end of the first session the psychologist gave Ron some questionnaires to complete before the next appointment. These included the State-Trait Anxiety Inventory (Spielberger, 1983) and a check-list of situations or events which Ron was required to rate as to how much anxiety he would experience.

At the following appointment, a week later, Ron discussed his responses to the questionnaires with the psychologist. On examining the check-list they noticed a pattern: Ron felt more certain that the symptoms would occur at 'important' social events (such as weddings) and when there were many people present. The State-Trait Anxiety Inventory revealed that Ron tended to be a generally more anxious person than average. These results provided information about the nature of Ron's anxiety and a baseline measure from which to evaluate whether or not treatment had been effective.

During the third session the psychologist asked Ron to keep a diary of situations in which he felt anxious. He was required to describe each situation in which he felt anxious and to record using a rating scale from 1–10 the amount of anxiety he experienced.

In following sessions the psychologist and Ron continued to review the diary that Ron maintained. The psychologist began teaching Ron a means of relaxing using a technique of progressive muscle relaxation. The psychologist explained that relaxation is incompatible with anxiety and would be used systematically to help Ron deal with situations in which he felt anxious.

With the information from the questionnaires and Ron's diary the psychologist helped him to draw up a hierarchy of situations (from least feared to most feared) in which he felt anxious. In sessions the psychologist assisted Ron in his relaxation then instructed him to imagine entering a situation low on the hierarchy. As Ron's anxiety increased while imagining this the psychologist instructed him to return to the relaxation exercises. This procedure was repeated until Ron could imagine a situation without experiencing any anxiety. Then they moved on to the next item on the hierarchy.

Owing to the fact that Ron reported always feeling some discomfort in social situations, with the psychologist's encouragement, he began to attend a group aimed at teaching people social skills, such as conversation and listening skills, and how to understand body language and posture. He was able to practise these skills during role-play exercises with other group members and to review his performance in video recordings.

As Ron's ability to manage his anxiety within the sessions increased the psychologist encouraged him to use the relaxation and skills he had acquired in the group in 'real' situations, starting with situations low on the hierarchy. Ron reported that on these occasions he had experienced some anxiety but he was able to limit it by using relaxation techniques and by telling himself positive messages the psychologist had encouraged him to develop. He said his anxiety did not reach a point where he had to leave or 'escape' a situation. Ron said that he felt this was helped by his increased confidence gained from learning social skills in the group. He completed the State-Trait Anxiety Inventory after entering each situation to provide a measure of his anxiety.

Over a number of sessions Ron was able to report that he had entered increasingly anxiety-provoking situations on the hierarchy. He did not move on to a situation provoking greater levels of anxiety until he had successfully mastered the preceding steps. After six months the psychologist felt confident that Ron could continue the procedure without his assistance and after discussion with Ron agreed to discharge him. At the last session Ron again completed the questionnaires he had filled out earlier. They demonstrated an overall decline in his level of anxiety and less anxiety experienced in particular situations.

Cognitive therapy

Before describing some of the cognitive therapies in use in clinical psychology it needs to be pointed out that the terms 'cognitive' or 'cognition' have been defined in various ways. In general these terms are used with reference to such concepts as attention, concentration, perception, memory and intelligence: as such they may be used as a synonym for 'thinking'. Such aspects of people's functioning are generally assessed by psychologists as part of a *neuropsychological* assessment (see Chapter 9).

In many clinical applications, however, the term 'cognition' is also used to refer to the *style* of thinking that an individual uses. Cognitive therapy aims to identify the mental processes which contribute to psychological problems, arguing that the way an individual views or *appraises* a situation or event and thinks about it will determine how they feel and behave (Beck, 1976; Brewin, 1988; Forsterling, 1988). This approach argues that many psychological problems are based in faulty or 'dysfunctional' core beliefs. These faulty core beliefs are often referred to as *schemata* which are said to develop early in life and remain relatively stable over time. These beliefs influence an individual's view of themselves, others, the world they live in and events in their lives. They are said to be reflected in how the person thinks, behaves and feels.

According to cognitive therapists these schemata generate *'negative automatic thoughts'* which have the following features: they are automatic in that the person may not consciously decide to think them; once started the thoughts may be difficult to stop or 'switch off'; they are biased or distorted because they are based on the person's schemata rather than an *objective* appraisal of a situation or event; they may be plausible enough, however, for the individual not to question them.

Cognitive therapists assume that, with guidance, individuals are capable of identifying the thoughts that contribute to their problems and are capable of learning to change or replace these thoughts with others that are less biased and that take into account a more objective evaluation of the world around them.

Therapy involves educating the client about the involvement of these cognitive processes in their disorder. Many people do not pay much attention to the thoughts they have in everyday life and how these influence them. They may view thoughts as the *result* of their difficulties rather than a possible *cause*. Very often they may have acquired false information about their disorder that contributes to the problem. For example, someone suffering from panic attacks may believe that they are the same as heart attacks – a belief that could contribute to their panic. Someone who repeatedly behaves violently may not distinguish between anger as an emotion and aggression as a behaviour. An important part of therapy is to correct these beliefs.

Next a series of goals and graded activities is identified (similar to the hierarchy discussed above) and the negative thoughts which may inhibit achieving these goals identified. The therapist assists the client to dispute, challenge or rebut these thoughts. The client may be encouraged to consider to what extent his or her negative thoughts are based in reality, to what extent they are logical and to what extent they are going to benefit the client and others (see Dryden and DiGiuseppe, 1990 for an illustration of how one type of cognitive therapy, Rational Emotive Therapy, utilizes this process). The last task is to challenge the *schemata* that underlie and generate the negative automatic thoughts.

Cognitive therapy was first applied systematically to people suffering from depression (Beck, 1976). In depression schemata tend to focus on the need to be loved, the need to do well at all costs, and the hopelessness of one's situation. The depressed individual may take a very biased view of past achievements in love and work and may feel hopeless about the possibility of any future success. A person suffering from depression might possess a number of core beliefs that contribute to their depression. These may focus on their need to be loved and the need to achieve. These schemata may generate negative automatic thoughts such as 'I am worthless', 'My situation is hopeless', 'I cannot do anything right' and others that occur at times of distress and difficulty. A cognitive approach attempts to disentangle genuine failures from imagined ones and to rectify the distortions in the client's thinking to assist them to take a more balanced view of themselves and their future.

Case Example: Mary, aged 39 and married with two children, was re-ferred to the psychology department by a consultant psychiatrist who assessed her on her admission to a psychiatric hospital following a suicide attempt. The psychiatrist noted on examining her file that she had had three previous admissions over the last four years, two of which were precipitated by suicide attempts. She had been consulting her GP, complaining of low mood, for nearly six years prior to this. The GP had prescribed anti-depressant medication.

The referring psychiatrist asked that Mary be assessed to consider her suitability for psychological interventions. A psychologist visited her on the psychiatric unit where she was an inpatient. She appeared tearful as she described her history and previous admission to hospital. She said she no longer wanted to die and felt very guilty about all the trouble her suicide attempt had caused. During the first session Mary completed a Beck Depression Inventory. She produced a score of 27 indicating that at the time she was feeling 'severely depressed'. From the first two sessions with Mary the psychologist felt the following factors might contribute to her low mood: low self-acceptance since her teens, isolation following the birth of her children 15 years ago, persistent concern regarding her ability as a mother, low self-confidence in social situa-tions, and a belief that nothing in her life could improve.

Shortly after the second session Mary was discharged from hospital be-cause she was considered well enough to return home. She continued to take anti-depressant medication prescribed by the psychiatrist and arranged to see the psychologist at an outpatient clinic. Before leaving the hospital the psy-chologist requested that Mary maintain a daily diary of her emotions. In addition to recording emotions the psychologist asked her to record the details of the situations in which the emotions occurred and any thoughts that accompanied the emotion.

At her first outpatient session Mary reported that she had had difficulty completing the diary as she was concerned she was not 'not doing it correctly'. She had, however, recorded several entries which the psychologist discussed with her. The first entry occurred after she mustered the courage to telephone a friend to tell her of her discharge from hospital. She said her friend could not speak for long as she had an appointment to attend. After the brief discussion Mary recorded thinking that 'not even my best friend has time to talk to me, she doesn't like me, I should never have phoned her then I wouldn't feel like this' and feeling 'hurt and sad'. The second entry occurred after her eldest son complained that his school uniform had not been ironed and had then hurriedly left for school. Mary recorded her thoughts as 'I must be a bad mother, I'm hopeless' but also 'how dare he after all I've done for him'. She recorded feeling 'angry, guilty and low'.

Through such exercises Mary began to associate particular thoughts with particular moods. With the help of the psychologist Mary devised a list of 'rebuttals' that she could use to impede the negative thoughts and their bias. These rebuttals included 'just because someone is unfriendly doesn't mean I'm a bad person' and 'My son is angry now but he'll get over it, it doesn't mean I'm a bad mother'.

Through continued use of mood monitoring and systematically countering the negative thoughts Mary reported some stabilization of her moods with fewer periods of depression.

Contact with the psychologist continued and began to focus increasingly on the underlying schemata producing the negative thoughts. By examining Mary's mood diaries she and the psychologist were able to identify several common core themes including 'I must receive love from my family and friends' and 'If I'm a perfect mother my children will love me'. It was noted that the negative thoughts arose every time Mary perceived these very rigid assumptions to be contested.

The psychologist pointed out to Mary that much of what she did in life was in pursuit of these needs and yet she had continued to possess a very low opinion of herself. In following sessions Mary was able to consider and address some of the causes of these assumptions including how her own parents had treated her in terms of put-downs and criticisms. The validity of these criticisms was challenged and Mary was encouraged to evaluate objectively her own worth as a person.

At termination of therapy Mary was able to report feeling less concerned about her abilities as a mother, and more confident at dealing with apparent rejection from friends. She reported, in fact, that her relationship with friends had improved from her being able openly to check out her anxieties with them and them being able to reassure her about these. This in turn enabled her to feel increasingly confident in social situations and she reported feeling less isolated.

The cognitive approach, outlined above, has been applied to a wide variety of problems and has been shown to be effective (Dryden and Rentoul, 1991; Marks, 1987; Rachman and Wilson, 1980).

Synthesis

Many psychological problems are complex in terms of their causes and presentations and such problems very often need to be addressed in more than one way (for example behavioural, cognitive, social). In practice most clinical psychologists are unlikely to restrict themselves to only one of these approaches. As mentioned in the introduction, part of the clinical psychologist's job is to tailor general techniques to the specific needs of the client. Clinical effectiveness may be strengthened by using a combination of approaches. A combination of behavioural and cognitive approaches is often referred to simply as a 'cognitive-behavioural approach' and is probably the dominant approach within clinical psychology at present.

An example of a cognitive-behavioural approach is the approach to anger management proposed by Raymond Novaco (Novaco, 1975; Novaco and Welsh, 1989) and commonly used by psychologists. This model considers the environmental factors emphasized by social learning theorists, the thoughts or cognitions mentioned by cognitive theorists, physical arousal and the behaviour itself, which has been the focus of behavioural theorists. Novaco's work (see also Howells, 1989) is a good example of a comprehensive broad-based cognitive behavioural approach to a clinical problem. Successful anger management first involves assisting the client to recognize and identify the stressors which precede anger, and to recognize the state of anger itself and what is occurring in their body. It then involves teaching the individual to distinguish between anger (the emotion) and aggression (the behaviour) and learning to control the physiological aspects through relaxation training. The next step is to identify the common thoughts that accompany anger and contribute to the behaviour. The client is assisted to change these and develop more adaptive cognitions through cognitive therapy. Finally the client is encouraged to recognize the difference between aggressive, passive and assertive behaviour and to develop means of controlling aggressive behaviour and enhance assertion skills through assertion and social skills training.

Other applications

Research on the treatment of personality disorders is in its infancy and research studies using scientific methods have been few and far between. There remains considerable dispute regarding the concept of personality and personality disorders but growing consensus that the definition provided by DSM IV (American Psychiatric Association, 1994) provides a useful starting point. DSM IV defines a personality disorder as 'an enduring pattern of inner experience and behaviour that deviates markedly from the expectations of the individual's culture, is pervasive and inflexible, has an onset in adolescence or early adulthood, is stable over time and leads to distress or impairment' (American Psychiatric Association, 1994, p. 629). A range of types of personality disorder has been described by DSM IV including the 'schizoid', the 'dependent', the 'avoidant', the 'compulsive' and the 'antisocial'.

There is a small but growing literature which demonstrates the effectiveness of cognitive behavioural therapy with individuals diagnosed as having personality disorders. As noted above the cognitive behavioural approach involves identifying the dysfunctional beliefs and maladaptive strategies that define the disorder. The schemas that contribute to these can then be identified and altered using the cognitive techniques described. Clinicians working in this area make the point that because the problems associated with personality disorders have, by definition, been around for much of the individual's adult life (at least) they should be expected to take considerably longer than other problems to respond to psychological interventions (Beck, Freeman and Associates, 1990).

While there is as yet no clearly established psychological model to account comprehensively for all the phenomena reported by those people who are diagnosed as having schizophrenia and while the concept of schizophrenia itself has attracted much controversy (Bentall, *et al.*, 1988), psychologists have identified a number of perceptual and cognitive abnormalities commonly associated with the disorder (see Bentall, 1991). Clinical psychologists have developed a range of techniques which have proved helpful in allowing individuals suffering from schizophrenia to control some of their symptoms. For hallucinations these methods have included assisting the client to moderate the level of sensory input they expose themselves to, developing behaviours which counteract hallucinations (e.g. reading aloud or listening to music through ear-plugs to inhibit auditory hallucinations) and self-monitoring and recording of hallucinatory experiences (Slade, 1990). Slade and Bental (1988) have suggested that the most successful of these procedures share the following common features: they assist the client to focus some attention on their hallucinations (e.g. through self-monitoring) they lower anxiety levels, and utilize distraction or counter-stimulation as techniques of managing hallucinations.

Clinical psychologists have also considered the attributional style of people who are considered to suffer from delusions. Some studies have shown that, for instance, those who suffer from the paranoid delusional belief that others are against them attribute bad events to external factors beyond their control which affect them globally (Kaney and Bentall, 1989). The application of cognitive therapy to these negative beliefs is currently being evaluated. Several authors have reported some success in modifying delusional beliefs using cognitive methods and this is likely to be an important area for future research and clinical practice (see Birchwood and Preston, 1991).

Finally, we have, inevitably, had to select just a few illustrative examples of the work of clinical psychologists in the present chapter. We have missed out many major areas, including work with people with learning disabilities and work with children and older adults. The focus for psychologists' work has in the past, and will in the future, change dramatically over time. As an example of this, we would point to the area of child sexual abuse. In the last 10 years there has been a massive increase in public and professional awareness of this social problem. Monitoring the effects of such abuse on mental health, providing treatment programmes for children and adults to offset these effects, preventative work, and the provision of interventions for perpetrators are all tasks that clinical psychologists have undertaken (Hollin and Howells, 1992). Undoubtedly the future will see other new areas emerge and established areas of work diminish.

References

AMERICAN PSYCHIATRIC ASSOCIATION (1994) *Diagnostic and Statistical Manual*, Edition IV, Washington, DC, APA.

ALLPORT, G.W. (1947) *The Use Of Personal Documents In Psychological Science*, New York, Social Science Research Council.

BANDURA, A. (1977) *Social Learning Theory*, Englewood Cliffs, NJ, Prentice-Hall.

BARLOW, D.H. (1988) *Anxiety and its Disorders*, New York, Guilford.

BARLOW, D.H., HAYES, S.C. and NELSON, R.O. (1984) *The Scientist Practitioner: Research and Accountability in Clinical and Educational Settings*, New York, Pergamon.

BECK, A.T. (1976) *Cognitive Therapy and the Emotional Disorders*, New York, Meridian.

BECK, A.T. and STEER, R.A. (1987) *Manual For the Revised Beck Depression Inventory*, San Antonio, TX, The Psychological Corporation.

BECK, A.T., FREEMAN, A. and ASSOCIATES (1990) *Cognitive Therapy of Personality Disorders*, New York, Guilford.

BECK, A.T., RUSH, A.J., SHAW, B.F. and EMERY, G. (1979) *Cognitive Therapy of Depression*, Chichester, Wiley.

BELLACK, A.S. and HERSEN, M. (1988) *Behavioural Assessment: A Practical Handbook*, 3rd ed., New York, Pergamon.

BENTALL, R.P. (1991) 'The syndromes and symptoms of psychosis', in BENTALL, R.P. (Ed.) *Reconstructing Schizophrenia*, London, Routledge.

BENTALL, R.P., JACKSON, H.F. and PILGRIM, D. (1988) 'Abandoning the concept of schizophrenia: some implications of validity arguments for psychological research into psychotic phenomena', *British Journal of Clinical Psychology*, **27**, 303-24.

BIRCHWOOD, M. and PRESTON, M. (1991) 'Schizophrenia', in DRYDEN, W. and RENTOUL, R. (Eds) *Adult Clinical Problems: A Cognitive Behavioural Approach*, London, Routledge.

BREWIN, C. (1988) 'Attribution therapy', in WATTS, F.N. (Ed.) *New Developments in Clinical Psychology*, Chichester, Wiley.

DAVIDSON, G.C. and NEALE, J.M. (1994) *Abnormal Psychology: An Experimental Clinical Approach*, 6th ed., New York, Wiley.

DRYDEN, W. and DiGIUSEPPE, R. (1990) *A Primer on Rational Emotive Therapy*, Champaign, IL, Research Press.

DRYDEN, W. and RENTOUL, R. (Eds) (1991) *Adult Clinical Problems: A Cognitive Behavioural Approach*, London, Routledge.

EYSENCK, H.J. (1952) 'The effects of psychotherapy: an evaluation', *Journal of Consulting Psychology*, **16**, 319-24.

EYSENCK, H.J. (1960) *Behaviour Therapy and the Neuroses*, New York, Pergamon.

FORSTERLING, F. (1988) *Attribution Theory in Clinical Psychology*, Chichester, Wiley.

HOLLIN, C.R. and HOWELLS, K. (Eds) (1992) *Clinical Approaches to Sex Offenders and their Victims*, Chichester, Wiley.

HOLLIN, C.R. and TROWER, P. (Eds) (1986a) *Handbook of Social Skills Training*, Vol. 1: *Applications Across the Lifespan*, Oxford, Pergamon.

HOLLIN, C.R. and TROWER, P. (Eds) (1986b) *Handbook of Social Skills Training*, Vol. 2: *Clinical Application and New Directions*, Oxford, Pergamon.

HOWELLS, K. (1989) 'Anger management methods in relation to the prevention of violent behaviour', in ARCHER, J. and BROWNE, K. (Eds) *Human Aggression: Naturalistic Approaches*, London, Routledge.

KANEY, S. and BENTALL, R.P. (1989) 'Persecutory delusions and attributional style', *British Journal of Medical Psychology*, **62**, 191–8.

KASS, F., SKODAL, A.E., CHARLES, E., SPITZER, R.L. and WILLIAMS, J.B.W. (1985) 'Scaled ratings of DSM III personality disorders', *American Journal of Psychiatry*, **142**, 627–30.

KIRK, J. (1989) 'Cognitive-behavioural assessment', in HAWTON, K., SALKOVSKIS, P.M., KIRK, J. and CLARK, D.M. (Eds) *Cognitive Behaviour Therapy for Psychiatric Problems: A Practical Guide*, Oxford, Oxford Medical Publications.

KOENIGSBERG, H.W., KAPLAN, R.D., GILMORE, M.M. and COOPER, A.M. (1985) 'The relationship between syndrome and personality disorder', *American Journal of Psychiatry*, **142**, 207–12.

MARKS, I.M. (1987) *Fears, Phobias and Rituals: Panic, Anxiety and Their Disorders*, Oxford, Oxford University Press.

MARZILLIER, J.S. and HALL, J. (Eds) (1987) *What Is Clinical Psychology?*, Oxford, Oxford University Press.

MILLON, T. (1983) *Millon Clinical Multiaxial Inventory*, Minneapolis, MN, National Computer Systems.

NOVACO, R.W. (1975) *Anger Control*, Lexington, MA, Heath.

NOVACO, R.W. and WELSH, W.N. (1989) 'Anger disturbance: cognitive mediation and clinical prescriptions', in HOWELLS, K. and HOLLIN, C. (Eds) *Clinical Approaches to Violence*, Chichester, Wiley.

OWENS, R.G. and ASHCROFT, J.B. (1982) 'Functional analysis in applied psychology', *British Journal of Clinical Psychology*, **21**, 181–9.

PILGRIM, D. and TREACHER, A. (1992) *Clinical Psychology Observed*, London, Routledge.

RACHMAN, S.J. and WILSON, G.T. (1980) *The Effects of Psychological Therapy*, 2nd ed., Oxford, Pergamon.

ROSENHAM, D.L. and SELIGMAN, M.E.P. (1989) *Abnormal Psychology*, 2nd ed., New York, W.W. Norton.

SHEA, S.C. (1988) *Psychiatric Interviewing: The Art of Understanding*, Illinois, Saunders.

SLADE, P.D. (1990) 'The behavioural and cognitive treatment of psychotic symptoms', in BENTALL R.P. (Ed.) *Reconstructing Schizophrenia*, London, Routledge.

SLADE, P.D. and BENTAL, R.P. (1988) *Sensory Deception: A Scientific Analysis of Hallucinations*, London, Croom Helm.

SPIELBERGER, C.D. (1983) *State-Trait Anxiety Inventory*, Palo Alto, CA, Consulting Psychologists Press.

ULLMAN, L.P. and KRASNER, L. (Eds) (1965) *Case Studies in Behaviour Modification*, New York, Holt, Rinehart and Winston.

WECHSLER, D. (1981) *The Wechsler Adult Intelligence Scale - Revised*, San Antonio, TX, The Psychological Corporation.

WOLPE, J. (1990) *The Practice of Behaviour Therapy*, 4th ed., New York, Pergamon.

WOODWORTH, R.S. (1992) 'The future of clinical psychology', *Journal of Consulting & Clinical Psychology*, **60** (1), 16-17. (Reprinted from *Journal of Consulting & Clinical Psychology*, **1**, 4-5.)

Chapter 13

Forensic Psychology

Clive R. Hollin

The application of psychology to law and criminal behaviour has been an area of considerable growth over the past decade (see Further Reading at the end of this chapter). Forensic psychologists have worked in such diverse areas as crime detection, police selection and training, courtroom dynamics, rules of law in mental health and juvenile and family legislation, the study of offenders, and the design and impact of crime prevention programmes. This chapter will concentrate on three areas – psychology in the courtroom, theories of violence and crime prevention – that illustrate the concerns of contemporary forensic psychology.

Psychology in the courtroom

The suggestion that psychology might have something to offer in the courtroom was made as long ago as 1908 by Hugo Münsterberg. Münsterberg suggested that psychologists have much to offer the court, both in terms of understanding courtroom dynamics and informing the court on matters psychological. In the years since, Münsterberg's suggestions have proved correct with studies, for example, of courtroom decision making, juries and the reliability of evidence. For present purposes I have selected the research on evidence to show how psychological research can be applied to the courtroom.

Eyewitness evidence

The study of eyewitness testimony, involving as it does the processes of perception and memory, is a natural topic for psychologists. Further, research in this area is relevant to a major concern of all those working in the justice system – the possibility of a wrongful conviction. Huff and Rattner (1988) have suggested that 'The single most important factor contributing to wrongful conviction is eyewitness misidentification' (p. 135).

The study of eyewitness evidence has generated a vast body of research which has shown that many variables can influence eyewitness evidence (Williams *et al.*, 1992). These variables are generally referred to in the context of the three stages of *acquisition*, *retention* (or *storage*) and *retrieval* tradition-ally used in memory research. Through research it has become clear that memory for real-life events can be significantly affected at all three stages. Thus, variables at the stage of acquisition, such as the length of time spent in obser-vation and the level of violence, can influence the accuracy of eyewitness recall and recognition. Storage variables, such as the length of time between viewing and recollection and talking with other witnesses, can similarly influence eye-witness testimony. Finally, retrieval factors such as the style of questioning used to elicit testimony and the impact of misleading information have been shown to play a role in the eventual accuracy of testimony. In addition, individual differences such as the age of the witness may play a role across all three stages.

While much of the early research pointed to the somewhat fragile nature of eyewitness evidence, this knowledge base proved to be the foundation for a further research effort aimed at enhancing eyewitness evidence. A body of psychological research has developed around, for example, the design and use of face recall systems such as the photofit and identikit procedures (Davies, 1983); the fairness of the identity parade or line-up (Cutler and Penrod, 1988); artist sketches (Davies, 1986); and improved interview techniques such as the cognitive interview (Fisher and Geiselman, 1992).

The law-psychology debate The psychological study of eyewitness evi-dence has led to three areas of debate. The first area concerns the theoretical interpretation of the findings from the research on the effects of leading ques-tions on recall from memory. Specifically there is a view that offering mislead-ing information during questioning can actually change memory, so that recall of the original event is impossible (Loftus and Ketcham, 1983). Alternatively, other theorists hold that the misleading information coexists with the original memory and can be accessed given the right retrieval cues (Zaragoza *et al.*, 1987). These different interpretations and the further studies they generate clearly act as a stimulus to theoretical discussions within cognitive psychology.

The second area of debate centres on the degree to which findings from mainly laboratory-based studies can be applied to, or can be *generalized* to, 'real-world' issues. Some psychologists argue that it is premature to apply research findings (e.g. Konečni and Ebbesen, 1986); while others maintain that the research evidence should be offered to the court (e.g. Loftus, 1986). This is an area in which the professional debate is set to run!

The third area of debate, linked to the second, concerns the presentation in court of the research findings. The argued lack of generalizability of the findings is said to restrict their usefulness generally, and may increase juror scepticism unduly resulting in wrong verdicts being reached. The suggestion has also been advanced that experts are not needed: it is argued that jurors have a common-sense appreciation of human behaviour that allows them to judge the accuracy of an eyewitness. Finally, psychological research findings have been a cause for concern as the results of experimental studies are based on probabilities, not statements of what is true or false. Thus psychological research cannot predict whether a particular eyewitness is correct or incorrect in, for example, their identification of a suspect. Williams *et al*. (1992) discuss these objections and conclude that confidence can be held in the reliability of the research findings; that expert testimony is needed to inform lay understanding of eyewitness testimony but that this does not adversely affect juror scepticism; and that probabilistic statements do not necessarily conflict with the role of the expert witness. It is unlikely, however, that this is the final word on the topic.

Confession evidence

Whatever the finer points of the debate, there is little doubt that psychological research has raised public concern about the reliability of eyewitness evidence. The same is also true with another form of evidence – confessional evidence. As with eyewitness evidence, confessional evidence often counts significantly towards a guilty verdict in the courtroom. However, several recent cases in England, including the Guildford Four and the Birmingham Six, have cast grave doubt on the value of uncorroborated confessional evidence. As with eyewitness evidence, psychologists have offered both empirical evidence and a coherent explanation for the phenomenon of false confessions (Gudjonsson, 1992).

Kassin and Wrightsman (1985) defined three types of false confession: (a) the *voluntary confession* offered in the absence of any external pressure; (b) the *coerced-compliant confession* made during police interrogation that the confessor knows to be false; (c) the *coerced-internalized confession* in which during interrogation the confessor comes wrongly to believe, either temporarily or permanently, that they committed the crime of which they are accused. While voluntary confessions may be a sign of psychological distress, it is the latter two types of confession that have attracted most attention from researchers.

The research into confessions has focused on two areas: (1) the tactics used by the police during interrogation; (2) the psychological characteristics of individuals most likely to give false confessions.

Environmental conditions   It is plain that the experience of police custody can be extremely stressful, thereby placing the suspect in a vulnerable position. As Irving (1986) remarked, 'Those people who haven't tried it should test the experience of being located in a small bare room, not knowing what's going to happen, or when they are going to get out. It has rather startling effects on some people' (p. 142). Recognizing this stress factor, sophisticated interrogational tactics and techniques have been developed to exert maximum pressure on the suspect to confess (e.g. Inbau *et al.*, 1986; Walkley, 1987). These tactics include the use of authority and power to exert social pressure on the suspect to confide in the interrogator; leading the suspect to believe that continued denial is futile, to the extent of displaying dummy files of 'evidence';

Table 13.1 *Psychological correlates of suggestibility*

Psychological factor	Relationship with suggestibility
Acquiescence	Positive
Anxiety	Positive
Assertiveness	Negative
Facilitative coping style	Negative
Fear of negative evaluation	Positive
High expectation of accuracy	Positive
Intelligence	Negative
Memory ability	Negative
Self-esteem	Negative
Social desirability	Positive

Note: A positive relationship predicts that, say, as anxiety increases so suggestibility also increases; a negative relationship predicts, say, that as assertiveness increases suggestibility decreases.

and suggesting that there will be rewards, both social and personal, for 'coming clean'.

Suspect factors Gudjonsson and Clark (1986) suggested that, in seeking to cope with the demands of stress and interrogation, some individuals will be coerced into making false confessions.

The *compliant* suspect is someone who seeks to end the interrogation by knowingly giving a false confession. This type of person is characterized by the traits of rather low intelligence, high acquiescence (i.e. a tendency to answer questions in the affirmative), and a high need for social approval. On the other hand, the *suggestible* suspect internalizes the interrogator's persuasive messages to the point of actually believing that they committed the crime. It then follows that they make a (false) confession. A summary of the experimental findings describing the characteristics of the suggestible individual, liable to make a coerced-internalized false confession, in shown in Table 13.1.

In all probability the same issues will arise here as in the law–psychology debate about eyewitness evidence. However, even to be debating the issues from a psychological perspective is progress given the recency of much of the empirical work.

Violent behaviour

The search for an explanation for criminal behaviour has a long history, with distinguished contributions from many disciplines including psychology

(Siegal, 1986). It is beyond the scope of this chapter to review in total the application of psychological theories to explain the phenomenon of criminal behaviour. Therefore, to illustrate current trends I have selected violent behaviour as an exemplar of contemporary theorizing in forensic psychology.

If we define violence as an action that produces damaging or hurtful physical (including sexual) effects on other people, the question is a simple one: why do some people hurt others? As you might expect, the answer to this question is far from simple (see Archer, 1994; Berkowitz, 1993; Taylor, 1993). Nonetheless, we can present a model that gives a framework by which to consider recent advances in understanding violent acts. This model has three components: (1) the characteristics of settings in which violent acts are likely to occur; (2) the profile of the thoughts and actions of the person who commits the violent act; (3) the impact of the violent act and the relationship of the impact to the future likelihood of more violence (see Figure 13.1).

Research conducted over the past decade has greatly enhanced our understanding of all three components of this model.

Situational analysis

Henderson (1986) conducted an analysis of the types of violent situation reported by a sample of adult male violent offenders. This study is of interest as it gives an indication of the settings in which violent incidents are most likely to be found.

The analysis revealed four broad categories of violent situation: violence in conjunction with another crime – sometimes intentionally as with robbery, sometimes in panic as when discovered committing a crime such as burglary; family violence directed towards both women and children; violence in public places such as clubs and bars; and violence in institutions (police stations and prisons in this study) directed towards fellow inmates and staff. While not part of Henderson's analysis, violence in institutions can be extended to other institutions such as hospitals; and to other professional staff such as nurses, social workers and probation officers.

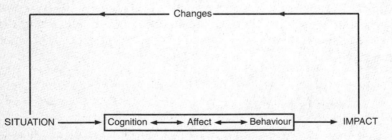

Figure 13.1 *Stages in the cognitive-behavioural model*

Henderson's study illustrates the distinction between premeditated or 'instrumental' violence, as in a robbery; and 'angry' or 'hostile' violence that is impulsive and unplanned. Situational analysis has also pointed to several factors that increase the likelihood of this type of violent outburst.

The first factor we can think of as *physical* in nature: this includes variables such as high temperature, air pollution and overcrowding. There is strong evidence to suggest that such situational factors are directly related to rises in the number of violent acts in the population (Anderson, 1989). The second factor is *social* in nature, including the words and actions of other people. Thus, the violent act might be made in response to verbal provocation, physical intimidation or the perception of another person breaking some social rule.

This reference to perceptual processes brings us to the next stage in the sequence: the individual's perception and evaluation of the events in which they are involved. Dodge (1986) has suggested four stages to this cognitive process: perception, interpretation, social problem solving, decision making and personal evaluation.

The person: cognition

The first part of the cognitive stage involves the person perceiving and interpreting situational cues, particularly the words and actions of other people. It appears that aggressive and violent people, perhaps especially aggressive and violent children and adolescents, perceive fewer social cues than non-violent people (e.g. Dodge and Newman, 1981). It is also clear that violent people are much more likely to interpret the words and deeds of other people in a hostile fashion (Slaby and Guerra, 1988). This hostile interpretation of social cues is a fundamental component of violent behaviour: a study by Stefanek *et al.* (1987) showed this to be the case even with young children. Stefanek *et al.* recorded the self-statements of groups of young children and found that children known to be aggressive were much more likely to describe social encounters in a hostile manner: 'That child doesn't like me', 'They want to take my toys'.

When it comes to the next part of the sequence – social problem solving – the aggressive person must decide what to do next. However, their decision will be based on a limited perception of the situation and a hostile interpretation of events. Effective social problem solving demands the ability both to arrive at effective courses of action, and then to select the most expedient solution. The research suggests that violent people generate fewer solutions to interpersonal conflicts and hence consider fewer consequences of their actions (Slaby and Guerra, 1988).

This cognitive sequence of perception, interpretation and problem solving may be affected by the individual's level of emotional arousal. The now widely known work of Raymond Novaco has suggested that there can be reciprocal relationships between environmental events, both physical and social, cognitive processes and angry emotional arousal. Novaco suggests that certain events can trigger angry thoughts, these thoughts heighten emotional arousal, in turn intensifying the angry thoughts; this interplay between cognition and emotional arousal may subsequently increase the likelihood of the individual acting in a violent manner (Novaco and Welsh, 1989).

Having appraised the situation, possibly in a hostile manner, the individual must then act. In taking a violent course of action, the violent person may see this as an acceptable and legitimate response to a hostile world. In addition, the violent person may lack the skills to behave differently. Some violent people lack assertion skills, suggesting that through a combination of frustration and an inability to act differently the individual resorts to violence to solve interpersonal problems (Howells, 1986).

Impact

The individual's behaviour impacts upon the world, changing the situation, principally by invoking a response from other people. Thus we have a dynamic, interactive system in which those involved are continually shifting and moving in response to each other's actions. It should be remembered that violence can be a highly rewarding course of action. Difficult situations can be avoided through threats and displays of violence. Similarly, violence can produce positive rewards, such as material gains and social status, along with a sense of excitement and enhanced self-esteem. These positive impacts are often highly rewarding for the violent person and so increase the likelihood of future violent behaviour.

Crime prevention

If we take the model shown in Figure 13.1 as a general model of criminal behaviour, what might it tell us about strategies to prevent crime? It leads, I think, to three strategies: (1) change the physical setting in which the violence occurs; (2) change the behaviour of the victims; (3) change the violent person. The first two strategies involve attempts to change the environment in which crime takes place; the third to change the person who commits the crime. The strategy of environmental change has become known as situational crime prevention; while changing the person is called offender rehabilitation.

Situational crime prevention

Situational crime prevention has become enormously popular over the last decade (Clarke, 1992). Simply, it holds that to prevent crime we must reduce opportunities for successful offending and/or increase the risk of detection. This approach to crime prevention has attracted a great deal of political interest over the past decade. As will be recognized from the discussion below, many of the initiatives that have sprung from this political (and financial) investment have become part of our everyday lives.

Reducing opportunity.   One way to reduce the opportunity for crime is known as *target hardening*. In practice this means physically strengthening the criminal's target or using security devices. The British Post Office, for example, adopted this strategy by replacing aluminum coin boxes with steel boxes in seeking, with some degree of success, to reduce theft from telephone kiosks. Similarly, car theft can be discouraged by using sophisticated door locks, lockable wheel nuts, security-coded sound systems and car alarms.

Similarly, *target removal* is aimed at reducing opportunity: payment of wages by direct bank credit, for example, removes the target of large amounts of cash being transported in public.

Increasing the risk of detection.   One of the most obvious ways to increase the risk of detection is to increase levels of *formal surveillance*, particularly in situations where there is an increased likelihood of crime. While a police officer on every street would reduce street crime, this would be extremely expensive. However, it is feasible for an increased police presence at sporting events such as soccer matches, and in video and amusement arcades where truants from school (a high crime group) may congregate during school hours.

Alongside a human presence, such as a police officer, shop assistant or car park attendant, technological advances have recently increased the potential for formal surveillance. Since closed circuit television (CCTV) was used to cut down crime on the London Underground (Burrows, 1980), it has become widely used in banks, shops and at sporting events. However, a recent technological advance lies in the procedure known as *electronic monitoring* or *tagging*. Tagging involves the convicted offender wearing on their body, usually their arm, ankle or wrist, a small transmitter. In one system the offender is required to log in to a central computer via a telephone link in their home: failure to log in would alert monitoring officers who are sent to investigate. Another system allows for constant monitoring via a device attached to the telephone system that picks up the transmitter's signals and relays them to a computer. If the offender moves out of a predetermined range from the telephone the monitoring officers are alerted. As observed by both British and American commentators, tagging has increased greatly in use over the past few years.

Given the high cost of formal surveillance, strategies designed to increase *informal surveillance* have also been developed. Of these strategies, there can be little doubt that Neighbourhood Watch (or Block Watch) has proved the most popular. Watch schemes have proliferated in North America, while Mayhew *et al.* (1989) estimate that more than two and a half million households in England and Wales are Watch members. The principle underlying Watch schemes is simple and neatly encapsulated in the much vaunted slogan 'Crime: Together We'll Crack It'. Thus, with the support of the police, people living in the same community take responsibility for the surveillance of each other's property, look out for suspicious characters, and report any sign of suspicious activity to the police.

Changing the behaviour of the victim.   Victims of crime can also adopt skills and strategies to lower the risk of personal victimization. A good example of this is to be found with the many professional people – nurses, police, prison staff, probation officers, social workers, forensic psychologists – who are regularly exposed to potentially violent situations. Several researchers have examined potentially dangerous face-to-face situations and have formulated various strategies that professionals can adopt to minimize the risks of their becoming a victim of a violent assault (Breakwell, 1989; Davies, 1989). Such strategies include personal skills such as perceiving the early warning signs of violence, 'talking down and defusing' the violent person, and coordinated team support in times of crisis.

Evaluation.   Does situational crime prevention work? The question is not easily answered and, in truth, the evidence is mixed, depending greatly on the operational definition of 'work'. There are undoubted successes, as with steering column locks on cars and the use of CCTV. In other areas the picture is more complex and less certain. In discussing the effect of Watch groups, Brantingham and Brantingham (1990) note: 'The weight of evidence accumulated through evaluation studies conducted in North America and Britain now suggests that Watch programs may improve participants' general attitudes about their neighbourhoods and may reduce participants' fear levels, but may not have much impact on crime' (p. 24). To complicate matters further, situational crime prevention initiatives may bring about the phenomenon of *displacement*.

Displacement.   Do situational crime prevention strategies stop crime, or do they simply move or displace crime to a fresh setting, a different time, or another victim? It is clear that displacement can occur: the evaluation of the introduction of CCTV on the London Underground suggested that crime had been shunted up the line to nearby stations without CCTV. Untangling the crime statistics is one of the major difficulties faced by researchers in attempting to establish whether a crime-prevention initiative has caused displacement on a large scale. Changes in numbers of recorded crimes can be caused by many factors, making it difficult to quantify displacement effects, if any.

Civil liberties.   Given that they change our environment, situational crime prevention measures raise questions about the society in which we wish to live. Thus there are issues about being recorded on videotape in stores, carrying a personal identification card, and the use of monitoring systems such as 'tagging'. Tagging crystallizes the dilemmas inherent in some situational initiatives: as a society do we want a criminal justice system that uses electronic monitoring of our fellow citizens? Technological advances may make it feasible to implant transmitters under the skin so that when used with CCTV the system would be in place to monitor and hence control an individual's movements with precision that previously was the stuff of science fiction (Nellis, 1991). Society has some hard decisions to make regarding the balance between crime prevention, tolerance of crime and preservation of existing freedoms.

Offender rehabilitation

In 1974 Robert Martinson published the paper 'What works? Questions and answers about prison reform' which carried the message that 'nothing works' in the rehabilitation of offenders. The view that nothing works has, in the time since Martinson's paper, become almost an article of faith, accepted by academics and policy makers alike. Why should this position, which is so pessimistic, have found such ready acceptance?

Researchers such as Don Andrews (e.g. Andrews, 1990; Andrews *et al.*, 1990) make the case that it is the focus on the individual, inherent in the concept of rehabilitation, that is the root of the problem. As Andrews suggests, this focus on the individual offender – in both a practical and theoretical sense – runs counter to the sociological and political theories that dominate mainstream criminology. The concept of rehabilitation, with its emphasis on understanding and working with the individual offender, stands in stark contrast to theories of crime that emphasize, for example, the role of economic factors in creating crime. Thus, the 'nothing works' position was in accord with theories of crime that minimize the role of individual differences and see no need for a psychological account of criminal behaviour. In other words, if the individual is not seen as a major factor in explaining crime, then changing the individual will not work in reducing crime; although, as West (1980) points out, the goals of social reform and individual change do not have to be exclusive.

The 'nothing works' view also received a favourable reception in the political climate of the 1970s and 1980s. The marked political swings to the right in the USA, UK and parts of Europe brought about changes in the criminal justice system based not on the 'soft' ideal of rehabilitation, but on policies steeped in the 'hard' line of the need for deterrence and justice through punishment (Cullen and Gendreau, 1989). There was a voice of opposition with some writers – most notably Paul Gendreau and Robert Ross (e.g. Gendreau and Ross, 1987) – arguing that effective rehabilitation was not an impossible goal and pointing to examples of success.

One problem faced by the advocates of rehabilitation lay in making a coherent, supportive case from a myriad of research findings. In the field of offender rehabilitation, reviewers are faced with evidence from studies that involve many different types of intervention, conducted in different settings, with different measures of 'success'. As there are hundreds of outcome studies, it is very difficult, if not impossible, to draw meaningful conclusions about what works, for whom, and under what conditions simply by pooling the results of all the studies and 'vote counting' as to who does best. Indeed, as Gendreau and Andrews (1990) note, such an approach can lead to the neglect of key information, the formulation of imprecise conclusions and even author bias. The development of the statistical technique of *meta-analysis* has, however, gone some way towards providing a means by which to produce a standardized overview of many empirical studies.

As Izzo and Ross (1990) explain, meta-analysis is:

'A technique that enables a reviewer to objectively and statistically analyse the findings of each study as data points. . . . The procedure of meta-analysis involves collecting relevant studies, using the summary statistics from each study as a unit of analysis, and then analysing the aggregated data in a quantitative manner using statistical tests'. (p. 135)

From such large-scale analyses informed conclusions can be made about whether treatment works, and estimates made of what type of intervention works best in what setting.

When considering the findings of the meta-analytic studies, it is important to make the distinction between *clinical/personal* and *criminogenic* outcome variables. The former can be thought of as some dimension of personal functioning, such as psychological adjustment, cognition, anger control, skill level and academic ability; while the latter refers specifically to variables concerned with crime, recidivism, type of offence and so on. As a generalization, rehabilitation programmes with specific clinical aims tend to produce beneficial clinical outcomes regarding personal change (Lipsey and Wilson, 1993). Thus, for example, programmes designed to improve social skills in offender populations do generally lead to positive changes in social ability (Hollin, 1990a). However, it is possible for programmes to produce significant outcomes in terms of positive personal change, but to have no impact on criminogenic variables (Hollin, 1990b; Hollin and Henderson, 1984). One contribution of the meta-analytic studies is that they allow us to begin to untangle the confusion in the literature between these two types of outcome measure.

In the field of offender rehabilitation there have been several meta-analysis studies reported over the past five years. The conclusions listed below are drawn from the two most recent studies reported by Andrews *et al.* (1990) and by Lipsey (1992). The Lipsey study in particular is a major piece of work, involving an analysis of 443 outcome studies in the field of juvenile delinquency.

The first point to emerge from Lipsey's large-scale meta-analysis is that there is a substantial variability of criminogenic outcome in the literature. As Lipsey notes, some studies show large and positive effects of intervention on recidivism; while other studies show either no treatment effect or even a negative effect. Given this variability it is understandable that different reviewers, depending on their sampling of the literature and their definitions of 'success', have arrived at different conclusions.

We know that psychological interventions can be successful in producing personal change, but what contributes most to changes in offending? The meta-analyses point to the characteristics of intervention programmes that show a high effect in *reducing criminal behaviour*.

First, indiscriminate targeting of treatment programmes is counter-productive in reducing recidivism: important predictors of success are that higher risk offenders should be selected, and that programmes should focus on criminogenic targets for change. Second, the type of treatment programme is important: structured and focused treatments, typically behavioural, skill-orientated and multimodal programmes are more effective than less structured approaches such as counselling. Third, the most successful studies, while behavioural in nature, include a cognitive component to focus on the attitudes, values and beliefs that offenders use to support and justify their anti-social behaviour. Fourth, regarding the type and style of service, Andrews *et al.* (1990) suggest that some therapeutic approaches are not suitable for general use with offenders. Specifically, they argue that 'Traditional psychodynamic and nondirective client-centered therapies are to be avoided within general samples of offenders' (p. 376). Fifth, treatment programmes conducted in the community are shown to have a stronger effect on delinquent behaviour than residential programmes. While residential programmes can be effective, they should be linked structurally with community-based interventions. The most effective programmes have high 'treatment integrity' in that they are carried out by trained staff and the treatment initiators are involved in all the operational phases of the programmes (Hollin, 1990b). Added to this list is the further conclusion made by Roberts and Camasso (1991), following their meta-analysis, that interventions specifically targeted at the family are also successful in reducing delinquency.

Overall, given the above conditions, the meta-analyses suggest that the high-effect programmes can produce decreases in recidivism of the order of 20 to 40 per cent over and above the baseline levels from mainstream criminal sanctioning of offenders. On this basis it is fair to conclude that it is not the case that 'nothing works' in attempts to rehabilitate offenders. Of course this conclusion has obvious benefits at every level: it can reduce victimization; it can take the offender out of the criminal justice system, to the potential benefit of both the individual offender and their family; and it can reduce the financial burden on taxpayers.

Conclusion

Through both their research and practice, forensic psychologists can have an impact on understanding the complexities of criminal behaviour and the criminal justice system. Further, forensic psychologists can realistically aim to reduce the pain and suffering caused by crime. While demanding of its adherents, there is no doubt that forensic psychology has become one of the major areas of growth in contemporary applied psychology.

Further reading

ANDREWS, D.A. and BONTA, J. (1994) *The Psychology of Criminal Conduct*, Cincinnati, OH, Anderson.

BLACKBURN, R. (1993) *The Psychology of Criminal Conduct*, Chichester, Wiley.

HOLLIN, C.R. (1989) *Psychology and Crime: An Introduction to Criminological Psychology*, London, Routledge.

HOLLIN, C.R. (1992) *Criminal Behaviour: A Psychological Approach to Explanation and Prevention*, London, Falmer Press.

KAGEHIRO, D.K. and LAUFER, W.S. (Eds) (1992) *Handbook of Psychology and Law*, New York, Springer-Verlag.

References

ANDERSON, C.A. (1989) 'Temperature and aggression: ubiquitous effects of heat on occurrence of human violence', *Psychological Bulletin*, **106**, 74–96.

ANDREWS, D.A. (1990) 'Some criminological sources of anti-rehabilitation bias in the Report of The Canadian Sentencing Commission', *Canadian Journal of Criminology*, **2**, 511–24.

ANDREWS, D.A., ZINGER, I., HOGE, R.D., BONTA, J., GENDREAU, P. and CULLEN, F.T. (1990) 'Does correctional treatment work? A clinically relevant and informed meta-analysis', *Criminology*, **28**, 369–404.

ARCHER, J. (Ed.) (1994) *Male Violence*, London, Routledge.

BERKOWITZ, L. (1993) *Aggression: Its Causes, Consequences, and Control*, New York, McGraw-Hill.

BRANTINGHAM, P.L. and BRANTINGHAM, P.J. (1990) 'Situational crime prevention in practice', *Canadian Journal of Criminology*, **32**, 17–40.

BREAKWELL, G. (1989) *Facing Physical Violence*. Leicester/London, BPS Books/Routledge.

BURROWS, J. (1980) 'Closed circuit television and crime on the London Underground', in CLARKE, R.V.G. and MAYHEW, P. (Eds) *Designing Out Crime*, London, HMSO.

CLARKE, R.V.G. (Ed.) (1992). *Situational Crime Prevention: Successful Case Studies*, New York, Harrow and Heston.

CULLEN, F.T. and GENDREAU, P. (1989) 'The effectiveness of correctional rehabilitation: reconsidering the "nothing works" debate', in GOODSTEIN, L. and MACKENZIE, D.L. (Eds) *The American Prison: Issues in Research and Policy*, New York, Plenum Press.

CUTLER, B.L. and PENROD, S.D. (1988) 'Improving the reliability of eyewitness identification: lineup construction and presentation', *Journal of Applied Psychology*, **73**, 281-90.

DAVIES, G.M. (1983) 'Forensic face recall: the role of visual and verbal information', in LLOYD-BOSTOCK, S.M.A. and CLIFFORD, B.R. (Eds) *Evaluating Witness Evidence: Recent Psychological Research and New Perspectives*, Chichester, Wiley.

DAVIES, G.M. (1986) 'Capturing likeness in eyewitness composites: the police artist and his rivals', *Medicine, Science and the Law*, **26**, 283-90.

DAVIES, W. (1989) 'The prevention of assault on professional helpers', in HOWELLS, K. and HOLLIN, C.R. (Eds) *Clinical Approaches to Violence*, Chichester, Wiley.

DODGE, K.A. (1986) 'A social-information processing model of social competence in children', in PERMUTTER, M. (Ed.) *Minnesota Symposium on Child Psychology*, Vol. 18, Hillsdale, NJ, Erlbaum.

DODGE, K.A. and NEWMAN, J.P. (1981) 'Biased decision-making processes in aggressive boys', *Journal of Abnormal Psychology*, **90**, 375-9.

FISHER, R.P. and GEISELMAN, R.E. (1992) *Memory-enhancing Techniques for Investigative Interviewing: The Cognitive Interview*, Springfield, IL, C.C. Thomas.

GENDREAU, P. and ANDREWS, D.A. (1990) 'Tertiary prevention: what the meta-analyses of the offender treatment literature tell us about "what works" ', *Canadian Journal of Criminology*, **32**, 173-84.

GENDREAU, P. and ROSS, R.R. (1987) 'Revivification of rehabilitation: evidence from the 1980s', *Justice Quarterly*, **4**, 349-407.

GUDJONSSON, G. (1992) *The Psychology of Interrogations, Confessions and Testimony*, Chichester, Wiley.

GUDJONSSON, G. and CLARK, N.K. (1986) 'Suggestibility in police interrogation: a social psychological model', *Social Behaviour*, **1**, 83-104.

HENDERSON, M. (1986) 'An empirical typology of violent incidents reported by prison inmates with convictions for violence', *Aggressive Behavior*, **12**, 21-32.

HOLLIN, C.R. (1990a) 'Social skills training with delinquents: a look at the evidence and some recommendations for practice', *British Journal of Social Work*, **20**, 483-93.

HOLLIN, C.R. (1990b) *Cognitive-behavioral Interventions With Young Offenders*, Elmsford, NY, Pergamon Press.

HOLLIN, C.R. and HENDERSON, M. (1984) 'Social skills training with young offenders: false expectations and the "failure of treatment" ', *Behavioural Psychotherapy*, **12**, 331-41.

HOWELLS, K. (1986) 'Social skills training and criminal and antisocial behaviour in adults', in HOLLIN, C.R. and TROWER, P. (Eds) *Handbook of Social Skills Training*, Vol. 1: *Applications Across the Life Span*, Oxford, Pergamon Press.

HUFF, C.R. and RATTNER, A. (1988) 'Convicted but innocent: false positives and the criminal justice process', in Scott, E. and Hirschi, T. (Eds) *Controversial Issues in Crime and Justice*, Beverly Hills, CA, Sage.

Inbau, F.E., Reid, J.E. and Buckley, J.P. (1986) *Criminal Interrogation and Confessions*, 3rd ed., Baltimore, MD, Williams and Wilkins.

Irving, B. (1986) 'The interrogation process', in Benyon, J. and Bourn, C. (Eds) *The Police: Powers, Procedures and Proprieties*, Oxford, Pergamon Press.

Izzo, R.L. and Ross, R.R. (1990) 'Meta-analysis of rehabilitation programs for juvenile delinquents: a brief report', *Criminal Justice and Behavior*, **17**, 134–42.

Kassin, S.M. and Wrightsman, L.S. (Eds) (1985) *The Psychology of Evidence and Trial Procedure*, London, Sage.

Konečni, V.J. and Ebbesen, E.B. (1986) 'Courtroom testimony by psychologists on eyewitness identification issues', *Law and Human Behavior*, **10**, 117–26.

Lipsey, M.W. (1992) 'Juvenile delinquency treatment: a meta-analytic inquiry into the variability of effects', in Cook, T.D., Cooper, H., Cordray, D.S., Hartmann, H., Hedges, L.V., Light, R.J., Louis, T.A. and Mosteller, F. (Eds) *Meta-analysis for Explanation: A Casebook*, New York, Russell Sage Foundation.

Lipsey, M.W. and Wilson, D.B. (1993) 'The efficacy of psychological, educational, and behavioral treatment: confirmation from meta-analysis', *American Psychologist*, **48**, 1181–1209.

Loftus, E.F. (1986) 'Ten years in the life of an expert witness', *Law and Human Behavior*, **10**, 241–63.

Loftus, E.F. and Ketcham, K.E. (1983) 'The malleability of eyewitness accounts', in Lloyd-Bostock, S.M.A. and Clifford, B.R. (Eds) *Evaluating Eyewitness Evidence: Recent Psychological Research and New Perspectives*, Chichester, Wiley.

Martinson, R. (1974) 'What works? – Questions and answers about prison reform', *Public Interest*, **35**, 22–54.

Mayhew, P., Elliott, D. and Dowds, L. (1989) *The 1988 British Crime Survey*, London, HMSO.

Münsterberg, H. (1908) *On the Witness Stand: Essays on Psychology and Crime*, New York, Clark, Boardman.

Nellis, M. (1991) 'The electronic monitoring of offenders in England and Wales', *British Journal of Criminology*, **31**, 165–85.

Novaco, R.W. and Welsh, W.N. (1989) 'Anger disturbances: cognitive mediation and clinical prescriptions', in Howells, K. and Hollin, C.R. (Eds) *Clinical Approaches to Violence*, Chichester, Wiley.

Roberts, A.R. and Camasso, M.J. (1991) 'The effect of juvenile offender treatment programs on recidivism: a meta-analysis of 46 studies', *Notre Dame Journal of Law, Ethics and Public Policy*, **5**, 421–41.

Siegal, L.J. (1986) *Criminology*, 2nd ed., St Paul, MN, West Publishing.

Slaby, R.G. and Guerra, N.G. (1988) 'Cognitive mediators of aggression in adolescent offenders, 1: Assessment', *Developmental Psychology*, **24**, 580–88.

STEFANEK, M.E., OLLENDICK, T.H., BALDOCK, W.P., FRANCIS, G. and YAEGER, N.J. (1987) 'Self-statements in aggressive, withdrawn, and popular children', *Cognitive Research and Therapy*, **11**, 229–39.

TAYLOR, P.J. (Ed.) (1993) *Violence in Society*, London, Royal College of Physicians.

WALKLEY, J. (1987) *Police Interrogation: A Handbook for Investigators*, London, Police Review Publications.

WEST, D.J. (1980) 'The clinical approach to criminology', *Psychological Medicine*, **10**, 619–31.

WILLIAMS, K.D., LOFTUS, E.F. and DEFFENBACHER, K.A. (1992) 'Eyewitness evidence and testimony', in KAGEHIRO, D.K. and LAUFER, W.S. (Eds) *Handbook of Psychology and Law*, New York, Springer-Verlag.

ZARAGOZA, M.S., McCLOSKEY, M. and JARVIS, M. (1987) 'Misleading post-event information and recall of the original event: further evidence against the memory impairment hypothesis', *Journal of Experimental Psychology: Learning, Memory, and Cognition*, **13**, 36–44.

Epilogue

Clive Hollin

Having read all the chapters in this book several times during editing I felt that it might be interesting to reflect briefly on my overall general impressions.

The first point to capture my attention was how almost all the contributors (myself included) wanted to place their subject-matter in historical perspective. One of my main tasks as editor was to encourage contributors to say a little less about the past and rather more about the present and the future. On the other hand, I had to do very little to get contributors to write about ideas, concepts and theories: to a person, the psychologists here wanted to talk about the ideas behind their research interests. This willingness to discuss history and theory stands in stark contrast with my views expressed in the Preface regarding the virtual extinction of the formal teaching of History and Theory in contemporary psychology courses. Perhaps with a little creative thought this might be gently weaned back into degree courses.

The second point to capture my interest lay in the way that many contributors were quick to point out the relevance of their topic to understanding everyday behaviour. Following from that, the natural step is to show how empirical research and theory can be translated into application, both to improve the quality of everyday life and to assist when things go awry. This is perhaps an important point to note at a time when academic researchers are under increasing pressure to justify their existence. It is, however, worth remembering that many of the advances made in applied psychology could not have taken place without the basic empirical and theoretical research that informs practice.

The third and final point lay in the sheer diversity of the subject-matter. While one implicitly accepts that the range of contemporary psychology is vast, it is only when reading work such as this that one realizes just how vast it really is and how much there is to know. I found this both exciting and daunting. Exciting because there is much to learn that might advance one's own thinking in one's own specialism. Daunting because it forces home the message that it is quite impossible to keep pace with every facet of one's own discipline. The answer to the problem, of course, is to edit and read books like this! I hope that five years down the line I am asked to do a second edition so that I can catch up once again with contemporary psychology!

Notes on Contributors

Ros Bradbury obtained degrees from University College, London and the University of Birmingham. She is a lecturer with special interests in cognitive and occupational psychology.

Kevin Browne has been researching family violence and child development for fifteen years and has published extensively on the subject. He is Chair of the Research Committee of the International Society for the Prevention of Child Abuse and Neglect (ISPCAN) and Co-Editor (with Dr Margaret Lynch) of *Child Abuse Review*, Journal of the British Association for the Study and Prevention of Child Abuse and Neglect (BAPSCAN). As a Chartered Psychologist and a Chartered Biologist, he is currently employed by the School of Psychology at the University of Birmingham, as a senior lecturer in Clinical Criminology and Research Coordinator for the Youth Treatment Service at the Glenthorne Centre, Birmingham. Publications include: Browne, K., Davies, C. and Stratton, P. (1988) *Early Prediction and Prevention of Child Abuse* (Chichester: Wiley); Browne, K. and Herbert, M. (1995) *Preventing Family Violence* (Chichester: Wiley).

Raymond Cochrane is Professor of Psychology and Director of the Graduate Research School at the University of Birmingham. His main research interests are in the processes of immigrant adjustment and social factors in mental illness.

Christine Griffin is a lecturer in Social Psychology at the University of Birmingham. Much of her research has concerned the transition to adulthood, especially for young women as well as work on men and masculinity, youth employment and the use of qualitative methods in social psychology. Her publications include *Typical Girls?* (Routledge and Kegan Paul, 1985), and *Representations of Youth* (Polity Press, 1993). She was also one of the founding editorial group members of the journal *Feminism and Psychology* (Sage Publications).

Gillian Harris is a lecturer in Developmental Psychology at the University of Birmingham, where she specialises in Infancy and Early Development. She is also a Principal Clinical Psychologist at The Children's Hospital, Birmingham, where she runs a specialist clinic for infants and children with feeding problems and eating disorders.

Mike Harris is a senior lecturer in the School of Psychology at the University of Birmingham. His research centres around the psychophysical and computational investigation of the analysis and possible uses of visual motion.

Clive Hollin is a Chartered Forensic Psychologist and a Fellow of The British Psychological Society. He is currently Senior Lecturer in Psychology at the University of Birmingham and Director of Research and Development in the Youth Treatment Service. His main research interest lies in the application of psychological theory and research to understanding criminal behaviour, particularly among young people. In over one hundred academic publications, he was written or edited fourteen books.

Kevin Howells is a chartered clinical and forensic psychologist. He has worked in several universities, including Birmingham University, where he was Professor of clinical psychology. He has also worked at the Reaside Clinic as a clinical psychologist, specializing in the assessment and management of anger and violence. He is currently based at the Department of Psychology at Edith Cowan University in Western Australia, where he is involved in postgraduate training in forensic psychology.

Glyn Humphreys is Professor of Cognitive Psychology at the University of Birmingham, having formerly been Lecturer, Senior Lecturer and Professor of Psychology at Birkbeck College, London. He works in the field of visual cognition, and has interests in neuropsychology and computational modelling. He is the editor of the journal *Visual Cognition*.

Koen Lamberts is a lecturer in Cognitive Psychology at the University of Birmingham. He studied psychology and philosophy at the University of Leuven, where he also obtained his PhD in Experimental Psychology. He worked as a research associate at the University of Chicago. His main research interests are human categorization and object recognition.

Jane Riddoch is a senior lecturer in Psychology at the University of Birmingham. Her particular research interests are the effects of brain damage on normal high level cognitive functions such as visual recognition, visual attention and movement. She has developed detailed assessments for deficits in these areas of functioning, and is currently investigating how rehabilitation may assist the everyday activities of people with cognitive disorders.

Philip Terry is a lecturer in Psychology at the University of Birmingham. His primary interests are in psychopharmacology and behavioural neuroscience, with particular emphasis on drugs of abuse and mechanisms of reward. He worked for four years at the National Institute on Drug Abuse in the USA, and before that at University College, London. He collaborates extensively with drug abuse researchers in Europe and the United States. He also has research interests in feeding behaviour.

Glyn Thomas gained his PhD from the University of Nottingham in 1971, and has held academic posts at the University of Stirling and at Bucknell University. He is currently senior lecturer in psychology at the University of Birmingham. His research interests include learning processes and cognitive development.

Patrick Tyler is a lecturer in Psychology at the University of Birmingham. He obtained degrees in psychology at the Universities of London and Illinois before completing his PhD in Psychology at the University of Colorado, Institute for Behavioural Genetics. He worked in Kentucky and Indiana before moving to Birmingham, where he currently carries out research into stress and coping in health professionals.

David Wales completed his clinical psychology degree at the University of Canterbury, Christchurch, New Zealand in 1988. He worked briefly as a clinical psychologist in the area of intellectual disability before moving to the United Kingdom where he pursued his interest in forensic psychology at Reaside Clinic, Birmingham. He returned to New Zealand in 1993 to take up his current position as Senior Psychologist at Kia Marama, a cognitive behavioural treatment unit for child sex offenders at Rolleston Prison.

Index

This item is due for return on or before the last date below.
It may be renewed by telephone, in person or via the internet at
https://librariesnl.northlan.gov.uk if not required by another borrower.

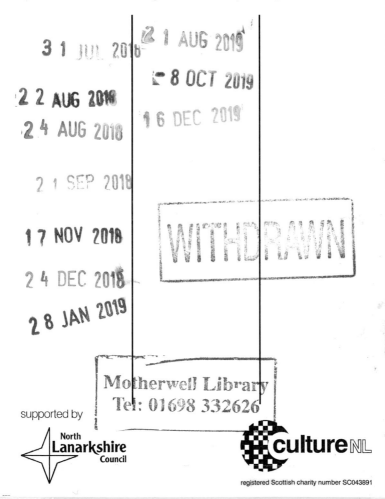

supported by

North
Lanarkshire
Council

cultureNL

registered Scottish charity number SC043891